The Manifestation of the Sons of God

2010-2012

*The Experience
of Romans 8*

This Book is Dedicated to
Rebekah, Chris & Amy
& to all of God's sons & daughters
who have come forth
for such a time as this

———————————————

And to John,
who is ever-present with us
as a guiding light

The Manifestation Of the Sons of God
2010-2012

The Experience of Romans 8

ISBN: 145378716X
EAN-13: 9781453787168
Library of Congress Control
Number: 2010913340

Copyright © 2010 by SonsOfGod.com
& L.Edward Kjos & J.Anne Kjos
Printed in the United States of America

All rights reserved. No part of this book may
be copied or reproduced for commercial
purposes without the written permission
of the publisher.

Edited by J.Anne Kjos

Published by
Sons of God.com
5699 Kanan Rd, Suite 145
Agoura Hills, CA 91301

www.SonsOfGod.com
Email: Edward@sonsofgod.com

The Manifestation of the Sons of God

Table of Contents

Romans 8 – An overview 8

Introduction 9

Section 1 – On The Front Line 13
    The Baton Has Been Passed To You 14
    The Front Line 19

Section 2 – The Emergence of Sonship 25
    Metamorphosis 26
    Sonship Is An Experience 32
    The Mark of Sonship 39
    The Path of His Cross 46
    The Ministry of the Sons of God 51

Section 3 – The Travail of All Creation 57
    The Travail of Sonship 58
    One Heart and One Mind 65

Section 4 – The Conjunction of Ages 69
    The Conjunction of 2 Worlds 70
    The One World of Christ 74
    Set The Captives Free 83
    The Elemental Kingdom 89

Section 5 – Prophet, Priest & King   95
    The Seer Prophet   96
    Dreams & Visions   106
    All Knowledge   112
    The Intercession of the Kingdom   117
    The Functioning Priesthood   124
    The Ark of His Presence   128

Section 6 – Administration of the Kingdom   131
    An Administration Suitable   132
    The Power of Oneness   138
    The Last Kingdom   143

Section 7 – Creative Word of the Kingdom   151
    In the Day of Thy Power   152
    The Creative Word of the Kingdom   156
    The Day of Reversal   164

Section 8 – What Delays the Kingdom   169
    Bonds & Vampires   171
    Are You Bonded to Your Concepts?   182
    Come Out Of Her   188
    Breaking the Ties to Ancestry   196

Section 9 – To Know The Lord   201
    Hunger   202
    To Know The Lord   207
    We Complete Him   214
    His Inheritance in the Sons of Light   217

Section 10 – Reality or Illusion?   221
    Is Your Reality an Illusion?   222
    The Process of Sight   230
    The Veil & One Step Beyond   235
    When You Make the Inner as the Outer   239
    The End of Illusion   243

Section 11 – The Warfare of the Saints   249
    The War Is Over His Word   250
    You Are The Fuse   257
    The Warrior Priest/Kings   262

Section 12 – In Pursuit of Resurrection Life   267
    Put on the Imperishable   268
    Resurrection Life   273

Section 13 – Quickening of the Mortal Body   277
    Come Alive!   278
    Integration of Your Spirit, Soul & Body   286
    Tracking In the Realm of Spirit   292

Section 14 – A Workshop for Seers   307
    A Workshop for Seers   308
        Breathing Techniques   312
        Diet & Your Spiritual Awareness   315
        Visualization & Imagination   320
        Simplicity   324
        Auras   326
        Journaling   328
        Worship   330

Conclusion   332

Index - Topical   333
Index - Scriptural   353

Romans, Chapter 8 Reference   357

Romans 8
An overview

All of creation is eagerly awaiting the final release and manifestation of the sons of God. Who are these sons? Those who have followed Christ through the open door that was made when He died on the cross; for Jesus Christ is the first born of many brethren.

- Romans 8 is a fascinating chapter, for buried within it is a clear picture of God's intent towards His sons for these final days.

- Romans 8 speaks of a deliverance from the bondage of the life of the flesh, and a birthing into a life and walk in the spirit.

- Romans 8 speaks of the anxious longing of all creation who eagerly await the deliverance of the sons of God.

- Romans 8 speaks of the travail that is being experienced in the earth right now; a travail to see the revealing and subsequent manifestation of the sons of God.

- Romans 8 speaks of the pre-destination of a people who will be conformed to the image of Christ - spirit, soul and body.

- Romans 8 speaks of the adoption of sonship; the redemption of your body, as you are glorified and brought into the transformation of resurrection life.

With the release of the sons of God comes the glorious freedom to all of creation; whether we speak of the elemental spirit world, or the Cloud of Witnesses. The earth is experiencing the travail of the sons of God; for it is the travail of Romans 8 and the birthing of the sons.

Introduction

Anne and I have watched and monitored closely the unfolding of the realm of spirit over the past 12 years - but especially the last 18 to 24 months - and it has become very apparent that many deep changes are happening. On a geophysical level, it does not take a great deal of perception to see this. But what is it pointing to?

There is a great deal of teaching in Christian circles that follow a belief in what we call the rapture or that follow a trend of eschatology concerning end time events. There is also a great deal of teaching emanating from the New Age movement that follow a myriad of different beliefs and perceptions, some very odd and very strange to say the least.

We have seen many Christians over the years become disillusioned with the path they were on. They were looking to experience a reality in a walk with God in the spirit, and only found dead rituals. If you have walked within religious circles, then you have seen the hypocrisy that exists so prevalently, holding a form or an acquiescence to the truth, but not walking in its power.

We have seen many turn to the teaching of the New Age movement because they have been looking for something more. The spirit within them was crying out, but the church was not providing an answer, so they fled to the New Age movement hoping to find some semblance of reality. But they are left woefully lacking.

God is not a respecter of persons for He is pouring forth of His spirit on the just and unjust alike, as it is referenced in the book of Joel.

So, what is happening? **The world is coming alive**. They are sensing changes that are coming, even if they do not know what to expect.

If you have been led to this book it is because there is a groaning and drive within your heart for something more. You have seen through the hypocrisy, you have seen through the forms and rituals of organized religion, or you have seen that the path of the new age movement and self-enlightenment is not the answer either.

For some the preparation has been through conventional church, for others perhaps the preparation has been walking in the path of the new age movement or within the eastern religions. It does not matter what the path for God is bringing His people into a realm of reality, and into the experience of sonship. Not theory, not doctrine.

God's sons have been scattered over the face of the earth and are in various walks of life, but the Spirit is calling them out. It does not matter what the faith is - or no faith at all - what matters is an openness of heart to be taught and brought into that which has been prepared for them.

Business is not as usual for we are talking about an experience of sonship, the embodiment of the Godhead within a people, a change of life and existence beyond what anyone has seen before this time.

Is this scriptural? Absolutely, for Christ was the first born of many brethren. And that "many" includes you.

We speak quite a bit about functioning in the realm of spirit and the conjunction of ages in this book, for God is bringing a merging of worlds. The world of spirit and the natural world. And God is bringing His people through this transition of time into a walk in the spirit beyond what eye has seen or has been perceived in the heart of man.

We have added a timeline to the title of this book which was only added at the last moment as the Spirit gave insight. Is there a tie in with the Mayan prophecies or Nostradamus? No, not that we are aware of. However, what we have seen unfolding over the past 18 to 24 months has been a significant ramping up in the realm of spirit of many changes - a precursor to many changes coming now.

We are at the door of change right now. We have entered a season that will see a whole new age of God's restoration in the earth, and I believe we will see these changes move exponentially forward over the next 24 months, for we are in the time that the man-child is coming to birth, as it speaks of in Revelation 12.

Throughout the book we speak of the travail of sonship. A travail that has only recently begun. What we have seen over the past several generations has been preparation, a preparation of God's kings and priests who have been in the womb of maturing until now. We are beginning to experience a transitioning, for it is the time for a delivery.

We also have addressed the issue presented in Romans 8 concerning creation, for creation is in travail with the sons to be set free from the futility they were subjected to ever since the time of Adam and Eve.

We will see a greater interaction of creation as the pangs of childbirth intensify. The earth changes that we will see are going to increase because the travail is going to get more intense. This can sound rather apocalyptic, and perhaps it is, but this is the time.

We are facing changes that are going to move forward exponentially; for one release after another will beget or empower the ability for subsequent releases to unfold even more quickly.

We speak about numerous issues and points throughout the book; bonds, revelation, the conjunction of ages, coming alive, functioning in the world of spirit, travail, the administration of the kingdom and so much more.

We are only touching upon the tip of the iceberg, for what God is restoring in the earth - both the physical earth we know and the earth of you and I - is so much more extensive.

There is so much unfolding at this time; we hope that we have effectively given you an overview or vista of what is transpiring during this season of change and a vehicle to accelerate your change and growth.

This book is dedicated to the sons of God, wherever you have been dispersed and in whatever form of belief system you may presently find yourself.

We bless this book to you; may it hasten your maturity into the full stature of sonship and the redemption of your spirit, soul and body, blameless before Him.

May these words equip you for the task at hand.

Edward & Anne

Section 1

On The

Front Line

- **The Baton Has Been Passed To You**

- **The Front Line**

The Baton Has Been Passed To You

And these all, having obtained a good report through faith, received not the promise: God having provided some better thing for us, that they without us should not be made perfect. – Hebrews 11:39-40

We have never seen a greater turmoil than what we are witnessing now. On every level, in the heavens or on the earth, the people who are blessed to live during this time will behold changes the likes of which no one has ever seen before.

We have come to a culmination or an ending of one day and the beginning of the next. As mentioned in Hosea 6:3, we have come to the third day, the day of spirit. We are walking in the time of the conjunction of 2 ages. One age is passing while another is coming forth. We are walking during a time that we will see a conjunction of 2 worlds; the realm of the spirit and this natural realm about us.

In many ways we are so much farther into this next order than we have yet had the eyes to see or the heart to understand. We are much deeper into the day of His kingdom and the time of His presence than we realize.

As a people we have been on a very long sojourn since we left the heart of the Father. We have been sent to see the completion of God's will in the earth during this time. Whether you began your walk with Him yesterday, or 80 years ago, you have been on a path of becoming and completing His will.

This sojourn takes us full circle. After we left the heavens, like Christ, we found ourselves in the form of a man; yet still residing in His presence. The difference was that our flesh had created a temporary veil, an illusion of separation, if you will, between us and God. But it has been only an illusion.

The Apostle Paul had an acute grasp upon the time in which he walked as he moved throughout the churches and later, as he functioned from his cell in the Roman prison. He understood the time and seasons that were before him; the challenge to see the church come forth and to see men come up higher to a plane of revelation and understanding. He faced the daily challenge to lay hold of that for which he had been called.

The church, the bride of Christ, once again faces the challenge of coming up higher. It is time to embrace the changes of a new order, a new way, a new baptism, and a new consciousness. This transition is dealing with a new order of creation that is coming forth, and that order concerns the establishing of a new race of people - the sons of God.

God is bringing His word to pass in this hour but the greatest challenge has been that His people have not been able to recognize the day of His appearing - the day of their visitation. This lag is being removed as the fire of His dealings and His deep work within the hearts of His sons have been turned up. It is no longer acceptable to just carry on, assuming at some point in the future that God will complete His plan.

You are His plan. You are pivotal in bringing to pass His will in the earth during this time, but you must see. There must be the removal of this lag that exists between God's moving and our recognition of His moving.

Within Christian circles there has always been this desire to define God; creating barriers and limitations of who and what God is by virtue of their revelation or present experience. But as God continues to move on, so does the expanding revelation of God and the unveiling of deeper truths in His word.

The challenge of change has always been to stay open, flexible and yielding to His demands. That is easier said than done for everyone brings with them baggage. That baggage is usually in the form of your personal concepts of God, and your pre-defined limitations of just how far you will go to follow after Him. If you have had a "position" in a church, then that becomes an even greater hurdle for you to let go of. We must hold nothing dear.

There is a time to walk, a time to rest, and a time to run. This is the time to run. As the prophet saw, there is yet much land to be taken (Joshua 13:1). We have come to a time of fulfillment and God has surely opened the portals of this new age to His sons.

It has been the Father's plan all along that He would bring forth His family - His sons & daughters - patterned after Christ their Lord. God never intended that you or I would see from a distance the promises and realities of the word, yet never enter into their fulfillment on this side of the veil. It is time to embrace the transformation of sonship.

What is coming forth now is a change that is complete and thorough; identical with Christ. With this change we will see the emergence of a race of people, the Sons of God, that truly embrace and manifest in their physical bodies both immortality and resurrection - on this side of the veil of death.

> **Therefore, since we have so great a cloud of witnesses surrounding us, let us also lay aside every encumbrance and the sin which so easily entangles us, and let us run with endurance the race that is set before us. - Heb12:1**

Hebrews 12 speaks of the men and women of faith - the martyrs that truly loved not their lives unto death - who followed the Lord. The book of Revelations speaks of those who follow the Lamb "whithersoever He goeth"; who also love not their lives unto death. We must realize that we have come into the company, as Hebrews speaks, of "just men made perfect" and to the myriad of angels and the Cloud of Witnesses.

We walk in the midst of a most holy company of believers who saw from a distance that which the Lord had prepared for these days; yet they did enter into it. The promise has remained that they, without us, would not be made perfect.

You are running the last leg of this race. You are holding the baton tightly for the baton has been passed on to you. The Cloud of

Witnesses is watching closely knowing that their release and the release of all creation is contingent upon you, and each of His sons, in completing this race. As Paul worded it - to finish the course. (Phil 3)

The admonition coming in the spirit is **"Break the tape"** my sons. There is a great deal resting upon your shoulders for God has chosen that you will be one of the anchor men in this last lap. What a privilege; what an honor.

Your heart is broken for you deeply feel the groaning of all of creation as you realize, "this last leg must be finished". It is up to you unto whom the baton has been passed.

To those who walk according to the flesh, these words, this stance of faith, could appear as arrogance. To those who have been given eyes to see, they see themselves as a reed broken by the wind; a lampstand which has been broken, allowing the light of Christ to shine through. God's sons in this day may appear many ways to different people, but what the Lord is creating is a humble people who have been brought low, so that the light of Christ might be fully revealed through them.

If you are wondering what you are experiencing, you are experiencing the beginning changes of sonship. You have been on a sojourn. It does not matter what appears to the eyes; how you may appear to people, or how well you have your "ducks in a row". It is not business as usual nor does it matter how we appear. What matters is that God is accelerating His work within each one of you. Your life is not about anything else but possessing that for which you have been chosen. You are the handful of seed scattered upon the mountain tops - the leavening that shall leaven this age.

We are further along and much closer to complete fulfillment than we have been able to recognize, for the kingdom that we seek is here. **It is within.**

If this calling of sonship is upon you, then you know that you have been walking on this path into His presence. It has probably been a long and lonely path, but it has been the path He has given you to walk - for this is why you are here.

God has most assuredly ruined you. He has ruined you for any other life short of complete fulfillment. You have seen and tasted of the powers of the age to come, and you cannot turn back. You have one reason for living; to follow Christ's path into sonship and to manifest the glory of God to a dead and dying age.

Whatever it takes, Oh Lord, do it in us. Whatever He requires, whatever He asks, our hearts are driven to be fully obedient unto Him.

We are not unwise as to the ways of the Lord, for we know that He will continue to stretch us beyond our limits. We know that the cost that will be levied is the elimination of the soul or adamic nature, but this is the path we have chosen - this is the path of sonship.

Make that pre-determined decision that no matter what He asks of you, no matter what He puts before you in the path; that you will give Him everything.

The Front Line

What does it mean to walk in sonship and to pursue God with all of your heart in this hour?

I thought about this word, "the front line", and thought about what it really meant. The term, "front line" was first derived from the battlefield, it was a term that described those individuals or that troop or regiment that had been sent forward "to the front". Sometimes they were sent in advance of the main troops, and on other occasions they were the ones that led the army into battle. They were the spearhead and their directive was to break thru the defenses of the enemy and establish a beachhead. Their lives were on the front line and they were expendable. They might have been living in trenches, but their lives were laid out on the line.

In this hour and at this time this would be a good description of the front line that the sons of God face. A whole new day and a whole new era is being established. It is the time for the kingdom of God to be established on every level; both in the heavens and on the earth. It is the time that every knee will bow before the Lord Jesus Christ. This is the time that the principalities and powers which have wielded such control over this world system are brought down. <u>This is the last beachhead</u>. This is the time of Christ's administration of the kingdom through His people; for to walk on the front line means to walk in this path of sonship and the calling of the sons of God.

We have seen numerous "front line" experiences of God's moving in the earth over the past several hundred years. God has brought many men on the scene to establish a break through or beachhead; as we have seen the progressive restoration of all things.

> **"and that He may send Jesus, the Christ appointed for you, whom heaven must receive until the period of the restoration of all things**

about which God spoke by the mouth of His holy prophets from ancient time." – Acts 3:21

We have been in a long session of the restoration of the kingdom which only now is coming to its zenith of fulfillment. During this time that we are walking we will see the manifestation of many sons that come to glory.

John Wycliffe, who lived in the 1300's, was the first person to translate the Bible into English for the common man. It was amidst terrific opposition from the Catholic church, yet Wycliffe established a beachhead.

John Huss in the 1400's, and John Calvin in the 1500's, continued to push against the resistance and restraints of their day to see the progressive restoration of God's truth in the earth.

William Tyndale, a contemporary of Martin Luther in the 1500's, was the first person to print the New Testament in the English language. Zwingli in the 1500's, Tyndale's contemporary, continued preaching the reformation of the Catholic church.

Martin Luther, also in the 1500's, lived on the front line as he came against the satanic manifestation of the Catholic church during his time. The Catholic church, so satanically driven, was set to control the minds and hearts of people. Luther, Tyndale, Huss, Zwingli and many others stood against this rising tide of evil and declared it was enough. They put their lives on the line.

Martin Luther is well known for his statement, "the just shall live by faith" - as he stood against the church and its practices during his time. A great beachhead was taken.

In the 1700's John and Charles Wesley came on the scene and continued to push against the resistance and limitations that existed at their time.

But the path of the righteous is like the light of dawn, That shines brighter and brighter until the full day. – Proverbs 4:18

Down through time there has always been a voice, a remnant that God used to change the age and bring the restoration of His spirit in the earth one more step. Many died as martyrs to establish a beachhead.

Over the past 100 years beachhead after beachhead has been established.

At the beginning of the 20th century, what has been called the Azusa street experience, came forth when God began to pour out the Holy Spirit. People began to be "born again" – baptized in the Holy Spirit. This was a tremendous beachhead that was met with very strong demonic resistance, yet the hunger and drive on the part of God's remnant overcame all odds to see the truth continue to come forth.

In the last 50 to 60 years we have seen the restoration of the 5 fold ministry of Christ; the apostles, prophets, evangelists, pastors and teachers. We have seen the movement of the Holy Rollers, the Latter Rain movement, the Pentecostal movement, and many others. There have been so many steps to restoration along the way, each the cutting edge of what God was doing during their time.

Each manifestation may have been unusual or soulish, but the believers were doing everything they could to walk in the light that was given to them at that time.

Unfortunately many casualties followed these movements because people built kingdoms around their revelation. We have seen the rise of one denomination after another. Rather than a testimony of the great spreading of the gospel to mankind it has been more of a testimony of man's rejection of God, for people would only go so far and then they would stop.

One man of God after another came on the scene and made a stand, embracing a whole new level of restoration. And another beachhead was established. As long as that man lived the church moved forward, but after his death the church would eventually stop and build a kingdom around that revelation or experience. We have seen this time and again, and so you had the rise of another denomination, each persecuting the one which followed.

The greatest persecution of God's move in the earth has always been led by those who stopped moving forward, and in turn persecuted those who continued to move on. These are rather strong words but if you look closely you will see, however subtle it may appear, that this has been so.

And so it is with what God is doing today. This time, however, there will not be that which looks back and says; "wasn't that great". "That was the 'Sons of God' movement". That was the sonship movement".

Now what is God going to do? What is the next thing?

There will be no "next thing". There will not be another move of God. We have come to the culmination of times, and this is why you are here.

You may look at your life and see issues that have no resolution. No answers. You could take this very personal, yet I believe God has tied you into something far greater than your own personal deliverance; He has tied you into the release of sonship. He has tied you into that which He is finishing in the earth.

What is the answer? The answer is sonship.

You are not looking for a little more power, a little more authority, a few more of the gifts that you might go out and work for Jesus. This is not about working for God. This is about manifesting God incarnate, through you, to this dying age.

As He opens the portals of this new day your eyes are seeing and you are tasting of the powers of His age that is here. Your spirit has gone into deep travail, a travail to see manifested within every aspect of your being the realities of sonship - that for which Christ died for and paved the way for you to follow.

There is only 1 thing that will satiate the drive and hunger He has put within you; <u>your full redemption</u>. This is the promise. He will perfect those things concerning you - spirit, soul and body.

The Cloud is linking hands with us, for it is the time for their fulfillment as well.

We are right here at the wall, and the demand is, "complete it now within us Lord". This is what the sons of God are all about. It is not about business as usual. We have come to the time of the complete manifestation of the Son within the sons.

<u>*This is the front line.*</u>

Notes:

Section 2

The Emergence of Sonship

- **Metamorphosis**
- **Sonship Is An Experience**
- **What is the Mark of Sonship**
- **The Path of His Cross**
- **The Ministry of the Sons of God**

Metamorphosis

The transition into a living reality of sonship in the earth, taking abode within a people, is a release that has not been seen since Christ's advent. God is taking a people into the reality of sonship and into the step-by-step changes that are necessary at this time.

When we stop and ponder what we are not only contending for, but what God has revealed for this time, and what He has emblazoned upon our hearts and minds, we realize what a miracle it is. It is something which has not been visited on this plane of life ever before.

> **2Co 3:18 But we all, with unveiled face beholding as in a mirror the glory of the Lord, are being transformed into the same image from glory to glory, just as from the Lord, the Spirit.**

We all have had concepts, perhaps visions, of what it means to change. As we stand before the Lord and behold Him, as the scripture says, "we are changed". But what is it that is really happening? What is it that we are experiencing? In many ways this change can be very difficult to perceive because we are straddled for the most part with our ongoing perception of ourselves.

God paints a very interesting picture when He speaks of change. Let's take a closer look at the literal Greek for the word "transformed". The Greek word for transform is metamorphoo, from which we get metamorphosis - the changing from one order of creation literally into something new. The best analogy is the change which occurs to a worm when it becomes a butterfly - it is a complete change in the order of creation.

In this scripture what God is conveying is that there is a change that is happening to His sons, a change so drastic and complete, that they are literally changed into a different order of creation. They are no longer patterned after the physical "Adam" but are created in the image of the "2nd Adam", Christ. (1 Cor. 15)

How is this happening? Up to this point it has been a gradual change, but the time is drawing to a close. There is the promise in Malachi that the Lord whom you seek will suddenly come to His temple. Who is this temple? We are, of course. We are His temple, a temple made without hands. We are the housing of His glory. Until the time of His final appearing within you, call it His "suddenly", or call it a change "in the twinkling of an eye"; until that time you are changing almost imperceptibly every time you come before Him.

Now let's go back to the Greek literal word - metamorphoo. You are changing, and this change that you are experiencing is changing you into a different order of creation. I know this can sound a bit strange, but the change you are experiencing as you walk in His presence is changing you one step at a time; literally changing you into His new creation.

You are literally changing from what you have known as life on this physical plane (at the base level of your essence, call it your DNA) into a new creation. It does not matter if you are at the initial stages of this change, what you have known of your human existence is changing, and it starts at the root level of all that you are.

You can look at yourself in the mirror. Yes, you look the same. Perhaps a bit older, maybe a bit more worn for the path you have been on, but still, it looks like you. And this is where you are wrong. This is where you must break the bonds or concepts you have had of yourself, because you are changing into a new order; you are becoming something new. As Isaiah the prophet spoke; "Behold I will do something new, will you be aware?"

We are talking about a change that is more than a mental paradigm shift; more than the experience of the renewing of your mind as Romans 8 speaks. Everything that you are experiencing leads to one thing; **an entire change of the structure of what you are**. Even though the final completion of what you are to be awaits a final appearing of the Lord to you, never-the-less this change is happening moment by moment - ***right now***.

This has been one of the challenges that the Lord has had to deal with concerning His sons, for although they are changing, they have not seen themselves as being any different. This inability to recognize these changes has limited God's sons from walking in and manifesting the deeper levels of spirit that God has ordained for them to walk in.

This is where God's sons are positioned right now. In all of the annals of history we have come to this singular time of God's completion within His people. This is not waiting for Armageddon, or some external event outside of us to occur. We are not waiting for His final appearing in the clouds. We have come to the time of completion and it is now – *and it is within you*.

So much of the thinking in this age in which we live conditions us to live in the future or in the past. As sons we cannot be caught living in a future or past tense mentality - always reaching but never obtaining. The closest parallel to this mentality is what is called the rapture theory which is so heavily fostered by the satanic and religious world.

I have never ascribed to this "rapture" theory - one moment you're here, the next moment just caught away – instantly. That totally circumvents the work of the cross that must be done as God's sons are purged, purified and refined, according to the Book of Daniel (Dan 12:10).

However, what we are dealing with is what I would call an exponential release or an exponential change. The more you change, the more you are able to change. The more you see, the more you are able to see. Do you understand? It is what I would call the "snowball effect". As that snowball begins to gain momentum cascading down the mountain, it gathers both in speed and mass. It experiences almost an exponential rate of speed and change as it cascades down that mountain.

This is what is happening within you as you are changing. The greater your exposure to the Lord, the greater your change. And the speed and momentum of this change just continues to expand. What is very unique is that you are not just "changing", you are "metamorphosizing". You are becoming a new creation that is unfolding at an exponential rate.

We can have all these concepts about what it will be like to walk in the reality of sonship, but when it begins to manifest, those concepts go right out the window because the reality is never quite what the mind of man can imagine anyway.

The sons of God have been in this work of the cross for a very long time, and the fruits of these changes are only now beginning to appear. There is a shift happening, a shift from walking as soulish Christians - as mere men - into walking as the spiritual sons of God that we indeed are.

God's sons are beginning to "see" with the eyes of their spirit and "hear" with the faculties of their spiritual hearing. These are no longer overshadowed by the soul's inputs or distortions. We are beginning to "hear" on a dimension that cannot be heard by the carnal mind. This transition is huge because this release is exponentially accelerating.

We have been partakers of a great takeover, the takeover of the spirit in ascendancy over the soul and the physical. All of the blessings, the endowments, the promises and prophecies are being fulfilled. These releases and these changes have their fulfillment and their reality first on the spiritual plane, then they filter down to the soul and physical body. As we continue in this process of the redemption of all that we are, we begin to understand that our spirit, soul, and body are being transformed and preserved blameless.

We are beginning to realize that we are a triune being having a spirit, a soul, and a body. We also understand that the demand in the spirit is to become a spiritual people who are led and directed by the spirit.

In Romans 8:14, Paul speaks..... "they that are led by the Spirit of God, these are the sons". We have taken that in times past to speak of being led by the Spirit of God, the Holy Spirit - Christ. But I believe we are missing this if we relegate that scripture to just this level of interpretation. I believe Paul is speaking about the sons that are led by their spirit, for to be led by your spirit, which is one with Christ and the Father, is to be led by the Holy Spirit. This really can't be separated.

So what is the point. Somehow we still have a way of relegating all of this to the future rather than understanding that you are living and walking this reality out, moment by moment. It is a deep recognition of not only the Christ in you, but the realization of who you truly are.

At what point do you begin to manifest the authority and control that begins to change things in this age? The answer is simple, at the point you begin to walk as the spiritual son that you are - at the point that the spirit takes ascendancy over the soul.

This has been a process which has not come easily. It has taken the deep work of the cross within the lives of God's sons that would finally bring them to the point where their spirit could begin to control the unction of their soul.

Let's take this up another level. Break the concept or bond of how you have seen yourself in the past. You are not your mind, your soul, or your physical. You are your spirit - that is really who you are. The more the cross brings to an end the life of the soul and physical, the more the spirit comes forth. Though your body has been a reflection of your soul and physical existence - to a large degree - the body of this new creation that you are becoming will reflect who and what you are in your spirit (1Cor 15).

We are talking about a change of identity. We are talking about walking in control. We are taking the "Pollyanna" out of our concepts and beginning to understand what it means to walk and manifest this change. We are one major step closer to the completion of this work and the laying aside of this earthly temple.

We are becoming a spiritual people who are starting to relate more and more to the spirit realm than we have to this natural level of existence. If we are to complete what needs to be done in the spirit, we must quickly come to the place where we relate to the spiritual world, and to the spirits which have governed, more than we relate to this natural plane.

When you move up into the realm of spirit what you have known as limitation, ceases. All limitation is bound up in the realm of the senses (soul), and in the realm of the physical. When you step out of the realm of the soul, you step out of the realm of limitation.

When you realize and grasp that you are truly unlimited, and that you have all knowledge; **this is where it all happens.** This is where we have come. This progressive unfolding of God's spirit within each of His sons is bringing them out of the realm of limitation and into the "freedom of the glory of the liberty of the sons of God" (Ro.8). We are led and driven by the very spirit that dwells within us, the very essence of who we really are.

This identifies the changes that are taking place as we enter into a level of sonship that we have not seen before, **and it all works because we are moving from our spirit.** The authority, control, and the seer ministry function from this point moving forward.

This deep change that is happening within you is gaining momentum. You are changing into a new order. This is the season of the fulfillment of Christ within the sons. As Isaiah the prophet spoke, "Behold I will do something new, will you be aware?" This is a new thing that God is doing. You are something new. You are a new creation. It's time to stop seeing men as trees walking and see the manifesting changes that have already come within you (Mark 8:24).

See it and Be it. It is the time.

Sonship
Is An Experience

The perception of the religious community and the new age community in many ways parallel themselves. Both have a measure of the truth but are so slanted that both are miles away from the truth. One accepts the reality of Jesus - but denies the power and all that Jesus in truth died to create. The other opens up wide to the principles of the psychic & spiritual realms, but denies the door, the Lord Jesus Christ.

Everyone is clamoring to find the door of entrance into the Kingdom and yet both sides have missed it.

The message of the Lordship of Jesus Christ has truly been lost or buried beneath a torrent of deception, propagated by the spiritual wickedness in high places. You either have those who are hopeless, believing for a rapture in their thinking, even if not in doctrine - or you have the self-realizationists, who are going to do it themselves.

The new age movement, although not new, has seen a gradual spawning of outreach since the late 1920's. Indeed, what we see unfolding in the earth right now is not new, but has been slowly emerging for the past 50 to 60 years. I am not saying that there is not a measure of truth in what the new age movement has tapped into, but without Christ, it is only a partial truth, and thus - a lie.

The teaching and doctrines of this day, devoid of the message of the Lordship of Jesus Christ, has become more and more palatable to Christians. Let's walk with Jesus, but keep Him at arm's distance. And it has been in this arena of complacency that we have seen so much deception propagated within the church.

What we have seen in the past 40 years in America is what I term the "demoralization of America". The TV, print media, and the internet has provided a huge platform for the dissemination of so much perversion and evil. More and more the American public has grown to accept immorality as morality, and unbelief as faith.

Interesting! Unbelief as faith! What do I mean - we have accepted a level of complacency as a faith that is holding fast, but in truth - it has been a level of unbelief that refuses to enter in to what God has spoken.

A mantle of sonship is beginning to rest upon a few; a calling to move into the highest level of life that man has known. Not a level relegated below the angels and below Christ, but a level in His presence - identical with Christ - who opened the door for many sons to come forth. "In my Father's house are many dwelling places....we know that scripture. Yes, there are many dwelling places, but we don't have to stay in the foyer. We can take the elevator to the top floor and live there. It is available for all, but very few have had <u>eyes to see</u> or <u>hearts to understand</u>.

The judgment that issues forth in this day is upon the deception in high places; those who have been specifically set to deter the manifestation of sonship within a people. Where do you find this deception? - propagated on every level through the religious spirit. What will it take to see the destruction of the fortresses of evil in the earth? Sonship. This is the only level that will accomplish the works of God in this hour. Nothing less.

In these days of the kingdom, God's message is one of authority and power, for the agency of the judgments of God in this hour will be His sons (Psalms 149:5-9). We are not tuning into what will come to pass and sending up a red flag; God's sons are creating - and will create - what is coming to pass.

There are not many believers, *nor do there need to be*, who understand that God's moving in the earth, during this time, is not a sovereign event. God has committed Himself to move through His channels, His sons. If Satan and the hosts of wickedness can dull your perception just a little, then you will not enter into this level. You can not enter into the portals of the kingdom without the ability to see it, for this is the level where sons make things happen.

There is no other message. Christ said in the New Testament, "I come not to bring peace, but I come with a sword" - *the message of this hour is one of moving in His power.*

The two revelations that the hosts of wickedness have been set to discredit and block are:

> **1. The revelation of Christ in you and**
> **2. The revelation that God is going to move through His sons to complete the judgments in the earth.**

The world is waiting for an appearance of the Messiah, Christ, coming in the clouds where every eye shall see Him (1 Thess 4:17). But the truth is that the appearing of God and Christ, in this hour, will first be visited upon the earth through His sons before the subsequent appearing where every eye shall see Him.

The judgments of God are being manifested in the earth and yet they are still to come. We are both in the process of their manifestation, yet we are at the door of so much that is yet to unfold. What His sons are beginning to understand is that what comes forth on the earth is a product of what is being created as Christ begins to direct and lead His army (Joel 2:11). God's sons are the ones who will bring the greatest expanse of this tribulation causing earth changes that have already begun.

His word has come to shake the heavens and the earth, and that word is the word through your mouth. Let everyone else discern the signs of the times, God's sons are the ones creating the times. Let everyone else get prepared for what is to come on the earth – God's sons are the ones creating it. The travesty is that very few have really understood this.

God has always moved through a remnant. It has never been about the multitudes - it was never about many. It has always been about the few, the remnant, through which God would move. If you recall the story of Gideon's 300 (Judges 7:7), God sifted an army of thousands down to a remnant of 300 who in turn thwarted an enemy of enormous size that was set against them. In Psalms 72:16 God refers to His people as a handful of seed, scattered on the mountains, the harvest which will shake the cedars of Lebanon.

You are the leaven that He has sent into the earth that will change this age. The Lord speaks of the weak who confound the mighty; the lame who shall take a prey and the downcast that are rising up to embrace their inheritance. Make no mistake, this is who we are - the sons of the Living God. And God's joy is to work through earthen vessels to bring forth a creation the like of which has never before been seen on this planet, or anywhere else.

There is a growing presence of many intelligences from other levels of existence who have come to behold what is taking place on the earth at this time. God is doing something new that no eye has ever seen. No one, especially the other intelligences and spiritual orders which have come to watch, understand just what it is that God is doing. But we know, for it is the mystery hidden for all ages - Christ in you (Ephesians 3). We are not talking about some new age "the Christed one", we are talking about God incarnate, Jesus incarnate, within us in a oneness that will please the Father. And everyone is watching - even the Angels - with awe, as God releases and finishes the creation of a new species of life - *the Sons of the Living God.*

Our thrones are being set in order and our crowns are being given to us. You must take that crown, accept it and wear it. You must know what it is that you have been given and what you have become. We may take our crowns, as the four and twenty elders in Rev. 4, and cast them before Him, but never-the-less, they are our crowns ... the crowns of the Kings and Priests of this age that we have become.

All throughout the scriptures you find numerous references to the "Army of God" going out in battle array. In the 149th Psalm it speaks about the execution of judgment that will come forth.

> **149:1 Praise the LORD! Sing to the LORD a new song, And His praise in the congregation of the godly ones.**
> **2 Let Israel be glad in his Maker; Let the sons of Zion rejoice in their King.**
> **3 Let them praise His name with dancing; Let them sing praises to Him with timbrel and lyre.**
> **4 For the LORD takes pleasure in His people; He will beautify the afflicted ones with salvation.**
> **5 Let the godly ones exult in glory; Let them sing for joy on their beds.**

> 6 Let the high praises of God be in their
> mouth, And a two-edged sword in their hand,
> 7 To execute vengeance on the nations, And
> punishment on the peoples;
> 8 To bind their kings with chains, And their
> nobles with fetters of iron;
> 9 To execute on them the judgment written;
> This is an honor for all His godly ones. Praise
> the Lord!

In the book of Joel reference is made to the end time army of God:

> 2:1 Blow a trumpet in Zion, And sound an
> alarm on My holy mountain! Let all the
> inhabitants of the land tremble, For the day
> of the LORD is coming; Surely it is near,
> 2 A day of darkness and gloom, A day of
> clouds and thick darkness. As the dawn is
> spread over the mountains, So there is a great
> and mighty people; There has never been
> anything like it, Nor will there be again after
> it To the years of many generations.
> 3 A fire consumes before them, And behind
> them a flame burns. The land is like the
> garden of Eden before them, But a desolate
> wilderness behind them, And nothing at all
> escapes them.

The book of Revelation is also full of references to the battle and war that is waged, on every plane of existence, as the Lord begins to subject every kingdom unto the Father.

We also read in 1Cor 15:19-26:

> 19 If we have hoped in Christ in this life only,
> we are of all men most to be pitied.
> 20 But now Christ has been raised from the
> dead, the first fruits of those who are asleep.
> 21 For since by a man came death, by a man also
> came the resurrection of the dead.
> 22 For as in Adam all die, so also in Christ all
> shall be made alive.

> **23 But each in his own order: Christ the first fruits, after that those who are Christ's at His coming,**
> **24 then comes the end, when He delivers up the kingdom to the God and Father, when He has abolished all rule and all authority and power.**
> **25 For He must reign until He has put all His enemies under His feet.**
> **26 The last enemy that will be abolished is death.**

It is in the plan and heart of the Father that every knee will bow before the Lord Jesus Christ. Every tongue will confess His lordship and every dominion will be brought down. Every kingdom will be subjected unto the Lord. It will only be after every knee has bowed before the Lord, that the Lord Jesus Christ will then hand over the kingdoms of this world to our God and Father.

Concerning the scriptures some have developed a rapture theory. A rapture that takes place before all of the judgments and the tribulation - the old "fire escape" mentality. But look around, we are in the midst of them right now. The truth is that God has brought forth His sons in this hour as instruments of His judgments. He has brought forth His sons to bring down one age and to create another.

There is a type of rapture, if you want to call it that, that is even now taking place within the hearts of those God has prepared for this day. It is what has been referred to in the book of Revelation (Rev. 12:5) as the man-child who is "caught up" to rule and reign with Christ. The man-child being "caught up" literally refers to the vibrational state of being that happens as the sons of God pass through the heavens, as Christ did, in their ascent to sit in the presence of the Father. Call it a vibrational shift, or call it dwelling in His presence; in either event the sons of God are indeed caught up into His presence into a realm of ruling and reigning with Christ.

The day of God's sovereign moving is largely over, for this is the day of the Body of Christ and the Day of His army, who are drawn out in battle array. And it will be through God's human "channels", His sons, that the kingdoms of this age will be brought down and subjected to the Lord Jesus Christ. This is a day of great battle and a day of great conquering for the destiny of the sons of God is a destiny of overcoming.

If you have lived your life on the cutting edge, always reaching more deeply into what the Lord has been revealing to you, then you are living on the front line. You are living a life of conflict and overcoming. For the conflict, though waged against you in the spirit realm, has always been a precursor to conquering. The destiny of God's sons in this day is to walk as the overcomers spoken of in the book of Revelation.

In the scriptures it speaks about the victory that was once and for all time won by Christ on the cross. The conclusion is already written. The victory has been won. It must be that a people will walk out and enforce that victory against every force which has withstood the kingdom of God on every plane and level of existence.

That which has withstood His Lordship is being brought down; whether it is the principalities and powers that exist, or the resistance within your own heart.

It is not a time to be at ease in Zion; it is a time that the violent will take the kingdom by force (Matthew 11:72) . These are all scriptures we have read before, but this day these scriptures are being fulfilled. You have been called and set aside for this day, as the warring <u>Kings and Priests of God</u>. You are the sons of God, and it is God's good pleasure that He shall bruise the enemy beneath your feet.

The Mark of Sonship

Everyone has their own perception of what the scriptures refer to when they speak of the *mark of the beast*, but what about the *mark of His sons*. Here is perhaps a different slant for you to consider.

> **"I advise you to buy from Me gold refined by fire, that you may become rich, and white garments, that you may clothe yourself, and that the shame of your nakedness may not be revealed; and EYESALVE to anoint your eyes, that you may see". – Rev 3:18**

The anointing upon the eyes speaks of an ability to see, and the ability to perceive accurately is one of the most critical areas that exist for the believer in this day. In the same breath it is also very important that we never take what we have from God for granted. In the moment that we feel we have God "wired" and fully understand just what He is doing, it is in that moment of jeopardy that you stand to lose what you have.

God is moving on, and so we too must continue to expand, grow, and stay pliable; *new wineskins able to bear the new wine that God would bring. (Matthew 9:17)* You can look back at the history of Christianity to see what a failure the church has been from that perspective. Every time God wanted to bring something new it always caused division; sides were taken, lines were drawn. The old order would invariably persecute those that continued to move forward into the new thing that God was unveiling.

Why is this?

Each new level in God requires a deeper level of submission and abandonment; a deeper work of His cross. For many the cost was too great. How much it has grieved the spirit of the Lord that this was the chosen path of so many for hundreds of years. And the testimony to this gradual yet seemingly perpetual apostasy? - the rise of church after church espousing one doctrine after another; divided and persecuting the very move of God that preceded them.

How many of you recall the spiritual breakthroughs that occurred at the turn of the century? It was about 1907, and although it began happening around the world, I recall it from the stories of how it happened in Los Angeles. There were groups of believers seeking God ardently for they knew there was something more that was available. God was doing something new. They were seeking the baptism of the Spirit, as the Lord had begun to reveal to them, based on the day of Pentecost. And so, in the early 1900's around a place called Azusa Street, an outpouring of the Spirit began that sent shockwaves around the world - shockwaves to those who were and were not prepared to embrace this new level that God was bringing. For years that followed those initial believers were branded as worshipers of the devil - so great was the persecution.

This "baptism" thing was labeled as of "the occult", yet believers around the world began to come alive to the Spirit; truly experiencing a day of Pentecost in their lives.

It took more than 30 years for conventional Christianity to open up and accept this baptism experience as being "of God". Yet to this day you still have many churches who will not accept this very basic experience that began more than 100 years ago.

Since the 40's God has continued bringing a restoration of many new truths for His people to embrace and, *more and more*, we have seen *more* churches and *more* belief systems arise. Why? Because people have a hard time accepting something *new*. They want God in a box, and God cannot be put into a box.

The travesty of Christianity is that you have so many groups believing so many different aspects of what they have seen of God; yet not willing to go any further. The rise in churches in this past 100 years is not a testimony to man's attempt to disciple the world, it is a witness of judgment against man himself for his choice in not following on after what God was bringing forth.

Your progress in God is directly related to your perception, and your perception is directly related to the depth of the work of the cross in your life. How does the scripture in the beatitudes go? "Blessed are the pure in heart, for they shall see God." (Matt 5:8) If you can't see the provision, you won't reach for it. If you do not know the hour of your visitation, you will not possess it. Perhaps in the final analysis it comes down to the choices and decision you make to truly follow on after the Lord.

Perception is a commodity highly revered in "spiritual circles"; one that is sorely in need. We are constantly admonished .... "guard what you have"..... for people would kill for it.

In the scriptures it speaks of the mark of the beast, and the mark of God's sons. Take a moment to read these scriptures:

> **4 And they were told that they should not hurt the grass of the earth, nor any green thing, nor any tree, but only the men who do not have the seal of God on their foreheads. Rev 9:4**

> **16 And he causes all, the small and the great, and the rich and the poor, and the free men and the slaves, to be given a mark on their right hand, or on their forehead Rev 13:16 (speaking of the beast)**

> **9 And another angel, a third one, followed them, saying with a loud voice, "If anyone worships the beast and his image, and receives a mark on his forehead or upon his hand, he also will drink of the wine of the wrath of God... Rev 14:9-10a**

> **4 And I saw thrones, and they sat upon them, and judgment was given to them. And I saw the souls of those who had been beheaded because of the testimony of Jesus and because of the word of God, and those who had not worshiped the beast or his image, and had not received the mark upon their forehead and upon their hand; and they came to life and reigned with Christ for a thousand years. Rev 20:4**

> **And I looked, and behold, the Lamb was standing on Mount Zion, and with Him one hundred and forty-**

> **four thousand, having His name and the name of His Father written on their foreheads. Rev 14:1**
>
> **and they shall see His face, and His name shall be on their foreheads. Rev 22:4**

Many of us have probably read these scriptures before but did you realize that they speak about perception? The forehead is an area of your body that is concerned with perception. The ancient Chinese and Middle Eastern religions speak of the "3rd eye". In "new age" circles today there is much talk about "chakras". What are chakras? They are energy vortex centers on your body where you process information. The area on the forehead is also referred to as the 3rd eye, or the 6th chakra. Yes, these are all eastern terminologies, but the fact remains that your spiritual eyesight is centered on your forehead.

Just as the mark of the beast is on the "forehead", so the mark of the sons of God is on the "forehead". The sealing of God's sons is through their **ability** to see and to hear. The sealing of the mark of the beast upon the apostate is their **inability** to see; their blindness. It is simple, but astounding. You will understand more and more the dynamics of the assault and persecution that will continue to unfold during this day because of this.

We see unfolding in the earth during this time those that walk in great light; yet we see many who walk in great darkness. This is a sign of the times we are in, and it will continue to unfold. We are walking in the simultaneous manifestation of great light and great darkness during this season.

What does this mean? Those whom God has called and sealed unto Himself will have a perception and level of sight that clearly separates them from those who have become darkened in their understanding. Realize, it is not enough to just go along with the crowd. It is not enough to attend church on Sunday. If you are called to this walk of sonship, then God has truly called you "outside the camp" (Heb. 13:13).

The whole issue in these days is a personal one between you and the Lord. An ability to see means so much more than just a nice revelation here and there; it is a deep understanding and ability to see the Lord on a dimension that will literally "change" you into His likeness. To those who walk with the mark of the beast it will not seem very apparent; void of perception, everything will seem just fine. To those who have been sealed on their foreheads by the Lord, will come a deep insight and ability to see. They will have more than just revelation, more than just insight; they will experience a walk of transformation as they are changed from glory to glory. The scriptures tell us that when you see Him as He is, you will be changed into His likeness (1Jn3:2).

We live in a time of great deception and that deception is directly related to the inability that people have to see. If you function from the soul realm, you are prone to the thinking of the flesh, and highly susceptible to deception which functions from the soul. The mark of the beast which is upon the forehead is the flip side of the mark of God's sons, for God's sons move with great clarity and sight, while upon those who are passing away there exists the darkness and inability to know the truth.

> **So I went to the angel, telling him to give me the little book. And he said to me, "Take it and eat it; it will make your stomach bitter, but in your mouth it will be sweet as honey." I took the little book out of the angel's hand and ate it, and in my mouth it was sweet as honey; and when I had eaten it, my stomach was made bitter. – Rev 10:9-10**

This scripture is one that most all of you have read, over and over, but let's look at it again.

The word - the revelation of Christ - is likened as to that which is "sweet as honey". We also understand that the process from the ingesting of the word to the manifestation of that word through us, can be compared to the "bitter". This process is the day to day dying out of the flesh and soul nature within; so that the word might be fully manifested in us. This is the process; a death, burial, and a resurrection born out of each and every experience of the word in us. Every time there is a death there will be a resurrection as you continue to spiral up higher and higher into His presence.

As much as you might want your family or your loved ones to really understand and embrace this new day that God is bringing, it really cannot be done without a commensurate preparation in the heart of every individual hearer.

How do you explain this walk in the spirit in this hour? You really cannot. No more than you can explain the existence of God or Christ. As the word portrays in 1st Cor 1:21; you cannot receive a revelation of God through the mental process of analysis, because nothing is going to make sense.

What is coming forth now is first born of the spirit; literally your spirit, as it comes alive to God on a level you never experienced before. We have yet to fathom the depths of what God is establishing during this time - for it bypasses the ability of our mind to understand.

> **Then there will be two men in the field; one will be taken and one will be left. "Two women *will be* grinding at the mill; one will be taken and one will be left. "Therefore be on the alert, for you do not know which day your Lord is coming. - Mat 24:40-42**

The traditional Scofield approach to this scripture is about the rapture.....one taken (raptured), another left. But it has nothing to do with a rapture, not in that context. This scripture actually speaks of the moving of God during this season of time and the one who is taken, is taken in judgment. The one remaining is the one whose heart has been prepared for this time.

We are talking about the mark of sonship; the mark that rests upon His sons. And this deals with the ability once again to see - those who are able to "see" the time of their visitation.

> **I advise you to buy from Me gold refined by fire so that you may become rich, and white garments so that you may clothe yourself, and *that* the shame of your nakedness will not be revealed; and eye salve to anoint your eyes so that you may see. - Rev 3:18**

As we continue to spiral up higher and higher into His presence we are in a constant process of buying gold, refined by the fire of His presence. We are continually experiencing a death, burial and a resurrection, and in some instances, daily.

God is doing a quick work in the earth at this time. He is bringing forth many sons to glory while the judgments simultaneously come forth.

> "**Who has heard such a thing? Who has seen such things? Can a land be born in one day? Can a nation be brought forth all at once? As soon as Zion travailed, she also brought forth her sons. - Isa 66:8**"

As Isaiah the prophet spoke, "can a nation be born in a day?" Yes; for God is birthing a nation of sons quickly as they step over the time barrier that they have known.

As each of you continue to go through this process of death, burial and resurrection, the scales continue to fall off. You are ceasing to see men as trees walking. You are beginning to see and walk by your spirit.

The door is open. May we all enter through this open door during this season of change. And may we be able to recognize just how rapidly each of us are changing right now.

The mark of the beast is becoming more and more prevalent upon those who are passing away, but the mark of sonship is radiating forth from a remnant; those who have been called and chosen for this hour of glorification.

The Path of His Cross

> "Truly, truly, I say to you, unless a grain of wheat falls into the earth and dies, it remains alone; but if it dies, it bears much fruit. "He who loves his life loses it, and he who hates his life in this world will keep it to life eternal. "If anyone serves Me, he must follow Me; and where I am, there My servant will be also; if anyone serves Me, the Father will honor him. – John 12:24-26

The journey into sonship and the path to a life in His presence is an unfolding experience through the daily application of His cross in our lives. As we die out to the soul and the flesh nature we find that we come more and more alive to His spirit. There is no other way.

For some time we have been aware that we are in a time of accelerated change. To that end we have dedicated and consecrated our hearts to the process and to the demands that the Lord continues to make upon us. It is time the sons of God push through the door that has been opened for them. How we do that centers around our ability to grasp and appropriate the completion of the work of the cross in our life.

To understand the work of the cross in your life, and to work synergistically with the Lord to see its completion within you, is absolutely necessary if we are to hasten the process.

> "Behold, I am going to send My messenger, and he will clear the way before Me. And the Lord, whom you seek, will suddenly come to His temple; and the messenger of the covenant, in whom you delight, behold, He is coming," says the LORD of hosts. "But who can endure the day of His coming? And who can stand when He appears? For He is like a refiner's fire and like fullers' soap. "And He

will sit as a smelter and purifier of silver, and He will purify the sons of Levi and refine them like gold and silver, so that they may present to the LORD offerings in righteousness. – Malachi 3: 1-3

God's process of refining, changing, and maturing the sons, is one of the greatest wonders of this age. It truly is one of the "greater works". We may have thought of Psalms 116:15 in a different light, but truly "the death of His godly ones" is precious in His sight.

Precious in the sight of the LORD Is the death of His godly ones. - Psa 116:15

We are right at the door of the most transformational change we have ever experienced in our lives. I have no doubt that we are at the tail end of a change that is opening the portals of transformation.

This is about more than just a work of the cross or another step in the purification of the priesthood; this is about completing His will within you and through you. We are talking about the glorification of the believer. We are talking about resurrection life, and it will only happen as we stand in His presence. "He is the way, the truth and the life" – John 14:6

For many the work of the cross can be a vague and esoteric concept. What does it mean to go through the work of the cross? What does it feel like? How do you know you are in the work of the cross? The key is to really understand what the cross is and to be able to identify the hand of the Lord as He is working within you.

We are in the time that God is completing this work of the cross in His sons. We want to work in unison with the Lord to hasten the completion of that which He has begun within each of us. To understand this process we need to understand that the work of the cross deals with the dying out of the soul; the seat of the mind and the emotions of an individual.

"But who can endure the day of His coming? And who can stand when He appears? For He is like a refiner's fire and like fullers' soap. "And He will sit as a smelter and purifier of silver, and He will purify

> the sons of Levi and refine them like gold and silver, so that they may present to the LORD offerings in righteousness. – Mal 3:2-3

As we enter this day of His presence, we experience the fire of God more and more in our lives. People have not understood what is happening to them and they draw back, complain and become bitter; imminently losing out in their walk with God.

> **BUT MY RIGHTEOUS ONE SHALL LIVE BY FAITH; AND IF HE SHRINKS BACK, MY SOUL HAS NO PLEASURE IN HIM. But we are not of those who shrink back to destruction, but of those who have faith to the preserving of the soul. – Heb 10:38-39**

Perhaps in times past we have all been a bit of a "cross dodger". Perhaps we have tried to take ourselves off the cross, without really understanding. It is important that we understand what the Lord is requiring and how we can work in concert with Him to see the cross completed and not protracted in our life. Whether we have understood it or not; we have come to the time where God is completing the work of the cross in our lives.

What has escaped our attention is just how far we have come and how close we really are to the completion of this work - so much closer than we have been able to see.

The death of the flesh nature is not a doctrine; it is an experience that God's sons live every moment. As Paul spoke, "always carrying about in his body the death of Christ". Paul was very aware that he was dying out to the soul and flesh nature as he became more fully alive to God.

We may not have understood that we have been experiencing a deep work of the cross – a dying out to our old nature. We need to understand that we have a great deal of leverage in seeing the completion of this work of the cross in our life. How? Through working in unison with the Lord, rather than fighting the process. It is time to put to death the last vestige of the flesh; the reactions, the murmurings, the complaining, and the unbelief. All of it. That we might **live** in His presence.

There is only one place, and one place alone that we die, and that is in His presence. The cross is not completed anywhere else but in His presence. Re-read Malachi 3.

The Lord has taken great lengths to position each of His sons in just the right atmosphere to accelerate the completion of this process. And He knows just how to do that! He knows how to position you in just the right dynamics of circumstances to put you through the fire of refinement. We must understand that in the final analysis He is looking for a total submission and abandonment of all that we are before Him.

We have been marked for sonship. We have been marked to enter through the portals of life, as we have known, into the unlimited reality of Christ and sonship. It is an incredible calling and your life is in the throws of tremendous change. The work of the cross is the only path to real change. We need to set our will to work with Him, and not against Him; for God is hastening the completion of the cross in your life during this season. He is cutting the time short.

There is a time at which all undergo the process of death. The only question is, do we partake of the death process on this side of the veil or must we pass over to the other side for it to be completed. If we fully partake of the death to our soul nature on this side of the veil, then we will partake of a resurrection on this side of the veil. With death comes resurrection.

Let me explain this further. While in this body we have the opportunity to undertake change much more quickly than if we existed as spirit only. This may be a unique concept to you, and one that I cannot quote you verse and chapter. However, I will tell you this, as long as we are here on this side of the veil we are able to change and mature much more rapidly. The minute we pass to the other side of the veil and the soul in effect "sleeps", as the scripture points out, our ability to progress and mature in God moves at a much slower pace. Why? Because as a triune being have a soul, spirit and physical body, the dynamics create a much greater potential for the cross to be hastened.

If we undergo the death process on this side of the veil we will possess resurrection life. If this process of the cross is not completed before we die, then we will experience a transition and the process must be completed on the other side of the veil.

I would much rather complete the process on this side of the veil, here and now; and enter into the resurrection of our spirit, soul and body. Our ability to grow and change by embracing the cross positions us to do just that.

Understanding the dynamics behind the work of the cross and being able to **identify** what the Lord is doing - and **giving** yourself to Him in this process - is a huge step. You will walk without walls, without reactions, without anger or resentment and without bitterness to the path He has chosen for you to walk.

There is no path to sonship in the believer's life that does not course through a deep and total work of the cross. The problem has been that we have generally not been able to recognize the process when we were in the midst of it. To understand the requirements and demands He is making upon you and to grasp the experience of the work of the cross in your life hastens your completion.

God is finishing the job. He is putting the fire to the last tidbits of the flesh nature that have hindered our ability to see Him. There is no other way. We are being ushered in to live in His presence, 24/7. This provision is a reality now. We don't have to be perfect to move into this day of His Presence, but as we press in His appearing to us will complete the work and transformation.

As we rise into His presence the dross of the flesh falls away - the judgments issue forth from His throne - and the greater works unfold.

The Ministry of
The Sons of God

The sons of God have walked in an anointing before the Lord similar to Joseph. Many words and revelations have come over those who have been called in this hour. Like Joseph, it can feel as though you have been sold into slavery and then thrown into prison seemingly preventing those words from coming to pass. Not having walked in Joseph's shoes, it can be difficult to ascertain all that he experienced as God prepared him for the role he was destined to fulfill (Genesis 39-41).

Like Mary, God's sons have pondered over the words deep within their heart which God has spoken to them; never letting go of the vision. They have stood resolute before Him, in spite of what seemed to be an apparent delay or reversal.

We know there is no roadmap to sonship, yet the signs are all around us. One simply needs to delve into the scriptures to see the path of God's anointed ones. Although there have been signposts along the way, we must understand that we are walking terrain that has never been traversed before. This is new ground. We are working with God to write the last chapters, creating a map that will help many follow as these days unfold.

When Christ came a whole new age began. This was new ground. There had been prophecies in the Old Testament concerning Christ, but very few really knew what to look for. The only ones who truly recognized Christ were those to whom the Father had revealed Him to. The day of Christ's appearance in the flesh created a new day and nothing happened according to preconceived ideas.

In this day of Christ's appearing within in His sons we find a new day dawning; and once again nothing is happening according to any of the preconceived ideas that we might have had.

Currently the term "Joseph ministry" has been coined, quite often, in the context of providing sustenance and provision on this physical level. When you think of the story of Joseph in the Old Testament, you remember how God used him to govern Egypt and store all of the grain and food for seven years. Joseph became the provision to supply food during the seven years of drought, not only to Egypt but to surrounding lands for God's people.

Joseph's ministry was a type or foreshadowing of the ministry of Christ in these last days; but perhaps not in the context that we so readily think.

Many of us have seen churches focus on survival for the days ahead: the saving of grain and food, and a general preparation to what is perceived as a time of very intense tribulation. I feel we are missing a greater anointing that is unfolding if we limit the Joseph ministry to just this level of fulfillment.

The anointing of the Joseph ministry in this hour concerns not what we see on the physical level of provision, but what God's sons are becoming in their spirit. We are a part of the great "Joseph company" which God is raising up, but the provision is what the sons have become – and are becoming. We are His channel for the word and the authority in this age. The real preparation that will see God's people through these days right in front of us will not be the storing of physical level provisions; it will be what God has become within them.

The true spiritual Joseph ministry in this hour is found within the embodiment of Christ in His people. I am not saying that God will not raise up those who will provide a level of release or provision for those earthly needs that may exist, but the greater anointing resides in God's sons who have become the bread for this age.

You are the Joseph company. You are His life, His water and His bread, which He has prepared for those who are transitioning out of this dying age.

> **As to this salvation, the prophets who prophesied of the grace that *would come* to you made careful searches and inquiries, seeking to know what person or time the Spirit of Christ within them was indicating as He predicted the sufferings of Christ and the glories to follow. It was revealed to them**

that they were not serving themselves, but you, in these things which now have been announced to you through those who preached the gospel to you by the Holy Spirit sent from heaven—things into which angels long to look. - 1 Peter 1:10-12

To us, upon whom the ends of the ages have come, rests a great responsibility. God has endowed His sons with a great anointing to accomplish what He has sent them to do. God's sons must walk in and manifest that anointing which has been hovering over them for such a long time. The fulfillment of every word or prophecy which has been uttered by the Holy Spirit from ages past now hovers over you. Every word and every prophecy concerning these days to which we have come - every promise spoken of a people that the Lord would bring forth in this hour - is hovering right now, waiting to be fulfilled within each of you.

Often during personal ministry you can visually see the cloud of glory or the anointing of the Spirit hovering over a person; yet they were usually unable to perceive how close they were to a release. It just takes reaching up by faith and a drawing down to embrace a release which has already been given. Experiences and fulfillments often hover over His people awaiting those with enough faith to see it, pull it down, and walk in it.

One of the greatest wonders we will behold as we continue to step through the barriers of this age is the embodiment of His word in a people who fulfill what they have been prepared for in this hour. It truly transcends what we can imagine.

Now these things happened to them as an example, and they were written for our instruction, upon whom the ends of the ages have come. – 1 Cor 10:11

In the book of Revelation it tells how the jaws of the dragon are poised to destroy the man-child, the son, before his final manifestation in this hour. Yet even in light of these words, we know that Satan and his horde of evil are but unwilling tools of God in bringing forth the sons of God. Even back in the days of Joseph the jaws of the dragon sought to destroy Joseph, but God used it to bring him forth (Rev 12:4).

It is no different now as God brings forth His sons.

Sometimes we can get a glorified concept of how the prophets walked before us. I think we may do them an injustice, for they walked - as each of us do in this day – bearing the reproach, confronted with fears from within and from without; often times wrestling over the promises and directives which God revealed to them. Joseph was tried until the day that word came to pass; as the psalmist in Psalms 105 spoke:

"until the time that his word came to pass, the word of the Lord tested him". - Psa 105:19

Upon each of God's sons rests a great endowment of grace, because the words and revelations the Lord has spoken over this generation of people have been beyond the scope of our faith, beyond the scope of our grasp or understanding. On the level of the soul it can be difficult not to stagger at the enormity of God's word.

It is now time for the word to be made flesh once again. Christ was the first born of many brethren, and God is at this time bringing many sons to glory. You have been given a new pair of shoes, only they may be a few sizes too big. You only begin to fill these shoes as the Lord brings you into the maturity of sonship.

The fight of faith is not about the day to day psychic or spiritual warfare we find ourselves drawn into. It is not about the daily pressures we may face. It is about reaching into or grasping that faith to see God's word and His prophecies that have lain dormant for several thousand years – fulfilled. And that time is now.

I encourage you to go through the New Testament and write down every prophecy concerning God's intent for His people in this hour. Go through the word, write them down, take them and meditate upon them. There are many, many prophecies and words over a people; a royal priesthood, that God is raising up in this hour.

It is the time that every word spoken of through the mouths of the prophets from ages past to have their fulfillment within you - now.

Christ is the first born of many brethren, and greater works than what Christ has done you will do. This is nothing new, this is scripture. The only difference is that we are addressing a reality that has come to its time of fulfillment.

It is staggering to realize how most of the Christian world has fallen short of becoming the Word, "once again", made flesh. The Word says, "will I find the faith in the earth". What is the Lord looking for? He is looking for His sons; those who decide it is time to stop the parade, and declare that not another moment will pass without that Word being fulfilled within them.

Sonship is one of the greatest promises concerning God's people in this hour (Ro. 8). Resurrection life is another. If you have truly heard these words, if you have truly heard these prophecies which have come by the spirit, then you have already been thrust into the travail of spirit to see them brought forth within you.

Is this comfortable? No, it is not. But is it necessary? Yes, absolutely!

Until these words, visions and prophecies come to pass within you, you will be tried. You will be purged, purified and refined (Daniel 12:10). There is no other path we can take to complete the glorification that God has destined His sons to partake of.

Faith does not stagger at the enormity of the words and prophecies that are destined to be fulfilled in a people in this hour, because this is His faith. This is where the warfare is truly centered. "Will He find the faith?" This is the Front Line.

The warfare and inner conflict you experience on a daily level can feel very, very personal. When you are in hand to hand combat, everything gets up close and personal really quick. The Christian world still lives with a Pollyanna view of reality, but the truth is that God is raising up His army.

Indeed - we are here, and we are pressing against the walls that have withheld the releases promised for this hour.

Notes:

Section 3

The Travail
Of All Creation

- **The Travail of Sonship**
- **One Heart & One Mind**

The Travail of Sonship

> For the anxious longing of the creation waits eagerly for the revealing of the sons of God. For the creation was subjected to futility, not willingly, but because of Him who subjected it, in hope that the creation itself also will be set free from its slavery to corruption into the freedom of the glory of the children of God.
>
> For we know that the whole creation groans and suffers the pains of childbirth together until now. And not only this, but also we ourselves, having the first fruits of the Spirit, even we ourselves groan within ourselves, waiting eagerly for our adoption as sons, the redemption of our body. – Ro 8:19-23

We are in a season of time upon the earth that is seeing all of creation experience a tremendous level of travail. As we read in Romans, there is a groaning and travail that is being experienced by the sons of God as they lean into this time of transformation and the culmination of all things.

Unless you have experienced childbirth, the term "travail" may be a bit foreign to you. Even if you are familiar with the term the actual experience of travail can be difficult to convey.

Women who have given birth to children understand travail and the pain and commitment that is involved. When you are pregnant and in birth you are completely committed to the process. Your body experiences travail as the baby is being delivered from the womb. This is the experience each of His sons are living during this time of the birthing of sonship within them.

We are only now beginning to understand the process of sonship and the travail that is involved to see the manifestation of the sons of God.

Just for the record, let's define travail:

1. Painfully difficult or burdensome work; toil
2. Pain, anguish or suffering resulting from mental or physical hardship
3. the pain of childbirth
4. To suffer the pangs of childbirth; be in labor
5. To toil or exert oneself.

This paints a fairly daunting picture, however this is what the sons of God are experiencing during this season. You are experiencing a travail to birth the Christ within you.

Romans 8 speaks of the travail of all creation. Creation, whether it is animate or in-animate, is in travail during this time; concurrently with the sons.

Even though Paul wrote the book of Romans under the anointing of the Holy Spirit a few thousand years ago, it has not been until this time that we could identify that the travail of sonship is truly in the earth. We are in travail, an aspect of the birthing process which is the point of no return; the point where the baby begins to emerge from the womb.

We know the jaws of the dragon stand at the door (Rev. 12), seeking to devour the man-child; but the man-child is caught up to rule and reign with Christ.

I don't know if we realize yet the significance of where we are now positioned, but this I know; travail has not been in the earth until very recently. What we have seen and what we have experienced over the past 30 to 40 years has been the process of the growth and development of the sons. Now things will begin to change dramatically.

All that we see unfolding in the earth today on the physical plane is a product of this travail which has begun. These travail pangs of birthing are also the travail pangs of His judgment in the earth.

With the birthing of the sons comes a commensurate judgment upon the powers of wickedness who have fought and resisted this release of the kingdom of God. There is no birthing without judgment.

The fulfillment of this travail that is being experienced both in creation and within God's sons, will see a level of authority and dominion come forth. The sons of God are being caught up to rule and reign with Christ; and with the release of the sons comes the release of judgment on a much deeper level than we have seen. They go hand-in-hand.

The signs of the times are becoming more and more blatant. The path of destruction America is on is like a freight train out of control. There will be no country and no government that will sidestep the judgments that have begun to accelerate at this time.

We have such a dichotomy within this generation. Everyone believes, as long as it is not "right now". The demons believe and shudder. Confront pastors and ministers about the reality of sonship and they will sidestep around that issue big time.

The reality of sonship exists in the realm of spirit, but it has been an "unrealized" potential until this time. This is the time that we will see the completion of what Christ set in motion so long ago.

Was it here 30 years ago? No, I don't think so. The baby was still in the womb, growing, becoming, getting ready for this time. The sons were not ready yet. Not until recently have we begun to sense that we have come to the fulfillment of this timeline.

When Paul lived and walked among the churches he understood the time in which he walked. He knew what the church was facing and yet he drove on in hope to possess that which Christ had called him for. This is a parallel time, for we are beginning to understand that we have come to the time of the birthing of the sons. We recognize the season which God's people have now entered.

Perhaps we have had some "Braxton-Hicks" in the past, (false labor pains), but the time of true labor is now here. God's sons have entered into travail; a travail that will see a son come to birth. The Son within them.

When people discuss earth changes, I don't believe they realize that they haven't seen anything yet. It is going to get very, very interesting because all of creation, ALL of creation is entering into this travail now.

> **And when these things begin to come to pass, then look up, and lift up your heads; for your redemption draweth nigh. – Luke 21:28**

Are we fearful or concerned? On the contrary as we see these things coming to pass we look up, as the Word states, "for our redemption draweth nigh". To those who walk in darkness it will be a time of great tribulation; they will seek shelter beneath the rocks for protection, as we read in the book of Revelation. But for the sons of God, it is a time of great release.

The judgments are in the earth and they are stepping up. How? Through the direct relationship of the change and manifestation of the sons of God. As they change, everything changes. They are the ark of God in this generation; they are God's instruments raised up for this time.

Perhaps now you are beginning to understand what has set you apart. It has been this insatiable hunger that has driven you on, in spite of all odds - in spite of your soul flesh or Adamic nature that has fought tooth and nail against what the Lord was doing within you.

We know the promise in Isaiah that as the sons come to birth that God will not shut the womb. Many sons shall come to glory. We have studied this and I believe we will see wave after wave of sons come forth during this time.

> **"Shall I bring to the point of birth and not give delivery?" says the LORD. "Or shall I who gives delivery shut *the womb?*" says your God.- Isa 66:9**

There are millions of Christians today, Christians that love the Lord, yet they do not seem to possess what it is that possesses you. Why is it that most people you have met do not understand what it is that is that drives you? It is because God has seared the vision you have seen so indelibly upon the fabric of your mind and spirit, that it has become all that you can do just to stay up with the urging and driving of your spirit that knows and recognizes the time to which we have come.

There is a groaning that we are experiencing at this time, a groaning as the scriptures state that is too deep to be expressed (Psalms 42:7). <u>It is born of the spirit within us that is longing for the freedom of sonship</u>. God has placed within you a spirit that is crying out for the adoption of sonship, for the completion of that which He has begun. We have been propelled into the final phases that will manifest in full and complete sonship.

This is the time that we are seeing a travail that will bring many sons to glory. The dragon may seek to devour the man-child, but the Lord is the fire around the child, and the glory in the midst (Zech 2:5). This time of travail will not cease without which we will see the full releases and fulfillments ordained for this day.

> **And the dragon stood before the woman who was about to give birth, so that when she gave birth he might devour her child. And she gave birth to a son, a male *child*, who is to rule all the nations with a rod of iron; and her child was caught up to God and to His throne. – Rev 12:4b-5**

If God has called you out to walk with Him in this new day, then do not think it strange as you experience this deep groaning and travail of the Spirit. Do not be discouraged, but recognize that the promise in the Word speaks that before Zion travailed, she brought forth (Is 66:7).

The sons God is bringing to birth are in travail. It has taken a long season of preparation; for the Christ within them was not yet ready. Yet it is not ours to judge how long this season has needed to last in order to see a completion within the hearts of God's sons.

We are in the stage of what is called, "transition", and this is the most difficult time of the birthing process because it cannot be reversed. We know the dragon stands at the gates intent on the destruction of God's sons; but what the spirit world is incapable of comprehending is that this mystery has already been completed.

When Christ ascended on high it was finished. The plan of God in the earth was set in motion awaiting the sons who would walk out the fulfillment which was finished and completed since the foundations of the earth.

It is finished, yet we are in travail to see it completed. This travail of the sons of God is genuinely a mystery, for this is not something that we have beheld before. This is not something that has previously been in the earth. Who can describe such a thing. Where in the annals of history can you go to look up and understand the travail of sonship?

God's sons are writing the last chapters.

For the first time in our years of walking with the Lord, I can truly say that this travail is here - it is being lived and experienced daily as the process continues forward to completion.

There are many sons coming to birth, and as the prophet Isaiah foresaw, this womb will not be shut up. After the initial release of sonship comes forth within those who are part of the first wave of this breakthrough, we will see wave after wave of the glorification of His sons that will follow.

The tragedy is that there have been many who have been called who have walked away rather than pay the price; for the demands of sonship are total.

There is much land to be taken. There is a life to be lived on a level you have never seen - a level of His presence which awaits you. God is bringing forth a people whom He has prepared to become the door openers to a new age. He is enlarging the scope of their understanding to see who they have always been, and what they have been sent here to do.

There are so many waiting for these first breakthroughs of sonship and the glorification of the believer – the cloud of witnesses, the elemental world, and so many other orders within God's creation. All waiting - all expecting. Even if they have not understood what it is they look for, and what it is they anticipate; they expect never-the-less.

We are so much further down the road than we have been able to perceive. The shackles are beginning to fall off and sight and illumination is coming.

All of creation groans and suffers these pains of childbirth simultaneously with the sons; for creation eagerly awaits their release from futility.

The Cloud of Witnesses are right here, right now. They are pushing us, helping us in any way possible to break the tape.

It's time to finish the birth. It's time for a son.

One Heart & One Mind

> When the day of Pentecost had come, they were all together in one place. And suddenly there came from heaven a noise like a violent rushing wind, and it filled the whole house where they were sitting. And there appeared to them tongues as of fire distributing themselves, and they rested on each one of them.
> – Acts 2:1-3

> When they had entered *the city,* they went up to the upper room where they were staying; that is, Peter and John and James and Andrew, Philip and Thomas, Bartholomew and Matthew, James *the son* of Alphaeus, and Simon the Zealot, and Judas *the son* of James. – Acts 1:13

When Christ ascended to the Father one of His last words to the disciples was to command them to wait for the "promise" that He would send them. They had no idea what was coming and they didn't know what to expect. But they waited.

As history reflects in the accounts of Josephus there were more than 300 who watched Christ ascend, yet only 120 remained after the 40 days following Passover. These were the ones who diligently waited for the visitation of the promise. And as they were gathered together, "in one place", as the scriptures state, the promise of the Holy Spirit fell upon the 120.

This is not a new story to most of you, but it is a snapshot in time of what was happening during those tumultuous times after Christ's death and ascension to the Father.

These days in which we walk are not quite the same, but there are a few parallels that we can draw from. During this time we are facing the glorification of the believer and the resurrection of his spirit, soul and body. Like the early disciples, we do not yet know nor have we experienced this transition of life. But it is coming.

We have been speaking about the travail that is resting upon both creation and the sons of God during this time. We are talking about a release of sonship and the transformation of this humble state of dwelling into the glorious likeness of Christ.

Perhaps we have had visions, revelations, or insights, where we have had a glimpse of this transformation coming. We know that God is doing a new thing. As the cloven tongues of fire was to the early disciples, so the transformation and change into sonship is to those of His believers in this day.

We are all aware of the experience on the Day of Pentecost, as it is mentioned in the book of Acts 1 and 2, that brought forth the cloven tongues of fire. This baptism inaugurated the church age in power with signs following.

> **When the day of Pentecost had come, they were all together in one place. – Acts 2:1**

In the book of Acts it speaks of the believers being in "one place", and we have interpreted that to mean a single room, and it could have been that. But more so, these followers, the 120, were in one place within their heart and the preparation of their spirit to receive the outpouring that was sent forth. Yes, they were in one place, geographically speaking, but what is more important is they were in "one place" within their heart. That was truly the upper room; for it was the state of their abiding.

In this day and during this time God is drawing His people into a plane of spirit, or abiding. It is the upper room of His presence. This upper room does not have a physical address for it is a level of abiding in the spirit, and it is not confined to location, for it spans the entire globe.

The Lord is calling out His people. He has been preparing their hearts and bringing a deep work of the cross to them. And His bride, the "called out" and the chosen, are not defined by organization, location, or even doctrine. They are the "called out". The Lord is bringing them into the upper room of His presence awaiting the next level of the restoration of His spirit in the earth; the manifestation of sonship. This knows no boundaries.

We know that we are living in a time of great change, a "season" of change as it were <u>that is predicated upon the ability of the believer to see</u> the time of his visitation. We are living in the time of His silent coming - it is the time of the wise and foolish virgins.

All of God's sons have been in school, a school of preparation. Everything which the Lord has brought to you during your present sojourn has had one goal in mind; to prepare you for your destiny. God has been preparing His army to complete His will during this time.

You have changed and learned a great deal. Perhaps you have had to learn some of your lessons a few times - but that's ok. We are approaching the time of graduation; for this season of preparation is coming to a close.

The promise is that He will do a quick work. As Isaiah spoke...Can a nation be born in a day? The breakthrough and transformation of sonship will probably go on for some time as we see wave after wave of His people transition. We are at the threshold of the first wave; we are right at the door.

The signs of the times continue to confirm what we have been feeling for some time; changes are in the earth and they are accelerating.

This time reminds me of Azusa street in the early 1900's. The believers at that time knew there was something coming although they had not yet experienced the change that God was bringing. Many probably had an idea of what it might be - this "baptism" in the Spirit - but it was still a new thing in earth. We know that the moving of the Spirit which occurred brought such radical changes and initiated a moving of God in the earth that had not been seen before. People had come to an end in what they could produce. There came a visitation from God that brought His church onto a new level. We are once again at this juncture, and the changes of sonship will usher in a new day that has never been seen before.

Here we are, the "upper room" or the "Azusa street" of this generation. We are aware of many changes that are coming and of which are slated for this time frame. We also understand that the depth of these changes and the depth of this transformation is still hanging as an unrealized potential, but it is here.

We have watched God progressively move to position His sons into a time of fruitfulness and fulfillment. Until the time set by the Father comes to pass, it seems that no amount of exertion will get you to the goal. However, when the time has come, and it is God's good pleasure to give His sons the kingdom, then your positioning before Him means everything. It is truly the parable of the wise and foolish virgins.

We have leaned into so much that the Lord is opening up, yet we have not scratched the surface. We know this is the time; the season of His appearing on a much greater level. And so we stand.

This next step into the kingdom is a huge one. *(I know, and you thought the last step you took was big)* In perspective it is the greatest step and transition you will ever take.

We are living our lives right now, moment by moment. We are living in the right now and Jehovah Jireh, (one of the many names of God), means "the God of right now". We are living with a "living" expectation of His appearing and the experiences of sonship which we know have begun.

> **"And the Lord, whom you seek, will suddenly come to His temple". – Mal 3:1**

We are in the season of this scripture's fulfillment. The Lord will complete that which concerns His sons. This is the season of His appearing within His temple on a level we have never seen before.

As His remembrancers we stand before the Lord and cry out with the Cloud of Witnesses, "How long O Lord". But we know the answer, for the answer is ***NOW.***

It's time to Expect the Unexpected for we have come to the upper room. God's people, as many as are prepared for this hour of His visitation, are being drawn into the upper room of His presence.

Section 4

The Conjunction
Of Ages

- **The Conjunction
  Of 2 Worlds**

- **The One World
  Of Christ**

- **Set The Captives
  Free**

- **The Elemental
  Kingdom**

The Conjunction of 2 Worlds

The world as we have known it has been going through changes; deep changes in fact. We briefly touched upon the travail that has been upon creation; but this is just the tip of the iceberg. All of God's kingdom is in transition.

God is bringing a conjunction of ages, or what we would call a conjunction of worlds. This is one of the themes we touch upon often throughout this book. This book is also about the changes happening within God's people; changes that are bringing about the manifestation of sonship.

As God brings forth His sons we are finding an increase in the turmoil within the world and within all of creation. Creation is in travail. And the world is in a state of upheaval that will only continue to get worse.

Is this about the pending and coming judgments of God? No. It is about the manifestation of the Father's family - the manifestation of the sons of God.

As this timeline progresses we are finding a shift that is happening; a shift that is affecting all levels of creation. The sons of God, (the man-child that is referred to in the book of Revelation), are being caught up to the throne of God. They are being brought into a level of ruling and reigning with Christ. But this is only one part of the shift.

In the same breath we are finding that the Cloud of Witnesses; those spoken of in the book of Hebrews who died in the faith, are also changing. Having seen from a distance the provision for this hour; they are now destined to enter into their release and their inheritance.

> **(*men* of whom the world was not worthy), wandering in deserts and mountains and caves and holes in the**

> **ground. And all these, having gained approval through their faith, did not receive what was promised, because God had provided something better for us, so that apart from us they would not be made perfect. - Heb 11:38-40**

The world of spirit and the natural world about us are coming closer and closer. We are beginning to see an overlapping between worlds. As the sons of God continue to come up higher, the Cloud of Witnesses are beginning to experience a shift or change in their vibration as well. We have watched as this energy of change has gradually been gaining momentum over the past 5 to 6 decades.

Will this be recognizable by all? Probably not, for you must have eyes to see to understand what is happening. In the midst of these changes there is a greater presence of the world of evil as well. Their presence may not be as difficult to discern. You can easily see that there has been a greater level of Satanic influence and appearing as they undergo a vibrational shift as well.

The world of evil is experiencing a different type of change. In the book of Revelation it refers to a "casting down" that happens to the satanic hosts that have dwelled within the heavens (Rev12:10). They are being cast down to the earth. There is definitely a measure of this happening, and it has been progressively unfolding over the past several decades.

Business is not as usual. Until this time, the realm of spirit has been able to operate behind closed doors, unseen and unknown by most. But all of that which has been hidden is now beginning to come to light. (Jn 3:20, Eph 5:13) This overlapping of worlds is bringing an exposing of that which has been done in secret by the world of evil.

We have spoken before about a level of dual-existence or dual-consciousness that is coming about during this time. This should be strongly anticipated for God has not ordained that His people live and walk without an awareness; an awareness of the Father, Christ and the entire world of spirit.

What we should expect in this day is a change of state; a change from living with an awareness that has been tied to the natural plane. The process of the purification of the believer and the subsequent appearing of the Lord are bringing about an entirely new state of abiding for God's sons.

who can stand when He appears, for He will be a smelter and purifier of the sons of Levi" - Mal 3:2.

Malachi prophesies about the appearing of the Lord to His people during these days - and that has been a challenge for God's people - because the Lord's appearing is that of a consuming fire. God is set to remove the last vestiges of the soul or Adamic nature. There is no other path into His presence and into the experience of this conjunction of ages without this purification by fire.

Everything being written in this book, "The Manifestation of the Sons of God", is about this transition; a transition from death into life. It is a conjunction, an overlapping or intersecting of 2 ages and 2 worlds; seemingly so distant and apart, yet separated only by vibration and individual awareness.

We have seen so many signs confirming this day to which we have come. Scriptures have been quoted about wars and rumors of wars, earth changes, and a rise of iniquity in the earth. Yes, there are certainly many signs pointing to this time that we have now come. <u>We are living in the time of a shift, and that shift is happening within you now.</u>

As we continue in this process of change we even find that our bodies are experiencing changes. There is a renewal going on, a renewal of the physical body and a renewal of the mind. Your energy or vibration is changing and you are becoming much more sensitive to the world around you. You are more aware of the spirit world around you, including the soul or psychic emanations that come from people towards you.

It is a whole new day.

Perhaps you haven't yet recognized that you have been in a shift; for we are usually the last to recognize the changes that have come forth within us. Often times we look for the fulfillment of our concepts of what it means to walk in the spirit, yet when the changes come - it is different than you expected. It may take a while for you to get your sea legs, and we must be careful not to be locked into our concepts.

The cunning work of the world of evil has sought to deaden your senses by overloading you with so much input (tv, radio, computers) and by defiling the food you eat. They are trying to destroy that innate ability to hear and see the realm which is just beyond this natural plane.

It is time to cease striving and carefully look and listen; a conjunction of worlds is unfolding right in your midst.

It is becoming increasingly important for us to interact and communicate with the Cloud of Witnesses. God has given them to help us complete the task set before us. Their closeness to us has become more than just a doctrine or wishful thinking; it is a reality waiting to be experienced.

We are realizing more and more that the wrap up will only be accomplished by both sides of the veil; working in unison with the cry, *"Thy Kingdom Come!"*.

We have entered into an accelerated period of growth where God is bringing forth a new day - a release of such magnitude, that Ezekiel's vision best states it .... "a river that could not be forded".

Again he measured a thousand; and it was a river that I could not ford, for the water had risen, enough water to swim in, a river that could not be forded. –Ezekiel 37:5

With this release there is a sense of urgency; **move forward as quickly as you can.** As Joshua admonished the children of Israel, **... there is much land to be taken and we must enter in.**

The One World of Christ

What we want to address in this word is the inter-connectedness of all creation with the travail, birthing and subsequent manifestation of the sons of God. These two aspects cannot be separated.

As the sons of God come forth during this season the effect of this change will reverberate throughout the heavens, the earth and all of creation. We are in the time of the Parousia - the appearing of the Lord - and it is through the agency of His appearing that the sons are changing and being completed.

The breakthroughs that are being experienced presently by God's sons are having a dynamic affect upon what is transpiring in both the earth and the heavens. What is happening is far more reaching than just experiencing individual releases. As the sons of God break through, the kingdom breaks through. As God's sons change, the kingdom changes; for they are the agency of change.

> **But we all, with unveiled face, beholding as in a mirror the glory of the Lord, are being transformed into the same image from glory to glory, just as from the Lord, the Spirit. – 2Co 3:17b-18**

The changes and deliverances unfolding during this time are not a singular or linear experience. They may appear on one level, yet they are having reverberating effects across the kingdom. Let me explain.

Imagine dropping a pebble in the water. What do you see? You see the rippling of the water as it radiates out literally to infinity. This example conveys the dynamic behind the changes that are happening within the sons of God, and the radiating affects these changes are having within all of creation; visible, or invisible.

It can be difficult to understand these dynamics when you still do not see them. For yet a season the eyes of His sons are still seeing in a glass dimly, as Paul speaks in the book of Corinthians (1Cor 13:12). But this will not always be the case.

Any release or deliverance that is being experienced at this time is inter-connected to every level of the kingdom, whether visible or invisible. Changes are happening on every plane of existence.

> **For the anxious longing of the creation waits eagerly for the revealing of the sons of God. For the creation was subjected to futility, not willingly, but because of Him who subjected it, in hope that the creation itself also will be set free from its slavery to corruption into the freedom of the glory of the children of God.**
>
> **For we know that the whole creation groans and suffers the pains of childbirth together until now. And not only this, but also we ourselves, having the first fruits of the Spirit, even we ourselves groan within ourselves, waiting eagerly for our adoption as sons, the redemption of our body.**
> **– Ro. 8:19-23**

Nothing should be taken too personal at this juncture in time, for the ministry of sonship is far more reaching than we have understood.

For some time now scientists have searched to find the answers to creation and to understand just what it is that holds everything together. At the most minute level of creation, what is it that holds everything in its order? What keeps it all together?

We know the answer, for that answer is God. Paul speaks of this in the book of Colossians, that all things are "held together in Him".

> And He is before all things, and in Him <u>all things</u> hold together. - Col 1:17

What this means is that within the very fabric of your being, at the most minute level of your consciousness; God is there. He holds all things in place. Interesting. At the most minute level of your existence or consciousness; God is there. He has always been there.

> **Thou dost know when I sit down and when I rise up; Thou dost understand my thought from afar. Thou dost scrutinize my path and my lying down, And art intimately acquainted with all my ways. - Psa. 139:2-3**

As the psalmist spoke, "He knows our inner thoughts, He knows when we sit down and when we stand up". Amazingly, every fiber of our being, every vibration of energy that we are composed of is held together in God. We can no more be separate from God than all of His creation can.

When we wait upon God, we quiet ourselves - we come into a state of listening. We go inside because there we find Him...not in the heavens, but in the deep recesses of our heart and being. God is always there, for we are never separate from Him. The enemy would seek to convince us that we must work up to God - that we must storm the gates of heaven so that He might listen and take account of us. But in truth He is as close as our innermost thoughts. **His energy rides upon the vibration of our very essence** - for without Him, we cannot exist.

We don't have to work up to God, but we must OPEN up to Him. We must realize how very, very close He is to us. He knows our struggles, our sorrows, our victories, and what path He needs to orchestrate to bring each of us into the fullness of sonship as a mature son.

Please understand, the Lord is the potter and we are the clay (Ro. 9:21). He is the master craftsman. It is He who is molding and shaping you. He has created a unique path, just for you. And it is designed for one thing; to bring you into your inheritance.

He knows what you need and He knows just how to get the results He is looking for. In some ways it may seem like you are just along for the ride, but we know it is a bit more involved than that.

Just for the record; God's dealings, His intent, and His plan for you is unique and it is created just for you. He is involved in every level of your life. He has sent you into the earth at this time in history to complete His will and manifest His glory.

There is nothing about your life that is happenstance or coincidental. As the scripture points out – "the steps of a righteous man are ordered of the Lord" (Ps 37:23). But you say, "I am not righteous". Yes you are, for you are righteous by faith. It isn't even your faith, it is His faith (Gal 3:11, Ro 1:7). Your steps are being uniquely ordered and tailor made just for you and no one else.

We are coming to realize that in Christ all things are held together; whether past, present or future. Whether principalities, powers, thrones or dominions; all things are held together in Christ.

This is important for us to understand because the true ministry of sonship in this hour is based upon this "inter-connectedness" of all of creation in Christ.

> **For the earnest expectation of the creation waiteth for the revealing** *(literal: manifestation)* **of the sons of God. For the creation was subjected to vanity, not of its own will, but by reason of him who subjected it, in hope that the creation itself also shall be delivered from the bondage of corruption into the liberty of the glory of the children of God. For we know that the whole creation groaneth and travaileth in pain together until now. - Romans 8:19-22**

In the book of Romans Paul speaks about the travail of all creation that is waiting for the release and manifestation of the sons of God. Perhaps you have read this passage many times before, however I believe there is something which has escaped our understanding with respect to the fulfillment of this passage.

As these days of the kingdom come into full view we are beginning to see that there is an intrinsic connection between the progressive manifestation of the sons of God, and the progressive release of all of His creation. With the mantle of sonship resting upon His sons we are beginning to know **"who we are"**, and we are beginning to understand **"what we are"** in Christ.

Let me explain...

We generally see ourselves as individuals who are walking with God. Our bodies we view as both the temple of the Holy Spirit and the housing of our soul and spirit. For the most part we have seen ourselves as a single entity, a unique individual in Christ. I do not believe that we have understood how inter-connected we are to all of God's kingdom.

As we become more fully identified with Christ, **in totality,** we begin to cease our existence as a singular individual. Do you understand? We are talking about a oneness at the core of our being with Christ and the Father. We are experiencing an absolute oneness or blending into all of that which comprises God's kingdom, and every level of creation that exists. How can it be anything less?

You are destined to walk with Christ and the Father and to experience deeper levels of change and transformation during this time. It is the season of what we call "the parousia", or His appearing. You must understand your change is creating radiating effects across the entire realm of the spirit.

The Ripple Effect

What happens when you drop a pebble in water? You have the radiating effect of wave after wave, literally to infinity. I call this the "ripple affect". We are beginning to understand that the progressive release of the sons of God is simultaneously creating a progressive release for all of creation. They go hand in hand.

There is no release, no deliverance and there is no judgment that you experience that does not have a ripple affect across every level of the kingdom. Your change brings with it commensurate releases and deliverances across the kingdom. Why is this? Because of the oneness with Christ that God is bringing you into.

Let me re-iterate. This is not about you. This is about Christ, and the affect that Christ and His progressive manifestation through you is having upon all of creation in the Father's kingdom. It is truly astounding. The manifestation of Christ in you, the mystery of the ages as Paul speaks of in Ephesians 3, is causing changes that is reverberating across every level and every dimension that has been created. We have only seen a measure of how these changes are beginning to impact an entire world of spirit.

When we talk about creation we are speaking of something that we may not yet truly understand at this point, for we are still seeing in part. God's creation, that which is both animate and inanimate, is so extensive - for there are many levels of dwelling within the Father's house (Jn 14:2). This speaks of a world of spirit comprised of many levels of life and orders of intelligences that are waiting for the release that will come with the manifestation of the sons of God.

As Christ ascended to the throne to sit at the right hand of the Father He passed through the heavens. You could call it "dimensions", "worlds", or other levels within the Father's house. Christ passed through the heavens and affected changes on every level of creation. The Word says that He "set the captives free". In similar fashion the sons of God are uniquely connected to the releasing of all of His creation.

The Father has done this. He has chosen that as His sons come forth, as they break free from futility, that all of His creation will experience the same freedom, and the same release.

What a destiny. What a calling. What an endowment. Until now we have not seen nor have we really understood, just how intrinsically connected we are with all of creation.

Let's look at this another way. Imagine a web that encircles the globe. This world and all that exists within this web are bound and interconnected together. One movement in the web affects movement in another sector of that web. It is inter-connected. Thus, as you change, as you walk free, you affect the matrix of this web.

I know I may be saying the same thing over and over, but as God's sons manifest, changes are happening on many levels. This "God level energy", Christ in them, is radiating out and reverberating across every level and dimension causing changes and releases.

> ***Even*** **the mystery which hath been hid from ages and from generations, but now is made manifest to his saints: To whom God would make known what *is* the**

riches of the glory of this mystery among the Gentiles; which is Christ in you, the hope of glory – Col 1:26-27

We have watched and studied the reactions and responses in the spirit world to prayers that are being made. Time and again we have seen an inter-connectedness between the changes that are unfolding in the earth and those prayers. Most often the fulfillment and releases appear unconnected from those prayers, because it cannot be perceived except from the realm of your spirit. However, the shift or deliverance affecting the sons in one area of the matrix was effecting changes in another area, simultaneously. Let me put it another way...

The releases and changes that you are experiencing are affecting changes on a global scale, yet that may be difficult to track on. It will take eyes to see, for without revelation it can be nearly impossible to recognize or discern the connection.

As human beings we have functioned too much through our mind, approaching things mentally, rather than from our heart or spirit. We have tended to think along linear lines, or 3 dimensional, rather than seeing things through the eyes of our spirit. There are a whole set of dynamics that we have not understood which are happening with every release and flow of judgment that we experience.

Nothing is a singular experience. As I have said before, our release, even incrementally, is affecting changes simultaneously in many different realms and on many different levels.

As the sons of God change *(it is the mystery of Christ within them)* so does this age change.

How can that be? As Christ in the earth, we are the energy and essence of the Father. As our oneness becomes complete, so the effect intensifies every time we change and come forth. Every word we speak, every aspect of our being, <u>even the slightest perceptions within our mind</u> has a rippling effect of energy that will see changes across every level of creation.

It is so vitally important that we see the final breakthroughs of the sons of God. As we have said, the release of the Cloud of Witnesses spoken of in Hebrews 11 and 12 is tied to the release and change which is happening within each of His sons, for they without us are not made perfect.

More and more we are seeing an interaction with the Cloud of Witnesses. They recognize it is the time; they sense that we are right at the door of the fulfillment of the Father's plan within the earth - <u>the earth of His sons</u>. They are groaning within, as well, for their release is tied to our release. We are one church, whether visible or invisible.

Let's talk for a moment once more about creation. The general perception of "creation" has been that which can be seen with the eye; the flora, the fauna, the earth etc.. But we are only now coming to understand that creation includes far more than just what our eyes might see. We understand that creation includes a spirit world, unknown or seen by most, but very much alive and active. This spirit world comprises many orders of creation; from the elemental beings that work in synergy to keep the earth in balance, to the Cloud of Witnesses who have died in the faith, awaiting their release.

When Christ died He passed through the heavens and sat down at the right hand of the Father. We have said this. Even as He spoke to His disciples, He said, "In my Father's house are many dwelling places".... And "where I go, I go to prepare a place for you, that where I am you may be also". This is all scripture. What Christ was speaking of is the many levels that exist within the Father's kingdom.

There are many orders of creation who are participating with us in these last days - for their release is tied to our release. We are aware that there are so many that have been awaiting this time; awaiting the changes and releases which have been prophesied over the sons.

It truly is the One World of Christ.

In a very mystical way we are part of all that God is. We are a part of every level, every dimension and every aspect of His creation. As He dwells within all of His creation, so do His sons. We are beginning to experience an inter-connectedness with every aspect of creation, of every aspect of life, intelligence and dimension.

In a very real sense we are entering into the order of Melchizedek; we have had no beginning and we will have no end. We are entering into the omnipresence of the Lord. This may sound a bit startling, but we are entering into Christ and His unlimited existence.

The sons of God are the leaven of this age. They are the handful of corn being cast upon the mountains; the harvest which will shake the cedars of Lebanon (Ps 72:16). They are causing changes across every level of creation and dimension.

This sheds a much greater understanding as to "what we are in Christ"; what our presence - the presence of His sons - truly means in this age and at this time.

> **In all wisdom and insight He made known to us the mystery of His will, according to His kind intention which He purposed in Him with a view to an administration suitable to the fullness of the times, *that is*, <u>the summing up of all things in Christ</u>, things in the heavens and things upon the earth. –Eph 1:8b-10**

We are seeing the summing up of all things in Christ, <u>because we are a fundamental part of that process.</u> We are the missing link or the key that is literally opening the door to the deep changes taking place in the earth during this time.

Now more than ever we understand just how dynamic and far reaching the ministry of Christ and the ministry of sonship is.

Now we begin to understand just what our presence in the earth at this time *really means*....

Set The Captives Free

A living word is coming forth in the earth embodied within a people whom the Lord has taken up His residence. This is not a new revelation for we have been aware for some time that this has been God's intent. The word is being made flesh once again within earthen vessels. We are only now beginning to understand what this really means, and what will be accomplished as the Word issues forth from the hearts of God's sons during this time.

Although His sons are at different levels of growth and maturity, the Word through their hearts will not be restrained; nor will it be limited.

A word is coming forth that is shaking both the heavens and the earth, and we are beginning to partake of a kingdom that cannot be shaken.

> **And His voice shook the earth then, but now He has promised, saying, "YET ONCE MORE I WILL SHAKE NOT ONLY THE EARTH, BUT ALSO THE HEAVEN."**
>
> **This *expression*, "Yet once more," denotes the removing of those things which can be shaken, as of created things, so that those things which cannot be shaken may remain. Therefore, since we receive a kingdom which cannot be shaken, let us show gratitude, by which we may offer to God an acceptable service with reverence and awe; for our God is a consuming fire. – Hebrews 12:26-29**

God is removing the hindrances, the blocks, and the limitations that have existed within you. He is removing layer after layer off of His sons.

As these layers are removed you will find an experience of knowing. You will begin to truly know and recognize who you have always been; it was just covered over by the debris and clutter picked up along the way in your sojourn.

God's sons have been on a course of deep change as they have seen the work of the cross go deeper and deeper. As this work of the cross has plumbed the depths of their hearts, the veils and the seals over them are beginning to fall away.

The experience of Romans 8 is right on course and right on time. It is the unveiling of the mystery of Christ in you, the revealing of all that you are and all that you have always been.

Romans 8 speaks of this revealing (in the Greek literal it is more accurately defined, "unveiling") of the sons of God. What this speaks of is a manifestation of something that has always existed. This is a revealing of something which has been hidden, not only to the powers of this age, but to the very vessels of God's presence in the earth today.

> **For the anxious longing of the creation waits eagerly for the revealing (unveiling) of the sons of God. – Ro 8:19**

We are talking about the revealing or unveiling of God's sons who have been here all along. So much has been hidden from the eyes of His sons until the time set by the Father for their unveiling.

> **Now I say, as long as the heir is a child, he does not differ at all from a slave although he is owner of everything, but he is under guardians and managers until the date set by the father. – Gal 4:1-2**

This is an unveiling of yourself - to yourself. You are beginning to recognize who and what you have always been. You have been hidden in Him; however we are now in the time of change.

God is peeling layer after layer off the sons of God; layers which have accumulated over this present sojourn which has created an illusion of separation. This unawareness of who you truly are is giving way. The sons of God are finally beginning to recognize who they are. They are beginning to perceive all that has been hidden beneath these layers.

The Cloud of Witnesses have longed for this day; for they without us will not be made perfect. They have waited for a people that would once again **become** the word.

> **And all these, having gained approval through their faith, did not receive what was promised, because God had provided something better for us, so that apart from us they would not be made perfect. – Heb 11:39-40**

> **All these died in faith, without receiving the promises, but having seen them and having welcomed them from a distance, and having confessed that they were strangers and exiles on the earth. – Heb 11:13**

We have believed in our oneness with Christ; but we have been a little behind in experiencing and understanding the reality of it. Christ, the Father, you or I, we are all one before Him. If you have seen me, then you have seen the Father, and you have seen Christ. If I have seen you, then the conclusion is the same. These are scriptures we have read and we have known in part; we are now entering into the experience of their reality.

During this season of time, as layer after layer is removed from God's sons, we are finding a capacity to see and to know. We are beginning to truly know one another after the spirit. This is a level of sight we have not experienced previously. True, we have walked in this - in the "day of the partial" - but I am speaking of walking in this in the "day of His fullness".

We are beginning to walk in the fulfillment of the prophecy in Joel where God's army walks shoulder to shoulder, seeing eye to eye, as God establishes Zion. This prophecy could not be fulfilled through a people who walked in the soul level; it remained for a people that would rise in the spirit.

Have we been able to truly see one another? In part, Yes. But the perfect is before us.

There have been very few who have been able to break into this level and walk in this; to truly know one another after the spirit. In this level exists oneness, a oneness amongst His people, and a oneness with Christ on the highest level. This has been a reality that can only be experienced in the spirit as the sons transition from life on the soul plane to a life in the spirit.

Christ is the Word, and the Word came and dwelt amongst us. This we know. But the point is that the Word is being made flesh once again - embodied within His sons. The church world may say a "yea and amen" to the idea of "Christ living in you", but when it comes to the reality of it - watch out - because they will vehemently resist it.

We are experiencing a release that is beginning to affect creation beyond what we can understand at this point. And this release is tied directly into the release of His Word - His sons - who are the physical and spiritual expression of His Word.

We know from the scripture that the Cloud of Witnesses without us will not be made perfect. We also understand that as we change, they change. And we understand that this change occurs within the realm of spirit. Now, let's look closer into this.

We have certainly been aware of a greater level of activity as the day draws closer. We are not holding séances, and we are not trying to contact them, but we are noticing that their presence, their vibration if you will, is coming closer and closer.

A word came many years ago that as we experience more and more breakthroughs in the realm of the spirit, the Cloud of Witnesses will experience this as well. It would be simultaneous; our change (from glory to glory) will affect a vibrational shift for them.

It probably sounds a bit unusual, but once again, "they without us will not be made perfect". In many ways, "we without them will not be made perfect either. We are tied together on this last leg of the race. We also know that God is empowering the Cloud of Witnesses to interact and participate with His sons to see the completion of God's will in the earth.

How is God "empowering" the Cloud to participate with us? It is tied directly into the release of His word within you.

As it was in the time of Christ, the Word which is coming forth now is being manifested in the physical realm. Christ was the Word then. His sons are the Word made flesh now. This is our identity. We are not "word-workers"; we are the manifestation of the Living Word - and this goes way beyond what we presently understand.

And who are the sons? They are the Word. We may not fully understand this yet, but this is what it means to be "identical with Christ". You become THE WORD.

There is a great deal of interest right now coming from the spirit realm, and their interest is increasing because we have come to the time of the WORD made flesh.

You are the Word, and you are entering into a destiny of the unlimitedness of Christ. The Word will not be bound, and the Word will not be limited. You may still feel a bit bound, I understand; but this is not your destiny, nor is this your reality. You may still be in the process of casting off your grave-clothes; but it's ok. God has a new set of clothes waiting for you. Paul calls it your "heavenly temple."

> **For we know that if the earthly tent which is our house is torn down, we have a building from God, a house not made with hands, eternal in the heavens.**
> **– 2 Cor 5:1**

Everyone and everything is tied into this manifestation of the WORD; the WORD which is releasing - the WORD which is shaking - the WORD which is healing and delivering, and the WORD which has begun to judge.

As you manifest the Word, you release creation. You are "unwrapping" them; tearing off the "layers" and grave-clothes and you are setting them free. The manifestation of this Word in you is reaching and touching every level of creation.

As God unwraps you; removing the scales from your eyes, peeling off the layers of limitation and tearing off your grave-clothes, you are doing the same for the Cloud of Witnesses. You are helping to pull off the remaining layers that still enshroud them and set them free!

When? Now. Now is the appointed time.

We must understand that the Word, this Living Word, is not relegated just to this level of the senses. As this word goes forth it affects every realm and every dimension of God's creation. His word knows no restriction, no limitation, and it is not bound. It is flowing forth and touching every aspect of creation. We are only now beginning to understand just how far reaching and expansive this change and experience is.

Make no mistake; you are the Word. What is your destiny? To walk as Christ and be the reality of the Word made flesh. This experience is unfolding as His sons are born running. This is what the manifestation of the sons of God is all about.

There is an unwrapping - a peeling off of the layers - a redemption that is happening for the Cloud of Witnesses. We have come to a very important time right now and we are running to catch up in our understanding of all that God is doing and has done. We are coming to the realization of what He has set before His sons in this hour to accomplish, and what the release of His sons in the earth really means.

The gospel of the kingdom is not about a level of "consciousness"; some sort of mass "prayer". The world is not going to be changed by a "collective consciousness". Change in this hour happens by sons who have become His word.

The Elemental Kingdom

> For the anxious longing of the creation waits eagerly for the revealing of the sons of God. For the creation was subjected to futility, not willingly, but because of Him who subjected it, in hope that the creation itself also will be set free from its slavery to corruption into the freedom of the glory of the children of God. – Romans 8:19-20

We have entered a time where we are witnessing a much greater participation of creation in the act of bringing forth the will of the Father in the earth, for all of creation is travailing and groaning together with us.

Creation has been caught in the birth-pangs of travail; for as the sons become free, so this freedom radiates out as it begins to progressively set all of creation free.

So exactly what is creation?

Creation is composed of the many entities and energies that comprise the Kingdom of God. There are many different orders. Those which we call "elementals" are those spirits which are responsible for keeping the earth in balance and function. When Paul refers to creation in Romans 8 he is speaking of a living and vibrant force.

For a long time the elementals that govern so much of the base order of creation have been under the canopy of the powers of this age. Often they have been goaded and manipulated, against their will, to do the bidding of evil. Yet during this season of change we are seeing a progressive release that has begun for them.

The escalation of severe weather patterns and diverse climatic changes in the earth have been increasing over the past decade. It has only begun, and it will continue to accelerate as this time of travail comes to completion. Why? Because what you see unfolding is in direct correlation to the increased interaction of creation as they wrench free from the control they have been under by the principalities, the powers and the rulers of this present darkness.

We are beginning to feel a greater connection with all of creation as they have become more involved in this travail that is upon the earth. It is part of what we would call a "conjunction of ages" or "realms" that we have spoken of previously. As the Lord brings a merging of the earth and spiritual planes we are finding a closer connection with all of God's creation.

This is not something that we seek. It is not a random tangent or some "new age" thing. As we continue to come alive to the world of the kingdom, God's kingdom - a kingdom of spirit - we come alive to everything within this dimension; including the many and varied orders of creation.

We must understand that the elemental spirits were created by the Father, not that we would worship them, but in a very real sense to function as servants of God with us. Their role concerns the maintenance of what we have known as the earth, and those aspects concerning the balance and proper functioning of this level of existence.

There are times when you experience a momentary breakthrough where you may see them. You may see them when you are in a vision or dream state, or perhaps out of the periphery of your eyes, or they might just appear to you. There are many ways they can reveal themselves, and as you continue to come alive to God, they will reveal themselves more and more to you.

The elemental kingdom is a bit nervous around the sons of God; for they have not beheld this "new thing" that God is doing. As much as they can control their ability to manifest themselves to you, generally, they will not do so. On occasion they have come; more out of curiosity than anything else. Some are a bit fearful for they sense the power and authority, yet they don't know what you are. One asked, some time back; "What are you? "Should we be afraid of you?" "What order of creation are you?" It was all I could do to still their fears; to let them know that we are here to work in synergy with them as God brings forth His kingdom.

The elementals are all a part of His kingdom and you will experience more and more of these interactions as you progress and continue to break through in the realm of spirit. As you enter more deeply into His presence, you will find that you will experience an ongoing shift in your vibration. You will begin to experience more and more connections from those who live and dwell in the realm of spirit, because we are in the time of an overlapping of ages.

You really can't have a selective awareness. The more you come into the presence of the Lord and of the Father, the more you will become aware of many different aspects of His kingdom. You need to stay open and teachable; for the Lord will bring this forth in His timing for you.

Understand, our pursuit is not a relationship with the fairy folk, the elementals or any other order of His creation. Our pursuit is a relationship with Christ and the Father. Their appearance to God's sons will generally be at their initiative, and for the purpose of changes that are unfolding.

We know and understand that the elemental world is under the futility which was placed upon all of mankind since the fall. They have been under the control and manipulation of the principalities and powers. We don't know yet the tremendous changes that we will see in the earth as the elemental spirits enter into the freedom coming to the sons of God, but we are beginning to see signs of these changes occurring.

There is a shift that is happening within the balance of power in the world of spirit. This shift has only just begun, and as this balance continues to change it will affect the elemental kingdom more and more.

There is a rising awareness on the part of so many levels of creation that changes are in the process. They sense that something is at hand. They sense a shift in the authority in the spirit realm. To them it feels like a changing of the guard, but they are not sure, for they do not really understand. We are monitoring and watching what is unfolding during this season, for the release of all of creation is tied into our release.

It doesn't take a great deal of perception to know that something significant is "afoot" in the earth. It is not business as usual. It is not "peace and safety". There are too many signs of the times that point to the changes that are becoming more and more prevalent.

Perhaps you think this word is a sideline to our main focus in this book, but what I want you to realize is that there is a whole world of spirit awaiting your change; awaiting your ascension into His presence.

While we are talking about this unique subject, we might as well touch on one other aspect. We are dealing with an entire world of spirit that is coming alive and is seeking to understand the dynamics of what is happening. These orders are not relegated to what we know in this dimension, for there is a growing interest and interaction from other orders of God's creation who dwell on many different vibrational levels.

As strange as this may sound, or as "new age" as this might seem, if you read the gospels Christ told the disciples that in His father's house were "many dwelling places". The old King James version says that "in my Father's house are many mansions". Many levels.

> **"Do not let your heart be troubled; believe in God, believe also in Me. "In My Father's house are many dwelling places; if it were not so, I would have told you; for I go to prepare a place for you. "If I go and prepare a place for you, I will come again and receive you to Myself, that where I am, *there* you may be also. – John 14:1-3**

There are many levels of the kingdom that are being affected right now, but we can only speak of that which we have seen or experienced. What we have seen is that there is a heightened interest and participation; orders of creation we have never known existed.

The Meneheune, as one example, are an order of creation that exists in the Hawaiian Islands; one of the very few that we are aware of who understand to some degree what is happening right now. They see the conflict and on occasion, have been able to help. They are watching very closely.

Although they exist in the Hawaiian Islands, they are by no means limited to that geography. They have come and ministered at pivotal times of change and are part of the force in the spirit to see the changes come forth that are slated for this season.

You have other orders that are more neutral in nature, neither good nor bad; neutral elementals whose job it is to maintain order within creation. The problem is that they are all affected by the reigning principalities and powers and can be goaded into doing evil.

These are a few of the entities that we are aware with. You must realize however, that all of creation is alive, or has consciousness. The rocks, the mountains, literally every aspect of creation, seen or not, has intelligence. The more you come up higher in your vibration, the more you will begin to see and interact with them as the Lord leads and directs.

This is about setting His creation free and the dynamics of what happens as His sons come up higher and higher in their vibration and begin to interact with creation.

All of creation is in the midst of deep changes, as we are in the midst of deep changes. We are truly beginning to see a releasing of creation, even though we have only scratched the surface in our understanding of how vast God's creation truly is.

We are talking about Romans 8. This entire book is about one chapter; Romans 8 - The manifestation of the sons God has longed for, and the subsequent release of all of His creation.

Notes:

Section 5

Prophet, Priest & King

- **The Seer Prophet**
- **Dreams & Visions**
- **All Knowledge**
- **Intercession of the Kingdom**
- **The Functioning Priesthood**
- **The Ark Of His Presence**

The Seer Prophet

> "He made known to us the mystery of His will according to His kind intention which He purposed in Him, with a view to the administration suitable to the fullness of the times that is, the summing up of all things in Christ, things in the heavens and things on the earth. In Him also, we have obtained an inheritance, having been predestined according to His purpose who works all things after the council of His will. Ephesians 1:9-11a

What Paul is referring to in this scripture concerns the empowering of the believer; with all authority, dominion, and power. We are only now beginning to experience the reality and provision of this word.

So much of the word is veiled, as the word says - veiled to those who are perishing (2Co 4:3). Yet, it has also been veiled to His sons until they come into the time of their maturing; the time set by the Father.

> but he is under guardians and managers until the date set by the father. – Gal 4:2

There is a great deal awaiting God's sons that has been held in escrow; waiting for the time of their maturing. How does the word go? ... "eye has not seen nor has it entered into the heart of man those things which God has prepared for those who love Him." (1Co 2:9). One very special aspect of Christ's ministry which has been reserved for this time of the maturing of the sons, has been the release and functioning of the seer prophet ministry in the earth.

The role of the seer prophet directly concerns the administration of the authority of Christ over the rulers and principalities of this current age. It is an aspect of the ministry of the kings and priests that the sons of God are being brought into.

The term, seer prophet, is not used in Christian circles much; nor is it a term that is readily understood. We were first introduced to the seer ministry in the Old Testament; for both Elijah and Elisha were seer prophets. Elisha saw into the realm of spirit; he knew what was transpiring behind closed doors in the king's bedchambers.

> **And the king of Israel sent to the place which the man of God told him and warned him of, and saved himself there, not once nor twice.**
>
> **Therefore the heart of the king of Syria was sore troubled for this thing; and he called his servants, and said unto them, Will ye not shew me which of us *is* for the king of Israel?**
>
> **And one of his servants said, None, my lord, O king: but Elisha, the prophet that *is* in Israel, telleth the king of Israel the words that thou speakest in thy bedchamber. – 2Ki 6:10-12**

What is a seer prophet? A seer prophet is one who sees the unseen, hears the unspoken cries of the people, and whose his heart is tuned to the voice of the Father. Like Christ, the seer prophet does what he sees the Father doing and speaks what he hears the Father speaking.

The seer prophet lives in both worlds simultaneously; the realm of the spirit and the natural plane. The seer prophet is both a king that administers the kingdom, and a priest, who intercedes before God in behalf of His people. This is a seer prophet, and the seer prophet ministry plays a crucial role in the establishment of the kingdom of God in this hour.

Who can be a seer prophet?

The seer prophet ministry is for every one of God's sons to walk in. It is not meant for just the pastor or the elder, or any other title within the church hierarchy that we may have known in the past. It is meant for each one to walk in.

And that has been a problem.

In the New Testament we read about the fivefold ministry of Christ; the apostle, the prophet, the evangelist, the pastor and the teacher (Eph. 4:11-13). They were given to bring forth the body of Christ into a place of maturity where the fivefold ministry of Christ would no longer be necessary. You might say they work themselves out of a job.

Right now what we see within mainstream Christianity is a great deal of control, position, kingdom built upon kingdom and a blatant, intended protraction of infancy. This has stunted the growth of those who have been specifically marked for sonship in this hour however, God is bringing His people out of what we have known as "mainstream" Christianity into a walk in the spirit. He is bringing them into a time of fulfillment and deliverance, and it will only be in this environment - an environment of freedom - that we will see the seer ministry established within His people.

In the days of the kingdom everyone shall know the Lord, from the least unto the greatest (Heb 8:11). And the knowledge of the Lord will cover the land as the waters cover the sea. (Isa. 11:9) These scriptures identify where we are headed, but we have a ways to go before we will see this experienced on every level. We will find, as we have mentioned previously, that there will be wave after wave of God's people who will be birthed into the changes and transformation of sonship.

The book of Joel paints a clear picture of what we see unfolding during this season as God brings forth His army. His army will be comprised of His seer prophets - His kings and priests. You will not have one telling another to know the Lord, for each one shall know Him and they shall walk together.

> **Blow a trumpet in Zion, And sound an alarm on My holy mountain! Let all the inhabitants of the land tremble, For the day of the LORD is coming; Surely it is near,**
>
> **A day of darkness and gloom, A day of clouds and thick darkness. As the dawn is spread over the mountains, *So* there is a great and mighty people; There has never been *anything* like it, Nor will there be again after it To the years of many generations.**

A fire consumes before them And behind them a flame burns. The land is like the garden of Eden before them But a desolate wilderness behind them, And nothing at all escapes them.

Their appearance is like the appearance of horses; And like war horses, so they run. With a noise as of chariots They leap on the tops of the mountains, Like the crackling of a flame of fire consuming the stubble, Like a mighty people arranged for battle. Before them the people are in anguish; All faces turn pale.

They run like mighty men, They climb the wall like soldiers; And they each march in line, Nor do they deviate from their paths. They do not crowd each other, They march everyone in his path; When they burst through the defenses, They do not break ranks.

They rush on the city, They run on the wall; They climb into the houses, They enter through the windows like a thief.

Before them the earth quakes, The heavens tremble, The sun and the moon grow dark And the stars lose their brightness.

The LORD utters His voice before His army; Surely His camp is very great, For strong is he who carries out His word. The day of the LORD is indeed great and very awesome, And who can endure it?
- Joel 2:1-11

There are many examples of the seer prophet in the Old Testament: Samuel, Elijah, Elisha, Jeremiah, Ezekiel and others. Each of them saw, and were led and directed to speak a word that brought down kingdoms and changed an age during their time.

The birthing or establishment of the seer prophet has been strongly contested over the past 2 to 3 decades. In the book of Revelation we are told that the dragon seeks to devour the man-child as he comes to birth. Who is this man-child that is coming to birth in this hour? We know the answer; the sons of God - His seers, priests and kings.

God is establishing a people who can see, function, and communicate in the realm of spirit - a people who truly come into a functional relationship in the spirit. When I speak of a functional relationship I am speaking about coming alive to a whole new world. When your senses are so in tune with God, you literally live with 1 foot on this plane of existence and 1 foot in the realm of spirit.

Once you have tasted of this existence, no other level of life will satisfy you. Sonship can no longer be a platitude; it must be a realized truth within your heart.

People think of heaven as some realm so far distant from them; in actuality it is only a different level of vibration. As Christ spoke in the gospels, He referred to His Father's house as being comprised of many dwelling places. He goes on to tell His disciples that it is His desire that where He is they shall be also (Jn 14:2). This is what I would call, "life on the highest plane". Until we reach that place of existence, we are on a sojourn or path that is taking us up higher and higher. - higher in vibration - higher in consciousness - deeper into a oneness with Christ and the Father.

There is such a deadness upon this age. There is a dullness, an absolute unawareness of anything spiritual; aside from what is termed psychic or soul. What should be "normal" is termed as "abnormal" and vice-versa. The "norm" of this age is to live a life void of perception. While the "abnormal" is to live with an awareness of the realm of spirit.

The promise in Zechariah 8 is that there will be a reversal of this downward flow - *The tables are being turned.*

What we face in this electronic age is excessive over-stimulation. As great a blessing as the computer is, it is also a curse. This age of information that we live in is making people more and more mental; as we constantly deal with more and more input. We are moving further away from the inherent sensitivity that we have had as part of God's creation.

People living today are becoming more and more like computers. They have become overly mental, over stimulated, and void of any real spiritual perception. There is an upward shift happening although; a change within the sons of God. As we ascend more and more into the presence of the Lord we are becoming more acutely aware of everything that exists within the realm of God's kingdom; for this is the realm and world that we are being drawn into. As these days continue to unfold we will walk more and more in the realm of spirit, <u>as the anchors of the soul that have held us back are removed.</u>

As we enter more deeply into the realm of God's kingdom, our awareness cannot become "selective". We are entering into an awareness of all of God's kingdom which includes many things we do not even have in our scope of knowledge yet. We must be careful to stay open to **all** that He will bring to us and continue to let go of the baggage of our concepts and pre-conceived ideas. We must stay open and let Him teach us.

There are many ways that God speaks to each of His sons; dreams or visions are but one way. The signs which come in your body as you continue to come alive to the spirit world, are another way. Until we come to the place of open vision - which will happen - we must work with what the Holy Spirit has given us to see what is transpiring in the realm just beyond our sight.

We must understand that the promises of God are available now. The more we realize that what we seek is here within our grasp, the more quickly we will reach in and take what He has already provided. It is time to stop hoping that God will hear, and realize that He not only hears, but that He has released all of those things concerning His sons. Every provision for your functioning as a seer prophet and a king and priest are resident within you.

We have spoken numerous times about the Azusa street experience back in the early 1900's, but let's look at it from another perspective. People were tarrying and waiting before the Lord because they realized that there was something more of God available than they had yet to experience. They had heard rumors of baptisms in the spirit that were starting to happen throughout Europe but nothing had happened here in America yet.

As they began to wait upon the Lord, believer after believer was baptized into an experience with the Holy Spirit. Others to whom this experience was still rather vague did not enter into it until they truly realized that the provision was right in their midst. When that light came on, they reached in and laid hold of the promise. It was that simple; but they had to see it for themselves.

I see a similar comparison in this hour. We are looking for something that has been released but we haven't quite seen it yet.

> **"It will come about after this that I will pour out My Spirit on all mankind; And your sons and daughters will prophesy, Your old men will dream dreams, Your young men will see visions. "Even on the male and female servants I will pour out My Spirit in those days. – Joel 2:28-29**

In the book of Joel the prophet speaks of the spirit falling upon both the believer and the unbeliever alike. What we must realize is that God is opening the doors of this age of the kingdom. There are many who are tuning into the realities of this Kingdom age; both the just and unjust alike. Many will try to enter in, but unless they enter through the door (Christ) no amount of perception or clairvoyance will make a difference.

We've seen a great influx in what has been called the "new age movement" over the past several decades. The growth of this movement gained a great deal of momentum in the early 1900's; about the same time as the Azusa street experience when God began pouring out His spirit - *This was not coincidental*.

The satanic world understood that there would be a time when God would open wide the door for His sons to enter new and deeper levels of experience. The metaphysical movement that preceded God's moving came to discredit the experiences of the baptism of the Spirit that God began to bring. The false came to discredit the pure thing which God would bring forth. It has been the same again during this time that we are in.

God is bringing a union of what I would call the church visible and invisible. He is enabling the Cloud of Witnesses, referenced in Hebrews, to come closer and closer in vibration to the church visible. As God's sons continue to rise in their vibration and oneness with Christ, they continue to experience more interaction with them. Some would say you are communicating with the dead, but in truth, there is an incredible corporal oneness that God is bringing His church into. For there is only one church, whether visible or invisible - for we are all one before Him.

This may sound a bit strange, but as the work of redemption and purification is completed within the believer, you will experience a shift in vibration. As you continue to let go of the weights, the sins, and the bonds that have held you back, the natural cause and effect is that you will rise in vibration and enter into a much deeper level of His presence. God is doing this as He begins to merge the church together; His complete bride.

We must realize that God has something far greater for His sons than what we've understood. Whether we are experiencing dreams or visions, the appearing of Christ, or traveling in the spirit; it is all a part of so much more that will be experienced as we enter into sonship.

Dreams and visions are an important aspect of the functioning of the seer prophet, for they are a steppingstone into the perfect - into the open vision that is coming. Although there have been many books and articles written about dreams and visions, most, if not all of them, address it from the plane of the human soul. None of them have any awareness of the realm of spirit.

Dreams and visions in this day are an avenue of sight; an ability that God is giving His people to see and hear as they come "alive". The more you seek His face the more you will understand that the dreams and visions of this day are a pivotal function of the seer ministry. They are a window of sight into the functioning of your spirit and an avenue of communication from the Lord to you.

To state this another way; the deeper levels of the dream and vision state are not a function of what you're going through in your soul, they are a way of hearing and seeing what the spirit is speaking and showing you.

As you continue to come alive you will find that your dreams and visions will become progressively more and more clear. They are a window of sight into what your spirit is doing as it goes about fulfilling the leading of the Lord.

What the Lord reveals to you in your visions and dreams occurs because there is dialogue that is opening up between you and Him. Everything we experience and everything we see is a result of our relationship with the Lord - that is what this is really all about.

You will find that you will come to a point where this transition is more complete, and what seemed as "dreams" will indeed become more clear to you. As you continue to transition more and more into a life in the spirit, you will understand more and more what you are experiencing. God is hastening the day of His appearing in you to see the complete release of the seer anointing.

As your body continues to come alive to the spirit realm you begin to experience what we have called "signs" within your body. One of those signs is the enlightenment of the eyes, as you begin to actually see in the spirit with your physical eyes. At first it may be glimpses, it may be shadows, you may begin to see the faint outlines of auras of people that are not there. But the more you practice, record and monitor what you receive in the spirit the more it will grow. If you respect and honor what the Lord is showing you and you are diligent to listen, He will bring greater levels of release to you.

As you continue going through the work of the cross in your life, you will continue to come up higher in your vibration, and your eyes will behold that which you have previously not seen.

> **"And although the Lord give you the bread of adversity, and the water of affliction, yet shall not thy teachers be removed into a corner anymore, but thine eyes shall see thy teachers." - Isa 30:20**

As we have mentioned previously, the Father's house is comprised of many dwelling places. As King James calls it, "many mansions". These different levels are separated only by vibration.

The satanic level dwells on a slightly higher vibration than the human, which is why there is such a great awareness of the demonic realm today. Even animals, if you watch them, are sensitive to spiritual things because their vibration is slightly higher than ours. The vibration of the electronic realm, the realm of computers, is very close to the demonic realm. This is why you find that your electronics can go haywire, or your computers will break down.

The only way the administration of authority will be successful in this hour will be through the function of the seer prophet – the sons of God. This is why there is a drive in the spirit to become. It is time for the sons of God to move into their inheritance, and this cannot be separated from the seer prophet ministry.

The first steps in walking into the deeper things of God involves simplifying your life, slowing down, and listening. Whether it's the television, the foods we eat, the bonds we still have, or the constant barrage of mental gymnastics that we live with day in and day out – all of these affect our sensitivity and alertness to the spirit.

Waiting on God, or meditation, is pivotal to a deep walk in the spirit. Simplifying your life on every level is imperative if you have decided to walk in those things God has prepared for you.

Dreams & Visions

The prophet Joel foresaw this day as a day of tremendous upheaval. It was a day of darkness stretching forth upon the land; yet it was a day of great light as the Father would begin to pour out His Spirit upon all of mankind. It was a day when the spiritual and physical dimensions that we have known would begin to merge or overlap.

> **Joel 2:28-29 " And it will come about after this that I will pour out My Spirit on all mankind; and your sons and daughters will prophesy, your old men will dream dreams, and your young men shall see visions. And even on the male and female servants I will pour out My Spirit in those days."**

Since the early 1900's we have seen a progressive outpouring of the Spirit upon all of mankind. God, who is not a respecter of persons, has poured forth His Spirit liberally upon the just and the unjust alike. We have seen both the godly and the ungodly begin to tune into the wonders of the age to come.

As a result of this outpouring, people are discovering and un-harnessing some of the latent powers within them. We have seen many begin to literally harness the power of the mind. We have seen a rise in healings; people being risen from the dead, and many other feats not thought possible, according to the limited understanding of man.

It has been in this climate of God's outpouring to an apostate age that we have seen the rise of what many call the "new age" movement. We have seen a restoring or returning to many of the capabilities that have been inherent within man since God created him.

It is during this time of God's outpouring that we are seeing the prophecy of Joel being fulfilled which speaks of the dreams and visions that come to a people in the last days. What exactly does this mean? That God is awakening His people to a world that they have been, for the most part, unaware of.

As God brings to pass the prophecies of Joel we must be very careful not to limit Him. We must not resist this *awakening* that He is bringing to us.

History has shown a pattern from which we can draw; that the false has always preceded the true. Let me be more explicit.

Before God brings forth something new, the world of evil becomes very active to discredit it. They create a reproach to what they perceive God is about to do. Unless you are walking in the spirit, you will not be able to grasp this new thing God is doing. It will just not be acceptable to the mind. In many ways this is a left-handed blessing as Satan once again becomes the unwitting tool of God, for you must move in the Spirit if you are to know.

When God brings a new level to His people it will often look similar to the false that had preceded it. The deception that was set in motion to discredit the true becomes another major obstacle for God's people to hurdle. This has been the pattern for hundreds of years.

An example of this would be the spiritualist movement of the late 1800's which carried thru into the 40's as well. You saw the rise of witchcraft, seances, speaking with the dead, levitation, and astral traveling; among other bizarre happenings. For what purpose and to what gain? ... to discredit the moving of God's Spirit as He began to awaken His people to the world of Spirit as the conjunction of ages unfolded.

This cross over between worlds and dimensions has continued to come closer and closer as God brings His people into their inheritance, for He is bringing His people into a true walk in the spirit.

As God continues to restore the experiences and truths for this new day, it can be challenging for His people; to say the least. You must be able to sift and sort through what is coming to know what is of God, and what is of Satan - lest you reject the new thing that God is doing.

Our concept of God's moving is usually far less than the magnitude of His provision. Even the Word speaks..."My ways are not your ways, neither are My thoughts your thoughts" (Isa 55:8). In our greatest moments of perception we are still unable to grasp the enormity of what God is doing and the provision that He has set aside for His people.

For since in the wisdom of God the world through its wisdom did not *come to* know God, God was well-pleased through the foolishness of the message preached to save those who believe. – 1Co 1:21

As we have just read; man cannot come to know God through the agency of his mind. To the mind God appears as folly, but when you walk in the spirit, however, you have the ability to see and to know the truth.

Although the false may have preceded the true, Satan has unwittingly set the stage that only the spiritual will know and will be able to see the hour of their visitation.

We are at the time of a conjunction of ages; a conjunction of the spiritual world with the physical world. This conjunction is not something that has happened over night. Since the early 50's we have seen a tremendous increase of the rate at which this restoration of God's Spirit has been taking place.

We are seeing a general awakening which has begun to happen to both the believer and unbeliever alike. The prophecy of Joel speaks of God pouring forth His spirit upon ALL mankind. What are the signs which follow? - the flow of prophecy, the flow of visions, and the flow of dreams.

It becomes important for us at this time to understand what is taking place around us and within us; that we might rightly discern the true intent of God's will for His sons.

We are not like the sons of the prophets in the days of Elijah and Elisha. They had a measure of perception and knew of Elijah's coming ascent, but they lacked the depth of revelation or understanding. Elisha knew what it meant, and he was driven to receive the double portion - (2Kings 2). Our destiny is to enter in and fully possess the promises and reality of sonship for which we have been called. We will not see this from a distance; sonship will be a reality possessed by His sons. This will be an ever-increasing and unfolding experience - not just a revelation.

In the book of Joel it speaks of an increase of the dreaming of dreams and the seeing of visions during this time. This experience represents more than just an increase in dream and visions; it represents a conjunction of dimensions or realms that is happening at an accelerated rate as God's sons come alive.

The veil which separates the realm of spirit from this realm of the physical actually does not exist. It feels like it does, because we still live with a great deal of unawareness. But this does not have to be. When Christ ascended to the Father He rent the veil. It was removed. This separation or veil has existed only as part of our belief system; but that does not give validity to it. The veil exists because we believe it does - but God is removing this out of our thinking. We are in an accelerated process of unlearning so much that we picked up along the way.

How does this increased communication from the Lord and those of the household of faith come to us? Dreams and visions are two of those ways. Until our personal vibration is high enough to see and hear the realm of the Spirit with our physical senses, we will find much of the communication coming this way. Often this communication comes in the time just between waking and sleeping, when your senses are heightened and sharp.

The dreams which are coming to God's sons in this day are not the same as what we have known of dreams in the past. We are experiencing an overlapping of realities at this time, and the dreams or visions have begun to take on a much more significant role. Let me explain.

Our basic understanding of communication is what we have experienced in the transmission of verbal words one to another. I speak to you, and you speak to me, and we have communication. Of course we understand that what people say is not always the intent of their heart. Oftentimes there are ulterior motives or hidden agendas behind their words. Bearing that in mind, people are beginning to realize that there exists a realm of soul where emotions and feelings can be transferred from one to another. You may say one thing, but that may not be your true intent or heart. The energy of your intent is broadcast much stronger than the concept of what you are speaking. I believe the world as a whole is beginning to recognize that communication deals with more than the transmission of words, but of energy.

Back in the days of the church at Ephesus the books of the occult were gathered and burned. Paul knew that there was an energy that could be conveyed just through the handling of these books. It is the same principle when Paul anointed the handkerchief with oil and sent it to the sick woman. The handkerchief carried the anointing and transmitted it to the woman; bringing a healing.

We are speaking about the same principle; we are talking about the ability to transfer or transmit energy. Whether it is an anointed cloth, or the pages of a book, everything is comprised of energy. We have spoken of this before; for we live and have our existence surrounded by a world of spirit - a world of energy.

Email is a classic example. It is one thing to receive a physical letter or some other item of physical substance - energy can easily be transferred. But in this day of spirit everything is shifting up a notch. The very intent of the writer of an email can be conveyed through that email, even though you will never physically touch a "letter". The thoughts and intent, at a molecular and spiritual level, are being conveyed, energetically, across the internet right into your inbox. What's the saying, "Watch out, you've got mail!"

In this day of spirit we are beginning to experience a communication of spirit to spirit. This is outside of the realm of the soul or emotions, or the realm of the physical and what we have known as basic audible communication. True communication is not the conveyance of just "ideas", "concepts" or "thoughts". True communication - in the spirit - deals with the ability to transfer or impart the essence of what you are saying. It is not about the words, it is about the energy or intent of your heart. As we mentioned, in the soul the energy that is conveyed can be freighted with a great deal of garbage. In the spirit, however, you are imparting Christ to one another.

Let me see if I can explain this further. In the realm of the spirit words are not generally the mode of communication. Communication between people is conveyed through the projection of your thoughts in image form. What you are saying is conveyed almost like a picture; not limited to the restrictive interpretation of words. In the same light, true communication also involves what I call a vicarious impartation from one to another. If I truly communicate with you in the spirit, then I am doing more than conveying my thoughts, I am imparting myself to you. Do you understand?

This is what is unfolding in the dreams or visions which are coming forth in this day. Spirit to spirit impartation brings blessing, life and change. When you receive a spiritual vision or dream, you are receiving an impartation. There is a conveyance of essence or spirit that literally changes you.

If you truly desire to walk with God on the highest plane, then you must gird your mind for what He wishes to teach you. Do not let the false which has paraded itself for generations as the "occult" frighten you away from what God is bringing you into. Learn to let go. Trust Him. Let go of your mind and your concepts and let Him establish something new in you. Even as Isaiah spoke, "Behold I will do something new, will you be aware?"

"Truly, truly, I say to you, when you were younger, you used to gird yourself and walk wherever you wished; but when you grow old, you will stretch out your hands and someone else will gird you, and bring you where you do not wish to *go*." - John 21:18

God is breaking through to you on new levels; and dreams or visions are just one part of so much that God is bringing in this realm of experience and change. Will you open up and step out on new waters and let Him lead you where you would not?

God desires to draw you up higher. Let go of your fears, and your concepts. Just let go. Will you let the promises only tease you, or will you possess them? Are you ready for a new way of life? I believe you are. There is a whole new world of spirit waiting to be experienced as God continues to pour forth His spirit and bring forth His sons.

All Knowledge

We have come to the time of "the period of the restoration of all things which God spoke through the mouths of His holy prophets from ages past." (Acts 3:21).

We are experiencing a release of knowledge on a scale that no one has ever witnessed before. God is bringing a restoration to His sons. This is the function of the Holy Spirit who brings to mind all of those things which have been previously given to us. The restoration of all things during this season of time involves so much more than we have understood.

We have entered a time where the knowledge of the Lord, *which includes the depth of knowledge that already resides within you*, is being released. You must understand that within the energy or fabric of your being exists an incredible amount of knowledge and understanding. Even though this knowledge is present within our spirits, we have not been able to access it until this time. God is beginning to bring to your recall all that you are and all that He has given you.

There is so much that God will bring to remembrance as we continue to mature into the full stature of Christ. We have not begun to tap into the depth of what resides within our spirit.

> **"where were you when I laid the foundation of the earth ... when the morning stars sang together, and all the sons of God shouted for joy ... you know, for you were born then.."** – Job 38:4a, 7, 21a

You may think this scripture refers to the "fallen angels", or perhaps the "angels" that reside in the presence of the Lord. But this scripture speaks of His sons (we were with the Lord at the dawning of creation); those whom He has sent into the earth during this time to fulfill a destiny and bring forth this new day of His kingdom.

There are many prophecies that speak of the release of knowledge and wisdom in this day; Daniel 12:34 and Isaiah 11:9 are but two of them. We know that knowledge is increasing and that the knowledge of the Lord is beginning to spread over the face of the earth. This is not the knowledge of man, but an awakening of a people that are coming into their inheritance.

As much as you have sought the Lord for a relationship with Him, He is bringing to your remembrance a relationship with Him that you <u>have always had since the foundation of time</u>. It has been the veil of this present incarnation that has prevented our ability to remember. But this veil is being removed within you, and what is coming forth is an ability to know, even as you have been known.

> **For we know in part, and we prophesy in part. But when that which is perfect is come, then that which is in part shall be done away. When I was a child, I spake as a child, I understood as a child, I thought as a child: but when I became a man, I put away childish things.**
>
> **For now we see through a glass, darkly; but then face to face: now I know in part; but then shall I know even as also I am known. – 1 Co 13:9-12**

We are writing the last chapters of this age. We are penning the last pages in concert with the Lord. These chapters have not been outlined in detail because God has been waiting for a people that would rise in the spirit and become.

We are living in the time of the wise and foolish virgins. Those who have prepared their hearts before the Lord are being endowed with the capacity to see and recognize the hour of visitation that has come upon the earth.

We have become more and more aware that we are part of a spirit world that is ever present around us. We also understand that we are more than just this physical presence we house, for we are composed of a spirit, a soul and a body; in essence a triune being.

We are, in essence, "energetic beings". We co-exist in both the spiritual and natural world, simultaneously. As we become more and more conscious of that existence, we will be more and more aware of our abiding and interaction within that realm.

Imagine with me a vast ocean. You stand, immersed in this vast ocean, at one with it. You sense it, you feel it, and it flows through you. This ocean is like the world of spirit that you have your existence in. You are a part of it, and every aspect of this ocean affects you and is a part of you. We live in this "ocean", or world of spirit, 24/7, but most have no awareness of this reality. We tend to view ourselves as having primarily a physical existence, yet we are more spirit than we have ever realized.

Within this realm of spirit exists the presence of God, the Father, and Christ; along with a host of innumerable angels and the spirits of just men made perfect (Hebrews 12). Within this realm of spirit exists all knowledge. And knowledge - <u>all knowledge</u> - exists in a state of fluidity and change within the spirit realm.

> **Seeing that His divine power has granted to us everything pertaining to life and godliness.**
> **- 2Pe 1:3**

When the Lord spoke that He "gave us all things pertaining to life and godliness"; there was a hitch. All things exist and have their reality in the spirit, but they must be appropriated. Yes, we are rich. Yes, we have all knowledge, and as the scripture says, we have need of no one to teach us. It will become our truth as we come up higher and find our level of existence more and more in the realm of spirit.

Let's look for a moment at a couple of scriptures.....

> **But the Helper, the Holy Spirit, whom the Father will send in My name, He will teach you all things, and bring to your remembrance all that I said to you. - John 14:26**
>
> **As for you, the anointing which you received from Him abides in you, and you have no need for anyone to teach you; but as His anointing teaches you about all things, and is**

> **true and is not a lie, and just as it has taught you, you abide in Him. - 1Jn 2:27**

None of you really have need for anyone to teach you. In truth this knowledge is at your disposal; if you only realized it. The Word says .... you have not, because you ask amiss, (or ask not); ask that your joy may be made full. (James 4:2) (Jn 16:24)

The problem is that we have not known how to ask, and we have not known what to ask for. That is the reason why we wait upon the Lord; this is why we are driven to stay in His presence.

Knowledge is being released into the spirit realm constantly. This knowledge is available to all, as the scriptures have pointed out; to the just or the unjust alike. We know the promises; that the knowledge of the Lord will cover the earth as the waters cover the sea, and that God has been pouring forth His spirit upon all mankind (Joel 2). These are the days that these words are being fulfilled.

> **And those who have insight will shine brightly like the brightness of the expanse of heaven, and those who lead the many to righteousness, like the stars forever and ever. But as for you, Daniel, conceal these words and seal up the book until the end of time; many will go back and forth, and knowledge will increase. - Dan 12:3-4**

Knowledge is increasing. You could call it an outpouring of His spirit, of His presence, and of His knowledge - a knowledge of the Lord that has only begun to spread; for we are only at the initial stages of this prophecy.

We have entered a heightened time of release, and as you continue to come alive to God you will find inspiration and impartation that will come to you from many different levels. In dreams or visions, you may often receive words of faith, or impartation from those of our brethren who live on the other side of the veil. At times our best encouragement in this race will come from them. This is all part of the release of knowledge that is flowing to God's people during this time.

On the flip side of this, we have seen glimpses of this in operation for hundreds of years within the demonic realm. So much of what is written and portrayed through the media and news today has its origins first from the spirit world. Why do books or movies just "catch on"? Is it because the author is so commanding? No, it is because the spirit behind the writer emanates through that medium.

But back to our focus. In truth you have need of no one to teach you. You may have questions, but the answers are right here. Know what you can do; know and understand the accessibility of this spiritual knowledge. God has not left His sons unprepared or lacking in any "good" thing. It's all provided; the wisdom, the guidance, the knowledge - it is right here. It hovers in your midst as a field of energy engulfing your very existence. Reach out and touch it. Bring it in. Just as God and Christ dwell within you - this knowledge is both in you and all about you.

The word of knowledge, the word of wisdom, and the word of revelation continue to pour forth releasing the seer anointing; releasing teaching and direction for this hour we are in. Knowledge is in a state of flux. It is increasing and it is becoming more and more accessible. All of the earth lies under a cloak of darkness; but you are the Sons of Light - a light that is shining in this darkness.

God is restoring all things. He is bringing His sons into a level of remembrance of who they are and who they have always been. God is releasing a level of knowledge in the earth; a knowledge that is resident within you, and a knowledge of Him that is beginning to fill the whole earth.

The Intercession
Of The Kingdom

> "But the Kingdom is within you, and it is without you. If you know yourselves, then you will be known and you will know that you are the sons of the Living Father. But if you do not know yourselves, then you are in poverty, and you are poverty." - *The Gospel According to Thomas.*

Prayer and intercession, as we have understood them to be, must change and become what is needed at this juncture in time.

Without question we have come to the time of the manifestation of the kingdom of God in the earth - "in the earth" of you and I. As Christ told His disciples when asked concerning the kingdom; His reply was that the kingdom of God was "within you" (Luke 17:21).

This manifestation of the kingdom within you is a prelude to everything else that will happen during this time. We will see every kingdom subjected to Christ; every dominion, every throne, every principality and power. All of the kingdoms of this age will be brought under complete subjection to Christ - **but first it starts with you** (Rev 11:15).

We are witnessing a swift change in our paradigm of reality where we have lived in the partial; seeing through a glass darkly. (1Co13:12). We are experiencing a shift from seeing the provision, outside of us - seemingly unattainable and at arms distance - into recognizing that it has "already been done."

It is for this reason that our intercession must make a radical departure from how we have viewed intercession or prayer in the past.

Much of our prayer and intercession has been along the lines of the woman with the unjust judge. We have gone before the Lord to hit

Him under the eye. We have persevered until He heard our prayers, heard our heart, and responded with answers (Luke 18:3-6). We have lived our lives crying out before Him day and night that He might avenge us speedily. Generally, we have seen the provision and promise existing outside of us - something we are reaching for - something we are believing for; yet something that we have not yet attained.

This where we have missed it. This modality or consciousness of prayer was fine for the day of the partial - the day of the church age; but not for this day of the kingdom. I do not fault the prayers or supplications or a walk with the Lord of a lesser day; on a level that was in the day of the "partial". The rules change, however, as we come into this day of His kingdom.

Intercession on this level of the kingdom involves something entirely different. Intercession and prayer in this day must come from a level of awareness; an awareness of what has already been done and accomplished in the spirit.

The scriptures of this day are not concerned with beseeching the Lord to move; rather, they speak of the reality of what He has already completed. (Eph 1:3, Jn 19:30, 2 Pe 1:3)

We have come to a time of change; the time of the bride and bridegroom. In scientific terms; we have come to a point of critical mass - a tipping point as it were – because of what is unfolding in the earth.

God is not going to do anything further than what He has already done. It is the travail and intercession of the sons of God that will bring forth the realities of what has already been accomplished - *onto this plane of existence*. God has already done it. Sonship is here. We have just not entered into the experience or reality of it – <u>the final seal of which is the redemption of this body.</u>

> The Book of Thomas has stated:
>
> **"His disciples said to Him: When will the repose of the dead come about and when will the new world come? He said to them; What**

> you expect has come, but you know it not."
> *Logos 51.*

> "His disciples said to Him: When will the Kingdom come? Jesus said: It will not come by expectation; they will not say; "See, here", or "See, there". But the Kingdom of the Father is spread upon the earth and men do not see it."
> *Logos 114*

What we seek is already in the earth; yet we have not been able to see it or recognize it. Our intercession or travail needs to come up higher. Rather than seeking God to do something, our intercession becomes a travail to see manifested within us that which He has already done. Although He has already provided everything pertaining to life and godliness, we find that we are still catching up to experience this scripture (2 Peter 1:3).

> **seeing that His divine power has granted to us everything pertaining to life and godliness, through the true knowledge of Him who called us by His own glory and excellence. – 2Pe 1:3**

If you have seen this, then your very "sight" has been the vehicle that has thrown your spirit into the travail and intercession of the kingdom for this day. You have begun to experience the travail or intercession that will bring forth, on this plane of existence, the realities of what has already been done. (Jn 19:30)

Our prayers can no longer be an expression of those who have no perception or who have no sight; not when God has provided it all.

The travail God's sons have been experiencing has begun to birth them into a deeper level of spirit. As you transition to higher and higher levels in His presence you will find that one level begets another. This is a process; but a process that increases exponentially as you spiral upward into His presence.

Where Christ is seated - at the right hand of the Father - is where you are destined to be. This scripture should no longer be viewed in the future tense, for we have come to the time for its fulfillment. This is the time of His appearing. Your travail and intercession is bringing forth the manifestation of that which has already been done. It is destined to be manifested within your physical body, here and now.

This becomes one of the greater works which Christ spoke of; an intercession and travail upon a people that literally create a level of sonship in the earth. This could not have been done by Christ alone. He opened the door, as the first born of <u>many</u> brethren, to pave the way for <u>many</u> to come forth in this hour. (Ro. 8:29)

<u>This travail or intercession is not complete until we see it manifested within the physical body</u>. The intercession of this hour is a cry, a groaning beyond words, that demands the manifestation of the truth within the very depths of each of God's sons. (Ro 8:26) That truth is the fulfillment of Romans 8 - Christ in you - the hope of glory.

It could seem like I am addressing 2 different issues; one concerning a kingdom level of prayer or intercession and another concerning the manifestation of sonship within our bodies. Really I am saying only one thing; you cannot separate the fulfillment of prayer, intercession, or the travail of sonship, from the direct manifestation of that prayer, intercession or travail **within you**.

During this time of change we are beginning to experience an interpenetration of all that the Father and Christ are with us. When the disciples came to Jesus and said, "Show us the Father". Christ's reply was, "Have I been so long with you and yet you ask me to show you the Father. If you have seen Me, you have seen the Father." (Jn 14:9) There was a complete interpenetration of all that God was within Christ. If you saw Christ, you saw the Father. That interpenetration was complete, and this is what we see progressively unfolding now.

If you are looking for another definition of sonship, this would be your answer ... it is the complete indwelling of the Godhead within the sons - Father, Son, and Holy Spirit.

We are just now beginning to realize how completely Christ can move through us. It is an interpenetration or oneness beyond what we have ever known. This is His will; a oneness with Christ and the Father - manifested in the physical form - within you.

We must also realize that there is no manifestation of the sons of God in this hour, without a corresponding manifestation of the Lord Jesus Christ within them. **It is one and the same.**

For some time now I have felt strongly that resurrection life is here even though we have not perceived the provision, truth or reality of that promise. We have still gone before the Father seeking for a release when it has already been given. The problem is that we have been functioning from a reality or paradigm of a level that is lesser, because our minds have not been able to embrace or comprehend the truth of this level to which we have come.

When the Lord reveals a promise, provision, or prophecy to you, it is at that very moment that you have been fully empowered to manifest the fullness of that provision on this plane of existence. It is no longer a promise or provision; it is truly a reality to be manifested in the "here and now".

In this hour the Word should not be read as a "Book of Promises", but rather, a **Book of Present Realities**. And the travail of the sons of God in this hour is a travail born out of the realization that these promises and these truths exist now.

So much can be implied in this word; take the scripture.... As a man thinks in his heart, so is he. (Prov 23:7)   There is only one way we can think; that we are complete in Christ, *here and now*. We have it all; we are prepared. We have what we have sought - we are the embodiment of Christ - we are one with Christ and the Father.

These are rather audacious statements, yet if you really believe the Word, then you realize that all that you seek is here. From the foundations of the world, it "has been done".

To fully embrace each and every word that God speaks we must truly "let go". Are you ready? We can't hold onto a perception, or limitation of yesterday; we must let go. We must let go of the lesser that we might receive the greater. We must stop the internal dynamics and just let go and accept what He has done. We must accept what He has said about us.

I am not saying you are perfect, but I am saying that you are complete in Him. Just let go. It doesn't work unless you really "let go". You have to trust Him.

This reminds me of a short story - a perfect example;

There was a man walking home from church one night and he fell off a cliff. On the way down he grabbed hold of a branch growing out from the side. He started to pray and said, "God, Save Me!" The next thing he heard a voice say, "Let go of the branch and I will save you". After thinking for a while, the man called up and said, "Is there anyone else up there?!".

We must let go of what we have had, that He might bring a new thing.

Christ said that He went to the Father, so that where He was, there we might be also. (John 14:3) Where is "there"? In the presence of the Father. Where do you dwell? The truth - in His presence. But "your truth" may be different. You may not have accepted this on this level. When Christ died on the cross, He said, "It is finished". And believe me, **It is Finished.**

This is not the day of the partial; oh sons, this is the day of His fullness.

You are a part of a royal priesthood; a mighty nation before God. When? <u>Now</u>. Now you are a king and a priest. You just need to see it . Read 1 Peter 2:9.

How do we intercede now? Our intercession is that which reaches beyond the veil, beyond limitations, beyond concepts and thoughts; an intercession that reaches in and touches the truth. Our intercession demands that this truth be fully embodied in each of us - here and now.

The enemy has fought to keep you unaware of your heritage, unaware of what you have become, and unaware of what you can do. The blessings and releases which He has already given are hovering over you - *just reach up and take them.*

In the book of Philippians Paul spoke about living on tiptoe (Phil 3:12). When asked if He had attained it, he said, "not yet", but he saw it and he was reaching to lay hold of that for which he was laid hold of. And so we too live our lives on tiptoe – there is no other way.

It is right here. Our intercession, our prayer and our travail is to manifest every truth, every provision, and the reality of sonship on this level.

The demons shudder; "Have we come before the time?"

No we haven't - because **it is the time.**

Actually it may be a little overdue, but now is the time that everything will be brought under the footstool of His feet. It's time to finish the job. Let's end this age.

The Functioning Priesthood

As we move more deeply into this time of His kingdom we find the Lord is re-writing and re-defining what we have understood of the functioning of the priesthood ministry of Christ. He is changing our paradigm of how we have perceived His word.

These days of the Kingdom are days of Spirit. When the early church was first formed; the laws, handed down by Moses and the prophets, dictated the way the believer walked. Everything was done by "the law". But when Christ came, He did away with the law and the decrees, and the believer found that the "just lived by faith" (Col 2:14, Gal 3:11).

As we transition into these days of the kingdom, once again, everything is changing. What worked on one level does not work on this kingdom level. What may have been effective in times past, has become an "Ichabod" - for the glory of God has departed (1Sam 4:21).

God is moving on and we are beginning to understand that the fulfillment of the prophecies of the Word are intrinsically linked to a level of spiritual abiding within the believer or son. As God's sons continue to come up higher, everything becomes more clear to them.

When you read the command in 1st Thessalonians 5:17 to "pray without ceasing", you realize you are utterly incapable of walking in that word from the level of the soul. This can only be achieved as you live in the spirit.

For too long we have not understood the inherent potential of "prayer". Because we have walked in a day of the partial, what we have known of prayer was limited. As we have said before; when you enter into this day of the kingdom, the day of the partial gives way to the day of His fullness.

When you grasp the depth of who and what you are in Christ, you begin to comprehend that you are entering into His omniscience – His unlimited-ness. You realize that only your spirit, through your intent, can alone sustain a level of praying without ceasing. You are entering into a oneness with our great high priest, who "ever lives to intercede" (Ro 8:34).

We must understand that one of the foremost callings of God's sons in this hour is one of "intercession". This kingdom level of prayer or intercession is truly Christ ministering through you as He ever lives to intercede for the sons.

> **Therefore He is able also to save forever those who draw near to God through Him, since He always lives to make intercession for them. - Heb 7:25**

In the priesthood ministry Christ ever lives to intercede through us. His intercession is from a level of knowing who we are, and what we are to do and to be (Hebrews 7:25). This aspect of the priesthood ministry of Christ is an example of how we must function - our prayer or intercession must come up higher. Once again, another paradigm or concept that we have had needs to change; we must let go of the lesser that He might give us the greater.

To have a revelation of your brother or sister in Christ, to really see them after the spirit, becomes the very catalyst of prayer on this next level of the kingdom. Without even an utterance of a word, your faith can literally "see" them into being. This is an entirely different mode of prayer. You are interceding or praying not born of your concepts or your soul's input and opinions. Your prayer and intercession is born out of what you have seen them to be in God. This is prayer "in the spirit", and it can only be fulfilled and manifested as you transition to a life in the spirit.

It is not too difficult to see each other after the flesh, after the personal issues each one has. If this is our level of awareness, then our prayer or intercession will create nothing but bonds and attachments. We will continue in the mode of supplicating the Father, rather than walking in the potential of being able to create and release one another. As we reach deeper into His heart, and see each other as Christ sees us - as we truly are - we find that we are linking hands with Christ and producing a powerful dynamic of spirit that creates. You are becoming co-creators with Christ; you literally create and release each other into all that He has and is.

This is the unspoken intercession; "a groaning too deep for words" that Paul speaks of. This is the relationship of the kingdom that is both creative and powerful. There must be a drive and demand to walk on this level of spirit and be the instruments of release that we are called to be. This puts a great deal of demand upon God's sons to become and to mature into the full stature of Christ.

We are talking about really experiencing "prayer in the spirit". As you transition to a life in the spirit, <u>everything</u> truly becomes new for you. What you knew and experienced in the day of the soul must give way to a fulfillment and reality born of the spirit. Your destiny is to walk in the realities of the spirit. You cannot force this new level of spirit into an old paradigm born out of the soul. You must be born into this new level. Do you understand?

In this process of becoming and maturing, each of His sons must enter into a realm of open vision and sight. You must truly know one another after the spirit. The relationship and unspoken word of faith you have for each other will create and draw out the fullness of Christ from within them..

The only way you are really going to help people, really set them free, will not be from a prayer level born out of yesterday's anointing; but by an intercession born out of a revelation of those with whom you walk.

We have come to the end of the "partial" - *the day of the soul, and the church age we have known*. To please the Lord we must walk in His fullness, no longer seeing in part; no longer seeing men as trees walking (Mark 8:24). The effectiveness of our prayer, of our faith, and of our intercession is commensurate to the spiritual level we are walking on.

We need to understand just what this catalyst is that binds the Word together with our faith to create the explosion. This catalyst has to do with how you see. Your understanding - your ability to rightly discern and judge - will affect changes on every level within the kingdom. This will create those whom God has led you to without even speaking a word.

In scientific terms you could say that when you are walking on a plane of spirit where you truly see, there is a unique vibration or energy that is different from anything else. This is more than a passive reflection, but an insight that the truth has a vibration to it. Christ is the truth, and it is the vibration of Christ that is emanating from you. You literally become the spiritual catalyst that releases the dunamis or "power". An explosion happens.

Do you recall the story of the woman who touched the hem of His garment? (Luke 8:44). There was a provision she tapped into that released the power of God. This is the same principle. This is the prayer or intercession that goes beyond words and releases the power of God from within you.

We are talking about a new mode of prayer or intercession. A kingdom level of intercession that effectively gets the job done. We are talking about really knowing as the Father and Christ know. In truly discerning one another after "the spirit", we are able to release each other into that which has been prepared for them from the foundations of the world (Heb 4:3).

We are linking into the vision of the Father about who His sons are; effectively creating and bringing forth each other.

How do you pray for your sons and daughters. **By becoming**. Your best intercession or prayer for anyone is in your act of becoming. That may sound a bit selfish; but it is absolutely true.

The man-child spoken of in the book of Revelation is coming forth. You are in travail, and you are bringing forth the kingdom. You are bringing forth the Christ company, God's sons and daughters. This is the travail, the intercession and the birthing of the sons of God in this hour.

The Ark

of His Presence

Several years ago a vision came which spoke of the Ark of the Covenant in this day. This ark was not an earthen box, rather this ark was our body. Within that ark were not the 2 tablets of stone signifying the covenant with the children of Israel; within this ark was the manifested presence of God. As this ark of His presence began to move throughout this age, changes began to happen. These changes came because housed within the framework of this "earthen temple" was the presence and power of God. Wherever this ark went; the energy and vibration of God caused deep changes within the earth.

As we move and function in this world we are finding more and more that we are bringing a confrontation to this age; because light and darkness cannot coexist.

The more you are given and surrendered to His Lordship and His demands, the greater His presence prevails within you. Whether we are aware or not, the energy of Christ and the Father is coursing through us and radiating out from us. The more His presence has free course through us, the more identical we are becoming with Christ. This oneness with Christ and the Father is confronting everything which comes into our atmosphere.

Your presence in the earth is beginning to evoke reactions and changes. You are becoming the ark of His Presence. If there is an openness to the Lord, these changes are positive; if not, these changes may be punitive.

Perhaps you have walked this way and never really understood what was happening. Perhaps you have been frustrated, yet in awe at the reactions that seemed to happen around you. This has been the path of His sons.

Why is this? Once again, this is because you are God's presence - His emissary in the earth. The energy of Christ is flowing through you, coursing through every fiber of your being - every molecule - every vibration. You are God, incarnate, and His energy causes changes to happen.

Some of the greatest intercession you can make is just by being who you are. Know it, accept it and allow the energy of all that He is to flow forth from you. Just stand, and be who God has called you to be. It is the greatest intercession you could make.

Expect the unexpected, for this is what His presence creates. The more you recognize your absolute identification with Christ, the more effective you become and the more the energy and essence of the Father is transmitted through you.

Let's talk about this for a brief moment.

The more you see who you are and what He is within you, the more you "untie" His hands; the more all that He is can flow forth through you. Whether we want to face this or not; our lack or inability of recognizing what He has become within us has held back the manifestation of the Lord through us. <u>We have tied His hands</u>. Your perception of yourself, if it is not born of the spirit - as Christ sees you - is the bond that ties His hand. This is changing; but it is important for you to understand that what is happening within you demands that you come up higher and truly see yourself as the Lord sees you.

To some this may appear arrogant. "Who are you to think so highly of yourself?" The truth is that we know we are just earthen vessels. It is not about who we are. It is about who He is within us. If our stance may appear arrogant to others; so be it. Unless someone sees you after the spirit, they will not know who you are anyway.

There is a drive in the spirit for you to come into a state of knowing or understanding. This is not passive by any means - this is very intense. The Word says that as He was in this world, so are we. What does it mean to walk this out; to experience this scripture? It means that you are to be the embodiment of all that Christ is. Your very presence will create changes wherever you go. This is a very present reality.

It can be very easy to quote these scriptures and banter them about, but God is demanding that His sons walk as the embodiment of His word.

Section 6

The Administration

Of the Kingdom

- **An Administration Suitable**
  to the Fullness of the Times

- **The Power of Oneness**

- **The Last Kingdom**

An Administration Suitable

..to the fullness of the times

> He made known to us the mystery of His will, according to His kind intention which He purposed in Him with a view to an administration suitable to the fullness of the times, *that is,* the summing up of all things in Christ, things in the heavens and things on the earth. In Him - Eph 1:9-10

The theme of the book of Ephesians speaks of the administration of the authority of Christ through the church. Paul talks about a "mystery" that God would establish in the latter days. This "mystery" concerns the empowering of the saints with an authority suitable to the times that they would face. The time that you and I have now come to.

> then *comes* the end, when He hands over the kingdom to the God and Father, when He has abolished all rule and all authority and power. For He must reign until He has put all His enemies under His feet. – 1Co 15:24-25

We know the promise that every knee will bow before the Lord. We also know that every kingdom will be subjected to the Lord; who in turn will give it back to the Father (Phil 2:10-11). We have known and read these scriptures often over the years, but it has not been until this time that we will see the fulfillment of these words.

What all of these scriptures speak of is the restoration of an authority in the earth that we have not yet seen; the restoration of Christ's authority. This authority will function through His church and will be suitable to the need of the times that we have come to.

We have passed through the time of God's sovereign moving in the earth. We have come to the time that what He will accomplish in these last days will be done through His human channels; the sons of God.

How will every kingdom be brought down and how will every knee bow before the Lord? This will happen - and has already begun - through the manifestation of the authority of Christ through the sons.

There has been a downward trend in the earth over the past several generations and it has grown increasingly worse. We have seen what I term the progressive "de-moralization of America". More than that, we have seen the countries of this world system overrun with a tremendous amount of evil. We have seen the love of many waxing cold. We have come to what is referred to in the Word as the "fullness of the times" - *for the iniquity has come to the full.*

There is a change happening, for we are in the time of the balance in the spirit world changing. The downward pull will be replaced with the upward pull to Zion, and that is scriptural. We are seeing a changing of the guard; a change from Satan's rule over this present age. As the manifestation of the sons of God come forth, the shift in the spirit realm will become complete, for it is the destiny of the sons of God to execute the judgments written upon this age.

We are speaking of a new administration with the anointing of the kings and priests of God; with all power, authority and dominion. A mantle of authority is beginning to rest upon His sons to complete the judgments that have been written from the foundations of the earth (Ps 149).

We must see the execution of authority at this juncture manifested if we intend to see the releases come to pass that are slated for this present time. It is apparent that the manifestation and wielding of Christ's authority is paramount to the ushering in of the kingdom of God.

The closer we come to the full release and manifestation of the word through His people, the greater the conflict has become. We know why - God's sons have come to the time where they are beginning to make a difference - they are beginning to affect a shift of power in the spirit world.

> **Do not participate in the unfruitful deeds of darkness, but instead even expose them; - Phil 5:11**

> **for it is disgraceful even to speak of the things which are done by them in secret. But all things become visible when they are exposed by the light, for everything that becomes visible is light. – Eph 5:12-13**

We are once again seeing the functioning of the seer prophet in the land as we did in the days of Elisha (2Kings 6:12). God has begun to expose that which is being done behind closed doors. All that has been hidden is beginning to be exposed. The Satanic cunning to destroy this age is being made known. That which has been conceived in darkness is being revealed by the Light.

Like Elisha, God's sons are beginning to learn how to control the spirit realm. As we move forward this will continue to bring more and more changes. We are seeing the administration of Christ's authority, and it is exposing and bringing judgment upon what has been done behind closed doors. This could not happen without the birthing of the sons and the anointing of the seer.

The Lord has brought word after word concerning bonds and the devastating effects they can have. We have watched this. We have seen how bonds continue to affect God's people. We have been concerned about how the witchcraft and transference comes through these bonds, but our greatest concern is the blindness that happens when bonds exist. If your sight is compromised, so is your ability to "hear". Spiritual vision or sight is very delicate. It takes very little to obstruct your capacity to see or to hear.

Authority is not that effective unless you can see. We cannot beat the air and hope to hit something (1Co 9:26). We must be able to clearly see if we are to be effective in administrating Christ's authority.

> **And Jesus came up and spoke to them, saying, "All authority has been given to Me in heaven and on earth. Go therefore and make disciples of all the nations, baptizing them in the name of the Father and the Son and the Holy Spirit". Matt 28:18-19**

This scripture speaks of a fulfillment on a level of spirit we have yet to see. In the past you might assume it is talking about saving souls, converting people and leading them to the Lord. We are missing it if we relegate it to only that level; for this commission in the book of Matthew has been reserved for this day. This is a word which is tied into the release and manifestation of the authority of the kingdom.

Christ didn't say, "go and convince them, pass out some tracts, talk them into it". No, He said, "<u>Go and Make Disciples</u>". You make them. Just do it! This is not possible without the authority to break the bonds, the hindrances and the oppressions over the nations.

We will not see the release of the kingdom, the release of resurrection life, or the evangelism of the kingdom completed, without we first see the absolute manifestation of authority and power that binds the strong man. We must see the judgment upon the principalities and powers that have held people in bondage. This is how we will manifest the kingdom. It is the same principle that was given when Christ spoke about plundering the strong man's house. (Matt 12:29)

The restraints are coming off, and we will see a level of financial collapse and devastation beyond what has ever been witnessed. This could sound a bit apocalyptic, but this is what has continued to come to us. The iniquity of this age has come to the full. As it was in the days of Sodom and Gomorrah, so it has become in this time, the time of the "Son of Man" (Luke 17:26).

> **And when the dragon saw that he was cast unto the earth, he persecuted the woman which brought forth the man *child*. –Rev 12:13**

Perhaps we have viewed this scripture as a past tense reality; that which happened when the angels fell from heaven. However, I believe this scripture has a present day application that we need to understand. The book of Revelation speaks about Satan being cast down as he goes to make war with the seed of Christ.

You may feel that at some point this scripture in the book of Revelation will happen, but we have been deeper into the unfolding of this reality than we have perceived. What we have seen for some time now is a deeper penetration of the demonic realm into this human plane. Not an overlapping, but almost like a "tear" in the barriers between levels.

Let me try to explain.

Christ said that in His Father's house were many dwelling places. He was referring to the many different levels that exist within God's kingdom. Each level of this house exists on a different level or plane of vibration.

> **In my Father's house are many mansions: if *it were* not *so*, I would have told you. I go to prepare a place for you. And if I go and prepare a place for you, I will come again, and receive you unto myself; that where I am, *there* ye may be also. – John 14:2-3**

We have spoken before that creation is comprised of vibration. Everything around you is vibration. The colors you see, the form and matter about you, and even your own essence. Everything is comprised of vibration. The more you come into the presence of Christ and the Father, the higher your vibration rises.

Satan and his cohorts are being cast down - their vibration is shifting. This "casting down" has been accelerating over the past several decades, as we have continued to witness progressively greater manifestations of devil power, devil worship and the manipulation of this world's scene through the channels of evil.

What we have seen happening has been an increasingly greater presence in the earth of the demonic world, for they are being cast down.

It is not that difficult to perceive the increasing tide of wickedness in the earth; for God is letting the iniquity come to the full. This increasing tide of wickedness is not random, it is occurring because of a greater degree of access that is happening between levels. The rise of witchcraft, especially as it has been fostered through the entertainment & literary industry, is staggering - yet people are clueless.

We are not that concerned with the plan of Satan. Granted he has a plan and a timetable to destroy mankind, but he is only the unwitting tool of God as God uses him to bring forth His sons.

You are in school. God is teaching you and bringing you into your inheritance as quickly as you are able to change. You have been in an advanced course coming forward in the spirit, for it is time to function and claim your place in His presence. He is creating you to be a new wineskin able to receive the new wine of this day, for His sons must understand how to operate and function effectively in the spirit in order to bring in the kingdom.

Please understand - there is no manifestation of His kingdom - there is no release of the elemental realm - there is no release of the Cloud of Witnesses - and there is no resurrection life - ***without judgment***. We must see the full enactment of the judgment spoken of in Psalms 149 - the judgments written which have been held in abeyance for this time. I doubt that the gods of this age may be too pleased about this, but this is the time of Christ's dominion over every kingdom of this earth. **The shift in the spirit is on.**

Even as the demons spoke to Christ saying, "Have you come to torment us before the "time"? Ahh... they knew there was a "time", a "time" set by the Father.

Once again the spirit world is asking the same question. They know there is a "time", a "time" that will see the judgments enacted. We have come to the threshold of this time. You are here now and now is the time of the administration suitable to the fullness of the times.

The Power of Oneness

We are seeing a visitation of power and authority which has not been in the earth before this time. We have seen a measure of power and authority, but until now, that is all we have seen - a measure; the partial. God is bringing forth a mystical oneness within His church, and this mystical union is going to bring about the release of power and authority that will be the fulfillment of Deuteronomy 32.

> "...could one chase a thousand, And two put ten thousand to flight ...-Deu 32:30

Everything in the spirit can be explained if you understand the workings or dynamics of the spirit world. God is very scientific. All of His creation function through the principles He has created - whether they are principles that govern the natural realm, or the spirit realm. There is much that we may see unfolding and equate it to "miracles", yet if we look closer they are just an operation of the principles that exist in the realm of spirit. Just like gravity is a principle in the natural world, so the functioning of the spirit also flows along the scientific channels of established principles.

It has always intrigued me to understand just what we were experiencing, from a scientific perspective, as we followed on to know the Lord. In the Old Testament the Word tells how the children of Israel saw the mighty acts of God, but Moses knew His ways (Psa 103:7). Moses understood the dynamics of God's ways and how they worked; he knew how it was done. The children of Israel only saw the manifestation.

There are times when you flow along with the spirit of the Lord as He brings changes; never really understanding the dynamics. Then there are times when He brings understanding to your heart and you begin to see things more clearly.

Perhaps this description of the power of oneness will shed some light on what God is establishing during this season of time that we call the "manifestation of the sons of God".

Anne's father was a very bright and scientific individual. He was an engineer and was involved with the development of the helicopter. We enjoyed sitting back and listening to his stories. He was also very analytical and was always looking deeper, trying to dissect and understand the moving of God. Here is a little snapshot of a discussion we had many years ago....

We're going to talk about frequency, harmonics and resonance; basic principles that operate in the natural plane. This will give us an insight into what we are experiencing during this season.

With a radio you are able to electronically tune into various frequencies. You continue to turn the dial until the electronic frequency of the radio is equal to what is called the RF signal or RF frequency being emitted from the radio station. When this happens they intermesh. There is a release of power and voila! - you can hear the radio transmission. Individually there appears to be no energy there, yet when these 2 electronic frequencies become one, they become harmonic - in the same realm at exactly the same frequency - and the power is released.

Another example of this principle of harmonics or resonance would be something which happened years ago when a new model of helicopter was being developed and tested. Some of the helicopters had experienced a resonant frequency that was so powerful that the helicopters blew up. They conducted experiments to find out what to do about it; how to change the design of the copter so that these frequencies would not become resonant.

When a helicopter does not have enough of what is called "dampening", then there is a tendency for that helicopter to reach a state of resonance. What happens when a helicopter reaches a state of resonance? A great deal! You might even say "it's explosive!"

To best explain this reaction would be to say that the frequency of the helicopter touching the ground (bouncing a bit), and the frequency of the main rotor blade, the transmission and tail rotor all end up vibrating or "resonating" at the same frequency . If and when this happens the helicopter is destroyed within micro-seconds. The helicopter literally comes unglued. Why? Because the frequencies overlapped and the exponential release of power absolutely unhinges the helicopter.

Resonant frequency is when 2 objects are vibrating at exactly the same frequency; they become "resonant". Their vibration overlaps and the atoms are transferred back and forth between those objects causing the power that is unleashed to go up exponentially. It goes straight up. If you graph it out, that line will go straight up - literally to infinity.

I realize this is a lot to grasp, but there is a point we are driving at here. On a scriptural level this would be a scientific explanation of what happens when you have people who are truly in agreement. One puts a thousand to flight, and two, 10,000. It is this principle of harmonic resonance as it is experienced within His sons.

It has always fascinated me to delve into the scriptures and really search to understand the ways of God; to ask God "just how does this work?" When He brings simple little explanations, or in this case, perhaps it is a bit technical, then it all comes together.

When we talk about oneness; this is what we are looking for. Not an "agreement of the soul", but an agreement or "resonance" of the spirit. This is a scientific definition of what happens when you literally achieve oneness. This breaks the religious concept of how we have looked at oneness and what we have thought oneness is.

What God is bringing in this experience of oneness is not an agreement born of the soul. We are not talking about a group of people all sitting around "agreeing" together. We are not talking about a prayer breakfast where they all come to a "decision". We are talking about a provision or reality that has been set apart for this day.

True oneness is a reality that can only be manifested from the spirit; by a people who walk in the spirit. What we have seen to this point has been a general level of agreement, born of the soul, that has achieved very little. But when God speaks of the power of oneness or the power of agreement, He is speaking of the potential that is unleashed when His sons truly achieve a resonant state of inter-connectedness. True "oneness".

In the book of Acts it reads that they were "all together in one room, with one mind", as they were seeking the Lord when the Spirit fell. I believe that there was something at work within the 120 that created a release on a much deeper level – very similar to this level of oneness we are speaking of.

Am I saying that the visitation of the cloven tongues of fire, and the baptism of the spirit came because the 120 entered a level of oneness that we are speaking of here? Yes - to a degree. Christ had already said He would send the comforter, but I believe the 120 helped to create the atmosphere for this outpouring by their synergy of oneness.

Joel prophesied about this level of oneness to come; a oneness that will cause the greater works. This oneness will create the open doors to see the kingdom established. By this oneness we will see the exponential release of the power of God on the earth on a level never before seen. How will it happen? I believe the sons of God will all vibrate on a similar spiritual frequency; spilling over into the natural realm creating a power like no one has ever seen.

We have had glimpses of this oneness, but we have only experienced the "partial". What we may have thought was oneness was more a level of agreement born of the soul. What we are speaking of is a oneness that will release the power of God, encompassing the greater works which Christ spoke of.

We know that God has brought His sons to this precise juncture in time, but we also understand that we must make the shift to this next transition. How quickly we are able to achieve this oneness is dependant upon how quickly we change.

The Sons of God are being trained in the ways of the Spirit; you have been in school. We have said this. This principle of resonating oneness will become an experience that God's sons will not only enter into, but they will know how they achieved it. They will live in it and be able to access this power of oneness anytime the Lord directs.

We have walked in a level of oneness born of the soul, but this is not the oneness that is coming. We can all be on the same page in our vision and our drive; all focused in the same direction, but that is not oneness. This is not what we are speaking of. That was the day of the Church Age, but we have come to the days of His kingdom.

We have been at this threshold for some time. Now is the time that we will enter through this portal into this resonating oneness.

When you achieve oneness, you will know it. The world will know it.

The Last Kingdom

We have entered a very precipitous time as we have seen the banking institutions and the economies of this world system shaken. It is one more sign of the days we are walking in.

There has been a fatalistic view in the rank and file of the religious community that God's plan for the last days has been precisely mapped out. I don't believe this is really the truth. There is much that will be determined as His sons work in concert with Him to see the wrap up of this age.

Throughout the scriptures, and especially in the book of Revelation, we get an overall view of God's plan for the latter days. However what is not spelled out as clearly is the path from point A to point B. It is the fine detail of how this all plays out in these days right before us that are still in a state of flux. The administration of God's plan in the earth is still largely dependant upon the actions and interactions of His sons; for God has limited Himself to move through human instruments. It is for this reason alone that the last chapters have yet to be written.

So often the word has come through in the Spirit during the early hours of the morning.....**Write the last chapters, my sons....**

We have a strong "inkling" of the mind and heart of the Father for the days ahead of us. We know that the judgments will come as a visitation of the fire of God (Isa 66:16), yet there is much to be determined concerning how this will all be orchestrated during this time.

It has been clearly evident that we will see a judgment upon the systems of this world that are in control. Whether it is the banking system, the media, or the structure of governments – all are being satanically driven and controlled by the hosts of evil. These agencies have manipulated a control over people far beyond what any have understood.

In Daniel 2 we read that God has decreed that judgment shall come upon this system that no amount of manipulation will be able to thwart.

> **Then there will be a fourth kingdom as strong as iron; inasmuch as iron crushes and shatters all things, so, like iron that breaks in pieces, it will crush and break all these in pieces.**
>
> **In that you saw the feet and toes, partly of potter's clay and partly of iron, it will be a divided kingdom; but it will have in it the toughness of iron, inasmuch as you saw the iron mixed with common clay. As the toes of the feet *were* partly of iron and partly of pottery, *so* some of the kingdom will be strong and part of it will be brittle.**
>
> **And in that you saw the iron mixed with common clay, they will combine with one another in the seed of men; but they will not adhere to one another, even as iron does not combine with pottery.**
>
> **In the days of those kings the God of heaven will set up a kingdom which will never be destroyed, and *that* kingdom will not be left for another people; it will crush and put an end to all these kingdoms, but it will itself endure forever. Inasmuch as you saw that a stone was cut out of the mountain without hands and that it crushed the iron, the bronze, the clay, the silver and the gold, the great God has made known to the king what will take place in the future; so the dream is true and its interpretation is trustworthy. Dan 2:40-45**

This vision pertains to the various world governments as portrayed by the Gold, Silver, Bronze and Iron. We know that many governments have come and gone; yet the vision of this last image speaks of the last days - the days which we have now entered.

The feet of this image is comprised of common clay and iron, and as the scriptures point out, the iron did not mix with that of the common clay. This "iron" signifies the seed of Satan which has attempted to mix and merge within the seed of man. As it mentions in the book of Daniel, this is a mixture that cannot blend.

This is the last kingdom which is yet to be dealt with. Every other kingdom in the vision of Daniel 2 has come and gone, but there is yet to be a fulfillment to this last one - the kingdom which is born of common clay and iron. We will see the judgment of this last image both in the spirit and natural plane as we have never seen before.

This is the kingdom which has spawned over the face of the earth today. It is not the United States, nor is it Russia, nor is it France, or Germany, or any other individual country. We are speaking of a "world system" which exists during these last days. It is the kingdom of this "world system" – that which exists within and throughout every government on the face of the earth at this time - which the vision of Daniel speaks of.

Unbeknownst to most, the seed and influence of this mixture of iron and clay has permeated every country, every government, and every form of media that exists today. This final kingdom is poised to be destroyed by the stone cut out of the mountain. This stone is destined to become a great and mighty kingdom, the kingdom of the Heavenly Father - His sons.

This mixture of iron and clay concerns the Nephilim; a pervading force in the earth today. For those of you who are students of the word, you probably have a cursory understanding of the Nephilim. But for those of you who do not; the Nephilim represent the seed born out of the unholy union of the fallen angels as they mixed with the daughters of men.

In the book of Genesis, in some translations, it refers to these fallen angels as the "sons of God", but this has no relevance whatsoever with what God is establishing within His people during this day. If you look on the internet all you see is more and more focus and propagation of lies concerning the "sons of God". There is a great deal of focus and interest in this evil seed, but little - if any - real perception concerning what God is really doing. We are speaking of the true Sons of God; those patterned after Christ as referenced in the book of Romans.

That which was born of this unholy union, the Nephilim, were known in the Old Testament as the "men of renown". These were men of great feats and capabilities. Who are they in this hour? They are the preeminent leaders, rulers, and men of power, wealth and influence that are in control - *mostly behind the scene.*

Joshua faced the Nephilim in the land of Canaan, and you can read of these "men of renown" throughout Greek lore. Many of these accounts were not mythical stories. These were actual accounts - on one level or another - of these "men of renown" who were born of this union of the fallen angels with women.

To this day much of our warfare in the spirit is dealing with these spirits, the spirits of the Nephilim, as they move within and throughout the "sons of darkness". Their mission - to manipulate and control the affairs of men in this day.

Where do you find men of such great evil and great capability? Where else but in government, banking, the media; virtually every venue that has the ability to control or manipulate the minds and hearts of the people that live in the world today.

Unless those days had been cut short, no life would have been saved; but for the sake of the elect those days will be cut short.- Mat 24:22

Their end goal? Of course - to destroy humanity.

In many ways we have been in a race; a race that God's sons have not known or understood that they were even in. It can seem as if there has been a race in the spirit to see who will control the destiny and affairs of this age. Who will manifest first – the satanic seed or God's sons? Of course we know the answer. We know what God is doing. Let the darkness pursue after themselves. We know we are but walking out a destiny and fulfillment that was completed so very long ago.

Understand that the Nephilim have been looking to establish a race of beings; call them the sons of darkness. This has been unfolding- the flip side - while the Father has been bringing His sons to birth; the sons of the Living God.

We know the promise or intent of the Father is that His instruments - His sons - shall bind and bring to judgment the principalities, the powers and the rulers of this present darkness. Their judgment has already been measured out. We are the executors of the Father's will. The satanic hosts have only been the unwitting tool of God in seeing His sons brought to birth, for we have come to "the time" - a time of finality and completion.

When Christ ascended to the Father's presence he saw Satan falling. The judgment upon the spirits of wickedness have been sealed. It was done – completed; however, the judgments have awaited the maturing of the sons of God who would enact and execute those judgments which have been written (Ps 149).

When Joshua and Caleb went into Canaan to spy out the land, they saw that the "shadow" or protection of the giants, the Nephilim, had been removed by the Lord. Read Numbers 13. The protection that was a covering to these Nephilim, this satanic seed of this earlier day, had been removed. They were now vulnerable. And so it is at this time. The protection of the Nephilim in the earth has been removed for their judgments have been sealed. It is at this time that we will see the judgment upon this last image, for judgment has begun to stream from Zion.

We are in the mop up operation of seeing the heavens and the earth cleansed of the filth and evil that has so saturated this world. It is time. And it is now. You will see and create the fulfillment of Daniel's vision as this last kingdom - the kingdoms of this world, - are brought down in judgment.

Daniel 7:21 and 22 also present another picture of what we are living and experiencing during this time.

> **"I kept looking, and that horn was waging war with the saints and overpowering them until the Ancient of Days came and judgment was passed in favor of the saints of the Highest One, and the time arrived when the saints took possession of the kingdom.**
> **- Dan 7:21-22**

We have been in a time where the warfare in the spirit has attempted to wear down the saints, yet we know that the judgments have been passed. His saints will possess the kingdom. This will not continue to seemingly stay "out of reach", for this is the time of possessing the kingdom.

We are in a concurrent time of prophetic fulfillment on different planes of prophecy and scripture. Whether it is Daniel 2, or Daniel 7, or the book of Revelation; it leaves no doubt that an acceleration of judgment and a release upon God's people has now come.

Now is the appointed time. It is the time for fullness; it is the time for judgment. Now is the time that we will see the fulfillment of Ephesians; <u>the execution of the administration of power upon this age</u>.

More and more we have been aware of the canopy of control that exists over the nations on the face of this earth by the principalities and powers of this present darkness. They have wielded a control over people far beyond anyone's recognition.

There has been an inability for people to change because of the veil of darkness that exists over this world system. This cloud of deception and restraint which has been perpetrated and fostered by the satanic hosts has literally created a veil over the perception of so many. This has prevented the sons from becoming. We have come to the time that the judgments of God shall break this strangle hold; the shackles over men's eyes shall fall, and His people shall see Him and they shall change.

The greatest evangelism to be experienced is yet to come forth. We have come to the day that the Sons of God will bind the satanic powers of darkness that have blinded the eyes of His people, and whole regions shall come alive to the Spirit. We are not speaking of one here, another there, but thousands. Literally whole geographic regions will change.

It is the time of the greatest change and transformation we have ever seen because this blindness that has existed shall be lifted. It is time that the spirits of wickedness and the sons of darkness shall lead the evil in a procession into the "pit of darkness" for which they have been destined.

Have you ever driven through an area and noticed the peculiarity of it? Have you sensed the changes in energy? If you have then you are becoming aware of the different spirits that exist in different localities. You can drive through a region where perhaps a tragic event took place and you will find that the signature of that energy still remains upon the land.

What I am talking about are the spirits that have governed and controlled whole regions of this vast planet we live on. What follows hand-in-hand most often are the restraints, the conditionings, and the oppressions which rest upon those who live within those areas.

The true "gospel of the kingdom" is not about sending out missionaries, sending out bibles, and distributing "tracks". The gospel of the kingdom - which for the most part has not yet happened in the earth - will happen in concert with the release of the power of God which will bind the kings of the earth. There is no gospel of the kingdom without the release of the authority and dominion of Christ as it is exercised through God's sons. Anything else is just partial at best.

We speak chaos, discord, and confusion into the camp of the enemy; for this is the day of judgment. As the Psalmist in the 149th psalm wrote…"to execute upon them the judgments written". The judgments have been written - from the foundations of the earth - but they have been waiting for a people who would rise in the spirit and become. They have been waiting for you. God's sons are arising and they will finish the last chapters of this book and complete the ministry of Christ.

You must realize that we are coming to live and function in and from a world of spirit. This is a whole new life and a whole new existence. The judgments of this day come forth as God's sons, His mouthpiece, usher them in.

Notes:

Section 7

The Creative Word

Of the Kingdom

- **In The Day of Thy Power**
- **The Creative Word of the Kingdom**
- **The Day of Reversal**

In The Day of Thy Power

There are a couple of scriptures that truly depict the heart and spirit of God's people during this day. Rev 12. - they love not their lives unto death. Psalm 110 – they shall walk as a freewill offering to the Lord, and Rev. 14 - they follow the Lamb wither-so-ever He goeth. These 3 scriptures capture the essence of what is being required to walk in this path of sonship and to deeply experience this hour of transformation.

> **And they overcame him because of the blood of the Lamb and because of the word of their testimony, and they did not love their life even when faced with death. – Rev 12:11**

> **These are they which were not defiled with women; for they are virgins. These are they which follow the Lamb whithersoever he goeth – Rev 14:4**

That "wither-so-ever" can be a rather all-inclusive word; for the demands of the Spirit are progressively greater and greater as we come into the time of His fullness. You could call it the progressive demands of discipleship, although the word discipleship has been over used and run into the ground by the religious spirit of this day.

The path the sons of Light have traveled has been a path of purification and refinement. The searchlight of the Spirit has gone deep within the hearts of His people. Malachi says it very well when the prophet spoke, "who can stand when He appears, for He appears as a refiner's fire, and He purges every son whom He receives (Mal 3:2)."

Few stand fast and allow this deep penetrating work of the Spirit to come to fruition. Unfortunately, most people want God on their terms; for there are limits to the price they would pay. There are times when the choices people make are limits they have set on a subconscious level. Even the act of not making a choice, of side-stepping around the issue that God has placed before them, is actually making a choice.

In your walk with God if you come to a point of decision, or a crossroads in your walk with Him, and you do not make a choice to move on with God, then you have in affect made your decision to stop.

God is moving on, and there is no such thing as "treading water"; you are either moving forward or you are going in reverse. The very act of God's movement forward has predetermined this. If you are following on to know the Lord, then you are in forward motion. But if you have stalled along the way - if you are not living on the edge - reaching in with every fiber of your being; then you have begun the slow descent backwards. There is no treading water with God.

Everyday people are being confronted in the spirit; will they walk on with the Lord, or will they reject the demands He places upon them. It is a fine line, because only you, within the depth of your heart, know the answer.

The spirit is deeply grieved at how closed His people have become. Even those who may appear so "open", are not really. They may walk in a form or appearance of discipleship, but it is only just that, a form - void of the real commitment of heart. So often people have their own agenda and as long as God's agenda lines up with theirs, then everything is just fine. This is what has become so prevalent in Christianity today. As the scripture goes; "following a form, but denying the power thereof" (2nd Tim 3:5).

What does this have to do with the release of the creative word of the kingdom? Everything. For Christ's authority to move through His sons, there must be an absolute abandonment of spirit. It reminds me of a book I read many years ago by Andrew Murray entitled; "Absolute Surrender". The title alone says it all.

"Thy people shall be a freewill offering in the day of Thy power.." -Ps110

So when is the day of His power? Perhaps at some distant point in the future? I don't believe so. The time of His power is now.

This "day of His power" is not about an external manifestation of signs and wonders; it is about the internal manifestation of the God-head - of Christ – within you. This is the day of His power; and it is to this day that you have now come.

The creative word of power is a word of authority. It is the word that will judge literally universes; that will subject every kingdom unto the Lord. With the commitment of authority comes great responsibility and accountability, for you become accountable for every word that you speak.

We are headed into a deliverance on a level we have never experienced before. There is not one person who can say, "I have need of nothing". God is undertaking a level of deliverance that will see the glorification of His sons and the commensurate liberty and freedom that ensues. This is the teaching of Romans 8. Before the deepest changes occur within the kingdom and the release of creation; there must first be the complete release of the sons of God. They must first be delivered from the futility within themselves in order that they might set all of creation free.

Is this happening? Yes, it has begun. At first it may seem to be slow and progressive; almost imperceptible to your own eyes, for we are generally the last to recognize the changes that are happening deep within us. Why? Because we are too bonded or attached to our perception of ourselves. We are changing, but we must not hold onto a concept of how we saw ourselves yesterday. This must go.

This is easier said than done for you must have a drive and an intensity to let go of your past perceptions. This will take a revelation from the Lord to your heart for this bond cannot be easily broken without the leverage of a walk in the spirit. You need to see yourself as the Lord sees you. That experience will shatter any limited perception you may have had of who you are.

God is birthing and bringing forth His sons into a "walk in the spirit". If you go through the scriptures you see the constant admonition; "walk in the spirit", or pray "in the spirit". When John was on the Isle of Patmos and received the book of Revelation the word goes... I was "in the spirit" on the Lord's day. I reference this because God is drawing you up into a plane of spirit; for fulfillment will be found as you walk in the spirit.

What we are looking for in the fulfillment of the ministry of Christ through us will only be achieved as we walk in the spirit. You must let go of the day of soul. As long as you remain bonded to past perceptions of yourself, then you are still walking in the soul. You must let go and cut the cords within your own heart. You are a son. And every word God has spoken to you is your reality. It does not matter how you feel, or what you see. All that matters is what He has spoken to your heart.

During this season of accelerated change and growth we have been in school. God has been training and developing our spiritual muscles. In whatever way God has been challenging you, it is all part of growing and developing, for God is equipping you to walk in the full capacity of sonship.

This change or glorification of the believer will see the emergence of a level of kingdom governance that neither the earth nor the spirit world has ever seen before this time. I love that term - kingdom governance - because Christ is taking over. First He takes you over, then we see the kingdoms of this present age brought down as He moves through you.

This is what it is all about. It is not about words or concepts void of experience. We are talking about possessing the reality of His word - and that makes a difference. You have been raised up to change this age. I know you have been fought tooth and nail. We know why – it is because this is the hour.

We have bitten the lie if we still accept restraint or limitation. We have bitten the lie if we believe that there must still be a process. And we have bitten the lie if we feel fulfillment is outside of us – relegated to a time in the future.

It is time to see the freedom of the sons of God manifested within and through a people. God has raised you up for this hour. Through you shall flow the effective judgments of the living God - for you have come to the day of His power. You have given everything, and He is committing the authority of the kingdom into your hands.

The Creative Word
of the Kingdom

Our concern for some time has been the release of the creative Word of Power, for God is bringing forth a level of authority and anointing that is beginning to break down the barriers existing literally between the veils. It is a word that destroys, as Paul calls it, "fortresses" (2Cor 10:4). This concerns what must happen "before" we move with the authority over the rulers of this present age. The word is coming that has begun to remove the limitations within our thinking of who we are, what we are, and what we have been given.

> **the weapons of our warfare are not of the flesh, but divinely powerful for the destruction of fortresses. *We are* destroying speculations and every lofty thing raised up against the knowledge of God, and *we are* taking every thought captive to the obedience of Christ, - 2Co 10:4-5**

As the walls and illusions that we have held onto continue to fall, we will see a rising tide of awareness within God's people. This is the prelude to the release of a living word of judgment for this hour; a word that will flow through His sons.

The gospels speak of the spirit that must reside within God's people if the changes that are slated to happen "within" them, are to begin. What is this quality of spirit? A drive or intensity that will not settle for anything short of the full release of the kingdom. As Christ spoke, it is the "violent who take the kingdom by force". For it is the kingdom - *within you* - that you are driven for; not an external kingdom, not yet - not at this point.

> **"And from the days of John the Baptist until now the kingdom of heaven suffers violence, and violent men take it by force." – Matt 11:12**

Is the kingdom brought forth by men of passivity or indifference, the very essence of this age? No. Is it brought forth by the "politically correct"? No. There must be an intensity, violence, drive, and demand born of the spirit within you. Perhaps you have only touched on it from time to time, but this is going to become your lifestyle. This has the address of the sons of God written all over it. We must make this shift if we are to accomplish what we have been here sent to do. It will take an abandonment of all that we are.

Can we sustain this type of drive? No; not after the soul or the flesh. Only by the spirit; the spirit within you. It is only by His grace that we are able to sustain such a drive, and that comes from the vision that He has written deeply upon our heart. This violence of spirit is at the crux of what it will now take to make the transition to this next level of the kingdom.

For the last several years the Cloud of Witnesses have been waiting - urging us on - urging us to lay hold of that for which we have been laid hold of in Christ Jesus. A number of times they have come; frustrated, concerned, and perplexed. They have not understood why we have we not been able to see how great an endowment that is resting upon us.

We have functioned too much as paupers, not yet recognizing the mantle and the endowment which has been given. We have been slow to recognize the scepter of authority which has been placed in our hands. We have seen only a trickle of the power or authority of Christ which has been already given to His sons; yet He has committed everything into our hands. Why is this? Because His sons are still in the process of having their eyes opened to see. The maturing process has perhaps taken a bit longer; but you are coming to the time of graduation.

We have been in a time of accelerated change and growth, as I have mentioned before, and the eyes of His people are starting to open. You may still see "men as trees walking", but God is opening the eyes of His seers and sons. He is removing the shackles around their ankles and the scales off of their eyes, and as these scales fall off they will experience a level of authority and control that they have not seen or experienced before.

God's sons are beginning to move into a level of control that will determine the future events that are to unfold during this time. This is being accomplished through the ability God has established within them to control the present.

Let me explain this further.

You may ask; "how does this happen?" It happens because the seer prophet in this day creates the present through his ability to see the future. This might sound a bit magical, but it is not; this is how Christ moved. What did He say; "I only do those things I see the Father doing".

As you see what the Father is doing, your intercession and your travail become the vehicle to bring it to pass in the present. By determining the present, you then control the future. You are co-creators with Christ and the Father.

This can seem like we have stepped out on the limb and cut it off, but we are talking about the functioning of God's seers and sons - we are speaking of the control that is beginning to be wielded over this age.

How do you explain something new? God is doing something new in the earth – the earth of you and I, and we will constantly be pressed for words to describe this experience of sonship. It is not in the dictionary.

We are in a shift, and the balance in the spirit realm is only now beginning to change, however slightly. This shift of balance in the spirit world will continue to unfold; as we have said this before.

There are aspects of God that have been deeply woven within the fabric of His creation, especially when you consider the scripture that "in Him all things are held together". We are only now just beginning to understand this.

> **For by Him all things were created, *both* in the heavens and on earth, visible and invisible, whether thrones or dominions or rulers or authorities—all things have been created by Him and for Him. And He is before all things, and in**

> **Him *(or through Him)* all things hold together.**
> –Col 1:16-17

Men of science, in their pursuit to understand what is at the base of creation, have been able to identify just about everything, but they have not come to an understanding or an agreement as to what holds it all together. We know; for it is the Father who is interwoven completely throughout all of His creation. He truly is the "cosmic glue" that holds everything in place and in order.

In this present incarnation, mankind has the innate ability to create what they believe in. This is something which sets us apart from other orders of creation. We have the ability, through what we voice and through our will and intent; to create. How is this? It is because we are talking about the interpenetration of all that God is; interwoven within the very fabric of your being - at the most minute level.

The strongly held belief system in new age circles today is that everyone is on a process of evolution; growing, changing and becoming – like unto a God. We have seen the continued growth of this movement, whether it has been furthered by the eastern yogis or the "power of positive thinking" movement. So many are convinced that they will be able to enter into their own state of perfection, completion, or "nirvana", by their own works. They may have experienced this latent power or capability within them, but without Christ, it will profit them nothing and they will not be able to pass through the open door – which is Christ alone.

Christ quoted Psalms 82:6 as He countered the accusations of the Pharisees, but He was making a point. That point had to do with the inherent "divinity" of man.

> **"Is it not written in your law, I said, Ye are gods?"**
> – Ps 82:6

The word speaks that man was created in the image of God (Gen. 1:27). This similarity has not really been understood very well, but it deals with an aspect of the creative nature of God. When man was created he was given authority to rule over creation. He was created in the likeness or image of God.

A common concept concerning this train of thought is that we are created in the image of God because we have been created as a triune being; spirit, soul, and body. Similar to the trinity or triune nature of God; Father, Son, and Holy Spirit. I do not disagree that we bear this similarity, but I believe that being created in the image of God deals more with Psalms 82:6 than we have understood.

What we are really talking about is the inherent ability within man to "create". God has placed within us a capacity to create, and this is what sets us apart from most of God's creation.

We create by our thoughts, by our intentions, and even more powerfully, through what we speak. Whether you are creating faith, fear or illusion, what you lend your mind and heart to - creates.

One simple scripture captures the essence of this truth, and that is the book of Proverbs 23:7. "As a man thinketh in his heart, so is he."

You are creating, literally, every moment of the day. You may not have realized this before, but never-the-less, whether you are creating faith, fear, or an adherence to an illusion; you are creating. In many ways you are a microcosm of the Father, for He has placed Himself deeply within you.

If you have studied the eastern religions or even orthodox Christianity, you would have noticed how significant mantras were. The practice of voicing in repetition (mantras) has a prominent significance within these religions. Why is that? Because there is an awareness of the power that each individual has to create through harnessing their voice, their mind and their intent - over and over. It is powerful, there is no doubt.

Furthermore what you focus on you can create. Some would call that "visualizing", which is another new age term frequently used. Visualizing deals with the power of imagery; the power of the mind to create by "seeing" what you want. Whether it is what you focus on, how you think, or what you voice - you are creating, *constantly*.

I don't think a moment passes by that we are not in some mode of the creative process. Whether it is your faith, your fears; or whether you are responding to the illusion, you are constantly creating.

A "Living Word"

Based upon what we have been talking about so far concerning the innate ability we have to create, I believe our concepts of a "living word" should have changed. We are not talking about the "Living Word" - the "Word of God", but we are talking about words that are "living".

It almost sounds sacrilegious to say that everyone is speaking a living word, but it is true. Unfortunate, but true. Every time you open your mouth you are creating, and that "living word" can be destructive or creative. The power of life and death is in the power of the tongue (Jas 3).

The more you are connected to the source, which is Christ, the "Living Word"; the more powerful and more creative the word becomes through your mouth. The more you have surrendered your life to Him (and let the deep probing work of the cross work within you), the more the fullness of Christ flows through you, and the more powerful and creative the word becomes that you speak. They go hand-in-hand.

Do you grasp the depth of this? You are in a constant mode of creating, whether you are aware of what you are doing or not. Whether you are aware of your thought projections or your perceptions - all of it has the power to create. This becomes even more critical for God's sons to understand because you have within you the power and authority of Christ.

Once you really understand this, you can see how much more dynamic the creative process is through you. The enemy knows this and that is why he is constantly hammering away at you to believe the lie; to respond to the illusion. He knows that you can create your faith or your fears. He knows that God has raised you up to be co-creators with Him.

It is of utmost importance that you understand the power that lies within your grasp; even in this temporary state of imperfection.

Having a present incarnation in the physical enables us to enter the creative mode with every agency at our disposal; **spirit, soul and body.**

What is it that really sets us apart from our brethren - the Cloud of Witnesses? *The ability to create on this level.*

The greatest advantage that we have living in the natural world, as we might call this, is our ability to create. This is what has set us uniquely apart from those who live within the spirit. You have the ability, even if you have not yet developed it, to utilize your spirit, soul and body in the process of creating. Your voice coupled with your will and intent - in synergy with your spirit - is very powerful.

We have spoken that one of the ministries of the sons is to see the release of the Cloud of Witnesses. This release is tied into our release from futility, but as well, it is tied into our capability to create. Having this present incarnation in the physical enables us to create and bring a bridging of the gap or an ending of the veil between this realm and the realm of the Cloud of Witnesses.

We are dealing with words that are creating life. What does the word say? Not one word that proceeds from the mouth of God will return without accomplishing the work for which it was sent.

And who might that "mouth of God" be that has sent forth that word? You. The more you continue to rise higher and higher into His presence the more the word you speak will be freighted with Him, and the greater will be the flow of His word through you.

You may recall the vision in Ezekiel concerning the waters flowing forth from the throne.

> **Then he brought me back to the door of the house; and behold, water was flowing from under the threshold of the house toward the east, for the house faced east. And the water was flowing down from under, from the right side of the house, from south of the altar.**
>
> **He brought me out by way of the north gate and led me around on the outside to the outer gate by way of *the gate* that faces east. And behold, water was trickling from the south side.**

> **When the man went out toward the east with a line in his hand, he measured a thousand cubits, and he led me through the water, water *reaching* the ankles.**
>
> **Again he measured a thousand and led me through the water, water *reaching* the knees. Again he measured a thousand and led me through *the water,* water *reaching* the loins.**
>
> **Again he measured a thousand; *and it was* a river that I could not ford, for the water had risen, *enough* water to swim in, a river that could not be forded. – Eze 47:1-5**

These waters represent the progressive unfolding of the flow of His word through you. It has been a process, but we know the word is coming and is now here that will change the course of events on the face of the earth.

That word is flowing from His throne and it will soon be a river that cannot be forded.

You are the Word, and you are creating the kingdom. And that is happening now as we speak.

The Day Of Reversal

> **And it will come about in the last days that the mountain of the house of the Lord will be established as the chief of the mountains. It will be raised above the hills, and the peoples will stream to it. Many nations will come and say, "Come and let us go up to the mountain of the LORD and to the house of the God of Jacob, that He may teach us about His ways and that we may walk in His paths. – Micah 4:1-2**

Right now there is a tremendous "downward" trend in the earth. There is a great deal of satanic activity and propagation of lies, deception and darkness that is spewing out of the mouth of the dragon in a concerted effort to destroy the sons of God. You can read of this in the book of Revelation (Rev 12:16).

> **But the earth helped the woman, and the earth opened its mouth and drank up the river which the dragon poured out of his mouth. -Rev 12:16**

We are not surprised with what we have seen unfolding in the earth during this time. This was prophesied to come prior to the final witness of judgment upon this age. We are in the time that the iniquity is coming to the full. How does the word describe this day? As it was in the days of Sodom and Gomorrah, so it will be in the days of the Son of Man.

We are seeing this beginning to unfold for we have passed beyond what I would call a "tipping point" or "point of no return" in this age. We are poised for the judgments that have yet to come.

As we have said before, the past 4 to 5 generations has seen the progressive demoralization of America. We have seen a change in the overall consciousness that exists in the world today, and it has not been good. The iniquity is most definitely coming to the full.

We have studied the vibration of the sounds coming forth right now, whether in the music and entertainment realm, or within the scope of communication and what we have known as dialogue. The sounds and vibrations that are coming forth during this time are not sounds of peace and tranquility; they are sounds which carry the vibration and energy of war and hostility, death and destruction. These sounds carry this level of consciousness, no matter what the "green movement" or any other "global consciousness movement" would lead you to believe.

The book of Micah, although, is pointing to a time of reversal that we will see as we enter more deeply into the days of the kingdom. The promise is that we will see a reversal of the trend and the tendency towards evil. Rather than this spiraling downward trend, there will be the emergence of an upward flow to Zion.

The train has been going full steam in a downward trend for a very long time. In many ways it may feel like it is taking everything to stop the locomotive that is plummeting toward disaster, but we are in the midst of a change that is beginning to happen in the earth. You can sense it. If you put your ear to the ground, you can feel the vibrations of a new day that is dawning.

What is that change? It is what this book is about; Romans 8 - the manifestation of the sons of God that are becoming the agency of change during this time.

The promise is that we will see a reversal of days. There is to be an upward flow to Zion. We will see the trend towards evil and wickedness - that is so prevalent in the earth right now - reversed.

This shift will not happen because of a collective consciousness of prayer or some other new age modality. This shift has only just begun, as imperceptible as it may seem, because God's sons are in the last stages of redemption.

The balance in the spirit world is shifting, and the more God's sons become, the more this age will undergo deep and tremendous changes; changes that perhaps on the surface may appear catastrophic. But don't get your eyes on what is happening on this temporal realm; it is all just a passing moment in time.

We have seen only a trickle of the releases slated for this day. We have lived in many ways like David, hiding out in caves. Saul, the false manifestation in that hour of God's true anointed, sought to kill and destroy David. It is no different now. The religious and satanic worlds have sought to destroy and hinder the release of the man-child, but God's will cannot be thwarted.

There has been a tremendous amount of misinformation and deception spewing from the mouth of the dragon; spewing from the "religious" leaders of this day. For one purpose, to confuse, distort and hinder the manifestation of God's sons. To restrain and box them in, to hinder their ability to see; in essence to delay the manifestation of God's sons and God's timetable in the earth. However, it is during this season that we will begin to see a reversal on every level.

> **The word that Isaiah the son of Amoz saw concerning Judah and Jerusalem. And it shall come to pass in the last days, *that* the mountain of the LORD'S house shall be established in the top of the mountains, and shall be exalted above the hills; and all nations shall flow unto it.**
>
> **And many people shall go and say, Come ye, and let us go up to the mountain of the LORD, to the house of the God of Jacob; and he will teach us of his ways, and we will walk in his paths: for out of Zion shall go forth the law, and the word of the LORD from Jerusalem.**
>
> **And he shall judge among the nations, and shall rebuke many people: and they shall beat their swords into plowshares, and their spears into pruning hooks: nation shall not lift up sword against nation, neither shall they learn war any more.**
> **– Isa 2:1-4**

What have we seen so far? We have seen futility. Your clothes have worn out. Your finances have been strapped. On every level we have seen impasse after impasse. But what is the promise?

> I have led you forty years in the wilderness; your clothes have not worn out on you, and your sandal has not worn out on your foot. – Deut 29:5

We have walked and lived much like the children of Israel, and we have been on a long sojourn. Since our sojourn began, it has been a long process coming into sonship. But come into sonship we shall; for this is God's plan which is unfolding. As it speaks of in Hebrews;

> All these died in faith, without receiving the promises, but having seen them and having welcomed them from a distance, and having confessed that they were strangers and exiles on the earth. For those who say such things make it clear that they are seeking a country of their own. And indeed if they had been thinking of that *country* from which they went out, they would have had opportunity to return. But as it is, they desire a better *country,* that is, a heavenly one. Therefore God is not ashamed to be called their God - Heb 11:13-16

We have entered a time of reversal. For the sons of God; those whom the Lord has called, change and the upward flow into His presence is the order of the day. This will not be the reality for the world as a whole, however, for God's sons it is to be a time of reversal.

> Be glad then, ye children of Zion, and rejoice in the LORD your God: for he hath given you the former rain moderately, and he will cause to come down for you the rain, the former rain, and the latter rain in the first *month*. And the floors shall be full of wheat, and the fats shall overflow with wine and oil.
>
> And I will restore to you the years that the locust hath eaten, the cankerworm, and the caterpiller, and the palmerworm, my great army which I sent among you. – Joel 2:23-25

You cannot talk about the restoration of all things without speaking of this reversal of days. The prophecy is that God will bring the restoration of all things as spoken of through the mouths of His prophets. We are talking about walking in the days of the overflow; walking in the word of Psalms 23:5.

> **You prepare a table before me in the presence of my enemies; You have anointed my head with oil; My cup overflows. – Psa 23:5**

As Joel prophesied, it will be a time that we will see a reversal.

> **Joe 2:23 Be glad then, ye children of Zion, and rejoice in the LORD your God: for he hath given you the former rain moderately, and he will cause to come down for you the rain, the former rain, and the latter rain in the first *month*.**
>
> **Joe 2:24 And the floors shall be full of wheat, and the fats shall overflow with wine and oil.**
>
> **Joe 2:25 And I will restore to you the years that the locust hath eaten, the cankerworm, and the caterpiller, and the palmerworm, my great army which I sent among you.**
>
> **Joe 2:26 And ye shall eat in plenty, and be satisfied, and praise the name of the LORD your God, that hath dealt wondrously with you: and my people shall never be ashamed.**

The days of lack and limitation are ending. We are entering the days of the reversal of this downward trend. First it begins within us, but it will gradually radiate outward and affect a change in the earth on every level.

We are leaving the days of "half-full" and we are entering the timeline that you will truly say, "surely my cup overfloweth, Oh God".

Section 8

What Delays
The Kingdom

- **Bonds & Vampires**
- **Are You Bonded To Your Concepts?**
- **Come Out of Her**
- **Breaking the Ties to Ancestry**

Anne and I would like to preface this section with a few thoughts.

We have studied the interaction of the spirit realm and the satanic intent to keep God's sons out of functioning in the realm of spirit. We have found that this issue of what we call "bonds" is of paramount importance.

As the sons of God we must walk free. We must understand how we have been fettered. We must be able to clear our own energy. We must be able to clear our spirit so that the issues we are dealing with are only ours.

As we have touched on in different areas of this book, the "free" spirit, (which is your spirit as it becomes liberated to function in God), can easily become burdened or weighed down by the transference or negative energy that it can readily pick up.

You must continue to clear yourself and stay free from the unequal yoking of relationships. This is one of the greatest hindrances to your freedom.

We approach this subject of "bonds" and how it has been pivotal in delaying the kingdom from several angles.

We dedicate this book to the freedom of God's sons.

Edward & Anne

Bonds & Vampires

We have come to a time in the earth where we are finding the iniquity coming to the full, and the love of many waxing cold (Gen 15:16, 2Th 2:17, Matt 24:12). We have touched on what we have seen unfolding in the earth as we continue to experience the overlapping of realms; a conjunction of ages. We are seeing the convergence of the spirit world as it interacts more and more with the natural plane, and this is creating a unique set of dynamics. This is something the Christian believer, or the sons of God, have not had to deal with before.

What exactly are we speaking of? We are talking about an access into the natural plane of the energy and intent of a spirit world; specifically the world of evil, that have been (and are being) cast down (Rev 12:10). They seek every opportunity to hinder the manifestation of sonship within God's people, while God simultaneously trains His sons for war (Joel 3).

The title of this word, Bonds and Vampires, is an interesting title. It never ceases to amaze me at the fascination people have with the occult and the dark side of human nature. So much of this fascination is created and fostered through the energy that is being generated and channeled literally from the spirit world; specifically the satanic hosts. That sentence says a great deal and it alone may change the way you view your reality around you.

Vampires within the realm of spirit do exist, however not in the conventional context. Certainly some demons you could say manifest that trait, and they are much more hideous to behold. But what I want to address concerns the act of vampirism that is experienced every day in the lives of God's sons and daughters - so often unbeknownst to them.

Perhaps the greatest deterrent to the manifestation of the kingdom of God in this hour can be expressed in a single word; <u>bonds</u>. Remember, we are talking about the kingdom of God within you. We are not speaking of an external kingdom; not yet. The existence of these bonds have been the greatest deterrent to the maturing and subsequent manifestation of the sons of God.

So what do we mean by "bonds"? Webster's dictionary defines a "bond" as that which 1. binds or restrains. 2. a band or cord to tie something. 3. an adhesive, cementing material.

Imagine a thin piece of metal cemented to another piece of metal. There you have a simple bond. However, the dynamics get interesting if you begin to cement one piece to another, to another and so on. You could go on to infinity, and yet you would find that the first piece of metal is linked to the very last in this long daisy chain of pieces. OK, so now it gets interesting. If you apply intense heat to the first item, you will feel the heat in the last piece of metal in that chain. That heat is literally transferred because of the existence of that bond.

Before we take this further, let's talk about the realm of spirit and the realm of the soul.

Imagine a vast ocean. Imagine yourself standing in this ocean, immersed in it, at one with it. You sense it, you feel it, and it flows through you. You are a part of it. Every aspect of this ocean affects you and is a part of you. This ocean represents the world of spirit that you have your existence in. We live in this world of spirit, 24/7, but most have no awareness of this reality.

This ocean, this world of spirit, is a level of reality that affects all things. You could call it a "field of energy" or "God", for it exists all around us and within us. The scriptures speak that in Christ all things are held together. Literally Christ is that "field of energy" that we live in. We are immersed in this ocean or field of energy.

Realize you are an energetic being vibrating at a unique frequency that enables you to have a physical manifestation on this plane of existence. If you could change your vibration, like a tuning fork, you could change the level of your abiding. Christ could do this as He passed through walls and walked on water. It was just a simple shift of His energy - the scriptures leave a lot unsaid between the lines.

> **and they got up and drove Him out of the city, and led Him to the brow of the hill on which their city had been built, in order to throw Him down the cliff. But passing through their midst, He went His way.** – Luke 4:29-30

We have tended to view ourselves primarily as having our state of existence and consciousness within this natural realm, but we are more spirit than we have ever understood.

Where is heaven? Light years away? Up around Orion or the expanse of space? No, heaven is only a level of vibration away from you.

Christ spoke to the disciples that the kingdom was within them (Luke 17:21). We are just now beginning to understand that the kingdom of God exists within. The kingdom is within you and it surrounds you - it is just a different level of existence or vibration. This is such a deep truth, yet we still live, for the most part, with an unawareness of this. We have not yet been able to comprehend the depth of this reality.

Remember Christ's words ... "in my Father's house are many dwelling places". That would be many dimensions - many worlds - many levels of abiding.

> **"In My Father's house are many dwelling places; if it were not so, I would have told you; for I go to prepare a place for you. And if I go and prepare a place for you, I will come again, and receive you to Myself; that where I am, *there* you may be also".** - Jn 14:2-3

When Christ died the word says He "passed through the heavens" (Heb 14:4). So, did He pass the moon, the stars, and the nebulae? No. He passed through the various dimensional levels that comprise all of creation - *our Father's house*. He sat down at the right hand of the Father, on the highest level, and He has beckoned you and I to come and be with Him.

Where am I going with this? Simply to establish one point - we have lived with an awareness of our lives primarily on one level.

The truth is that we have our existence in a realm of spirit, and we are living, interacting and responding to stimuli that come to us from many different levels.

You are affected by that which comes not only from the physical realm but the spirit realm and the soul realm simultaneously. On the flip side, you can affect the realm of spirit and the realm of the soul as well. It goes both ways.

Let's do a brief visualization. It is important that you grasp and understand just what we are dealing with within the realm of bonds, contacts, and attachments. This is at the core of so much that is restraining and must be removed for you to walk in the freedom God has for you.

Visualize 2 people, standing next to each other. Now, visualize a cord emitting from one and attaching to the other. Let's put those 2 people on the opposite sides of the planet, and no matter where they are; that cord cannot be not broken. That cord may stretch across continents, or even through the veil, but that cord remains.

To see this in the realm of spirit would be to see very fine strands of light. They connect individuals together. People live their whole lives with hundreds of these "strands" connecting them. These strands or cords represent your relationships, contacts, or associations. They are not limited by distance; and they know no barriers. No matter where a person goes, these cords are always in tact.

In the scriptures you will find scripture after scripture that reference the "cords of the wicked". The promise is that the Lord will cut in two "the cords of the wicked". Psalms 129:4 is just one of numerous references in the scripture to "cords". We are talking about "cords" that bind; "cords" that prevent you from becoming.

> **The plowers plowed upon my back; They lengthened their furrows. The LORD is righteous; He has cut in two the cords of the wicked. – Psalms 129:3-4**

Do a concordant study on the word - cords or cord. It is an eye-opener.

Now let's go back to the initial example of the metal that is bonded to another piece of metal - into infinity. Bonds function much like that example. Bonds exist, without limitations, and can be a source of blessing, yet equally, a source of great hindrance and oppression.

Now, visualize these cords as conduits of electricity, except what is traveling on these cords are not electrical currents to light a house, rather they are energetic (eg: spirit/soul) currents conveying thoughts, emotions, feelings and oppressions from one individual to another. Now, multiply that by hundreds, or even thousands. This is a picture of what exists in the realm of the spirit, and the realm of the soul.

Whether we are dealing with the prayers of the saints, or the transference that is upon the judgment of the wicked, this gives you a clearer grasp of how energy flows and moves in the spirit realm. This gives you a quick picture of what a bond looks like in the spirit, and how devastatingly effective it can be.

This is also a picture of how transference can work.

To really understand transference, we must understand what Christ accomplished through His death on the cross. When Christ died He transferred our sins upon Him and His righteousness upon us. That was transference. That is the scripture. He took upon Himself the sins of humanity, and He opened a door that all of His righteousness might flow to you. It's truly wonderful. How are we righteous? We are righteous by virtue of Christ's blood that was shed; opening a door for the transference of all that He is to be given to you. What a gift. That is transference.

According to Wikipedia, transference is defined as; "a phenomenon in psychoanalysis characterized by the unconscious redirection of feelings from one person to another". It is interesting that even the world is beginning to recognize the principle of transference, if only on the soul level.

As a people we are called to be "in the world", but "not of it". We are also admonished to be "all things to all people", yet neither of these are possible until we have understood and experienced the realm of bonds and transference.

The more we understand the principles that govern the realm of the spirit; the more we will move into a functional relationship in the spirit.

This principle of transference is how the spirit world functions; for everything in the realm of the spirit and the realm of the soul function through transference. Transference can be used to send a blessing, or it can be used to send or convey oppression. Christ understood this principle clearly when He said that He gave Himself to no man (John 2:24). He knew what was in man. He also clearly understood the principle of transference.

Now let's talk about bonds, because it is through incorrect bonds - or bonds of an "unequal" yoke - that negative transference can flow. And this is our concern.

Bonds that exist between people can be a source of some of the most detrimental transference that we have seen. Bonds are a function of your soul, and that is what makes them so dangerous. Bonds are created through sympathy, obligation, expectation, fear, physical exchanges, anger, and a host of other emotional responses or reactions. Even the simple act of breaking bread with another creates a bond.

> **"Do not think that I came to bring peace on the earth; I did not come to bring peace, but a sword. "For I came to SET A MAN AGAINST HIS FATHER, AND A DAUGHTER AGAINST HER MOTHER, AND A DAUGHTER-IN-LAW AGAINST HER MOTHER-IN-LAW; and A MAN'S ENEMIES WILL BE THE MEMBERS OF HIS HOUSEHOLD. - Mat 10:34-36**

What is Christ speaking of here? He is speaking of bonds; of the relationships born out of obligation and sympathy. He is also addressing the principle of being unequally yoked. He is speaking about the detriment bonds can have; for a man's enemies will be the members of his household.

You may think that Christ meant something more "literal" with this scripture; that it could literally be your own household? Very possible; however what Christ is really addressing are the bonds and relationships that we have - specifically the unequally yoked relationships of the soul.

Instead of carrying the power to create and release, soul-bonds carry the ability to demean, intimidate and destroy.

> **But if you bite and devour one another, take care lest you be consumed by one another. But I say, walk by the Spirit, and you will not carry out the desire of the flesh. Galatians 5:15-16**

Paul was dealing with severe issues in the Galatian church because the relationships that existed in that church were on the wrong level. The bickering and arguing began to take a toll on the people within that church. You had those who were reaching into a deeper walk in the spirit, only to find their energy siphoned off by those walking according to the flesh, or soul. This problem faced Paul not only in Galatia, but in most of the churches.

The title of this word, **Bonds and Vampires**, certainly conjures up a few images. When you think of Vampires; what do you see? I see that which sucks the blood and life from another - one that lives by feeding upon another's life. That would be the mythical creature called a Vampire, but this closely describes what happens when soul-bonds are created and allowed to exist.

When an individual passes through the veil (death), there are instances where he cannot go on unless their partner (the one left on this side of the veil); lets go. You have probably heard of these instances; people transitioning after death could not go on without someone on this side letting go of them. It is interesting because bonds exist without limitation. You can literally bond to someone on the other side of the veil, but that is a very different dynamic and not what we want to focus on right here.

Most everyone living today functions from the soul; people don't really know any other way of relating. What is the buzz word used so often these days ...."bonding". "Having a time of bonding". There has not been any real understanding or teaching of the difference between spirit and soul.

It is rudimentarily simple; if you walk in the spirit, as the word speaks, then you truly will not fulfill the lusts of the flesh (Rom 8:4). Your relationships and the mode of your relating will be spiritually grounded.

For those who are walking into this day of spirit, there is a growing awareness and sensitivity coming. People are beginning to become more aware of this issue of bonds. They are beginning to sense and feel the existence of bonds within their life, even if they have not known what to call it, or how to deal with them.

Paul saw the great jeopardy of bonds within the churches.

> **Do not be bound together with unbelievers; for what partnership have righteousness and lawlessness, or what fellowship has light with darkness? Or what harmony has Christ with Belial, or what has a believer in common with an unbeliever? Or what agreement has the temple of God with idols?**
>
> **For we are the temple of the living God; just as God said, "I WILL DWELL IN THEM AND WALK AMONG THEM; AND I WILL BE THEIR GOD, AND THEY SHALL BE MY PEOPLE. "Therefore, COME OUT FROM THEIR MIDST AND BE SEPARATE," says the Lord. "AND DO NOT TOUCH WHAT IS UNCLEAN; And I will welcome you. "And I will be a father to you, And you shall be sons and daughters to Me," Says the Lord Almighty. – 2 Cor 6:14-18**

There is no bond that is good, for bonds are a function of the soul - not the spirit. As long as bonds exist then your ability to see and to hear are blocked. It is really very simple. If you are not able to effectively deal with the bonds in your life, then you will be constantly hindered with the oppression of another that hinders your spiritual sight. You cannot carry the baggage of the soul and enter into a spiritual oneness with Christ. If you want to be one with the Lord then you must break the bonds you have had that you might rise and experience a "spiritual oneness" with Christ.

Literally, a bond is the devil's highway right into your spirit. Until this revelation hits you, you may not give that much credence to the importance of eliminating bonds. Until you pass through this step, your progress will be hindered.

We have spoken many times about knowing who you are. This is crucial because the Lord wants you to know who you are; who He is within you. The tremendous jeopardy of bonds is that they bring you to the point where you cannot know yourself. Why is that? Because bonds block your spiritual sensitivity. It is like taking a walk on a beautiful day except the clouds are out blocking the sun.

So often the thoughts you carry are not yours. The oppression you feel - *not yours*; you are carrying that which has been transferred upon you. Your ability to see the Lord and commune with Him is hindered to the degree that you are still fettered with the bonds you carry. As shocking as this may sound, the truth is that the majority of your problems are not yours. You may think not; but you haven't realized how much you have been under as the world of evil has sought to keep you under a cloud of oppression.

Our progress in God is not as dependent upon our effort "to become" as upon our ability to cut the cords and the anchors that have held us back. What are these cords and anchors? - The bonds we carry. Do not strive to "become", endeavor to eliminate the chords that have bound you.

Let's go back to the scripture in 2nd Corinthians for a moment.

> **Do not be bound together with unbelievers; for what partnership have righteousness and lawlessness, or what fellowship has light with darkness? Or what harmony has Christ with Belial, or what has a believer in common with an unbeliever? Or what agreement has the temple of God with idols?**
>
> **For we are the temple of the living God; just as God said, "I WILL DWELL IN THEM AND WALK AMONG THEM; AND I WILL BE THEIR GOD, AND THEY SHALL BE MY PEOPLE. "Therefore, COME OUT FROM THEIR MIDST AND BE SEPARATE," says the Lord. "AND DO NOT TOUCH WHAT IS UNCLEAN; And I will welcome you. "And I will be**

> a father to you, And you shall be sons and daughters to Me," Says the Lord Almighty. – 2 Cor 6:14-18

Paul was pointing out the problems with bonds. As long as your relationships are born of the soul – born of insecurities, needs, wants, expectations, or obligations; then you have linked yourself to those individuals and all of the baggage that they carry.

Remember the first visualization I gave - the bonding of metal to metal, to metal? Well, you are not only bonded or tied to the baggage of the immediate relationship; you are vicariously bonded to that persons baggage, and the baggage of the next person, and so on. That is a bit sobering!

> **Draw near to God and He will draw near to you. Cleanse your hands, you sinners; and purify your hearts, you double-minded. – James 4:8**

So, what do bonds do? They cloud and inhibit your awareness. They block your oneness in the Spirit. They yoke you into the double mindedness of the very one with whom you are bound to. It may not be your double mindedness, but that does not matter; if you are bonded to them, then it will have your address on it as well (Jas 1:8).

It can seem relatively easy to discern or identify the obvious relationships you have that are incorrectly feeding off of you; but the real issue lies at being able to discern the bonds that you are not aware of. This takes some real perception to understand how you are relating and how you are allowing yourself to be related to which is creating these relationships on the wrong level.

If bonds continue un-checked and un-dealt with, then you can count on the fact that your ability to see and function in the realm of spirit will be hindered. For those who have not had much teaching on the existence of bonds, it can be very difficult to discern them. That is how subtle this is. That is why you must guard your eyesight - for walking in the spirit takes a great deal of sight.

We are beginning to understand the far reaching ramifications of bonds or soul-level relationships and how easy it has been for the satanic powers to hinder and significantly delay the manifestation of the kingdom, within you. We are not talking about an external fulfillment; the fulfillment of the kingdom in this day is **within you**.

As long this issue is kept on the sidelines, or hidden, then there will not be an acute understanding of the far reaching effects that the existence of bonds have. They are singularly the most deadly force that prevents the release and manifestation of the kingdom – *within you.*

If you are running this race anchored and fettered, then no matter how hard you run it will be very difficult for you to break the tape. We know there is a direct correlation to "seeing the Lord" and "being changed"; and until you deal with the bonds in your life, you are not going to be able to see clearly. If you do not see - you will not change.

The minute you start to break free is when you really find out what spiritual warfare is all about. Why? Because your progressive freedom empowers you to function and see in the realm of spirit. You are able to walk as the authority that you are. Your presence and the words you speak will do more than tickle a few ears; they will destroy fortresses. Your words and your presence will destroy principalities, powers, thrones and dominions.

Where are we headed? We are headed into clarity and into a level of life free from bonds and free from attachments - literally free from this age.

We are called to be "in the world" but not "of it". This cannot happen until you are able to cut the moorings of the bonds and attachments of the soul and walk as the spiritual person you are.

This issue of bonds is the basis of all effective spiritual warfare against the saints, and it is also at the crux of why God's sons are not becoming more quickly.

Are You Bonded To Your Concepts?

> **Hereafter I will not talk much with you: for the prince of this world cometh, and hath nothing in me.**
> **–John 14:30**

Christ spoke to the disciples that when the prince of this world would come, that he would find nothing in Him - nothing within Him, on any level. This will become – and is becoming - our own reality as well. We are walking a similar path – identical with Christ – in this experience.

There must be nothing within us that holds on to the past; whether it is to relationships born of the soul or a way of life that was part of our sojourn in the day of the partial. Nothing can remain within our thinking that is still born of the influence and conditioning of the rulers of this present darkness.

This teaching may seem strong and difficult, yet this is the path of sonship that you are on. This teaching on bonds is preparing us to move into the next level of the kingdom.

> **But Jesus did not commit himself unto them, because he knew all men, - John 2:24**

Christ gave Himself to no man, for He knew what was in man. We have spoken of this, and this will become our experience as well. More than we know, we have given ourselves to relationships and obligations born out of our misperceptions and lack of understanding. In essence; our immaturity. We have been growing and maturing in Christ, and we have walked as children - *but now we are to walk as sons.*

We are beginning to understand the dynamics of bonds. We are realizing that when a bond exists that we have, in affect, taken upon ourselves the same oppressions that are resting upon that individual. In truth, a bond is one of the most direct accesses Satan can have to you; for when a bond exists you have created a backdoor entrance into your very own being. I understand these are strong words, but we are headed into the freedom of sonship.

When you understand the full import of what a bond is, you begin to see how deep the inroads or limitations are that can be transferred upon you. God's sons have been running this race, baton in hand, yet handcuffed and weighted at their ankles.

We have mentioned previously that the majority of your problems are based upon transference that is working through bonds. As long as these "soul" bonds are allowed to remain; then there will be no fulfillment of Romans 8 and the freedom of the sons of God. Like everything else in a walk with God; this must be experienced. No one can tell you or convince you; you must experience this first hand.

For too long we have walked before the Lord with a bag with holes. He has desired to pour forth a deeper measure of His spirit, yet we have not been able to contain the releases and blessings. The bonds and attachments have siphoned away the blessing.

I don't know if you have ever experienced a real release and blessing from the Lord. Then immediately went out and shared this blessing, only to find that almost overnight it just disappeared. We have. When Christ healed the blind man He told him to "tell no one" (Matt 8:4). There was more to it than Christ wanting to keep a low profile. Christ knew the principle of transference; He knew there was a jeopardy involved and what this man was given could readily be taken from him. It is no different now.

What we need is a paradigm shift.

> **Do not be bound together with unbelievers; for what partnership have righteousness and lawlessness, or what fellowship has light with darkness? Or what harmony has Christ with Belial, or what has a believer in common with an unbeliever? 2Cor 6:14-15**

The word admonishes us not to be yoked together with unbelievers, yet have we really understood what this means?

If I were to define an unbeliever - in the most severe instance - I would say anyone outside of the immediate sphere or level on which you walk. This sounds very stern, but it is the truth. If another is not on the same level of sight and vision - comprehension and understanding - that you are on; then what you are facing is a level of an unequal yoke. And that unequal yoke can affect you far more than you may have been aware of in the past.

You may have to re-define your concept of what an unbeliever is. In the least you will have to be much more careful to what you are open to.

Your most precious commodity is your ability to see. If you compromise that by allowing bonds, relationships and attachments born of the soul into your life, then you have just compromised your greatest gift. You have compromised the very aspect that will carry you into the deeper things of the Lord; your ability to see. A walk with God is not born of liturgy or doctrine, it is born of experience; a daily unfolding experience of living in His presence.

Why are you admonished not to be bound with unbelievers? Is it because of some type of judgment you will incur *by association*? In a way, perhaps, but that is not the point. The blindness that rests upon the unbeliever, and that includes your dear brother or sister in Christ as well, can be transferred upon you in a moment of time. Transference through the bonds of sympathy and relationships of the soul is deadly. The clutter, confusion, and blindness that might exist on your brother or sister can be so easily "dumped" on you. We all know the term, "dumping". How people can dump their garbage on another. It is a crude term, but I believe we understand how easy it is to transfer the oppression off of one individual onto another.

In many instances we are dealing with a judgment that is resting upon the "old order", those who chose not to walk on into the deeper things of God. The anointing leaves and what is left are the dealings of God upon an apostate group, or individual. These are hard words, but the concern is that ye "be not a partaker of her sins". To those who have chosen a different path, who have determined the cost was too much to pay, there exists a judgment or dealing of God. If you are not careful, you too will become a partaker of their sins - by association - through the operation of soul bonds and attachments that you allowed to remain.

We are dealing with a spirit world - the realm of spirit. We are dealing with those entities and energies, whether angelic or demonic, who are set to help us; or who are set to significantly try to hinder what God is establishing.

You have to understand that at any juncture the spirit world will take full advantage to hinder your progress and growth if at all possible. What is the greatest way to do that? Transfer the blindness of another upon you. I am speaking of bonds, for bonds are deadly; because your vision, and your sight - a commodity so precious - can be lost. You can lose your sight and not even know you have lost it. This alone should keep us on our faces before Him.

The word speaks of Samson who knew not that the glory of the Lord had departed from him. It is a warning to us. You can walk with God for your whole life and yet not realize that at some point, due to choices you may have made, that you just stopped "seeing". Yet, you think you are doing fine, but you wist not that the glory of the Lord had departed.

Samson experienced this:

> **And she said, The Philistines *be* upon thee, Samson. And he awoke out of his sleep, and said, I will go out as at other times before, and shake myself. And he wist not that the LORD was departed from him. Jdg 16:20**

That is probably the bottom line for many of the evangelical and electronic church leaders today. They are walking in the light they had, yet they have no idea that they have become blind; leaders of the blind. They know it not.

> **"Many will say to Me on that day, 'Lord, Lord, did we not prophesy in Your name, and in Your name cast out demons, and in Your name**

> perform many miracles?' "And then I will declare to them, 'I never knew you; YOU WHO PRACTICE LAWLESSNESS.' Mat 7:22-23
>
> Because you say, "I am rich, and have become wealthy, and have need of nothing," and you do not know that you are wretched and miserable and poor and blind and naked.. Rev 3:17
>
> "For whoever has, to him shall *more* be given, and he shall have an abundance; but whoever does not have, even what he has shall be taken away from him. Mat 13:12

It does not take much to miss the mark, for every bond you carry distorts your ability by that much to see clearly. The more you are bonded, the blinder you become. The more baggage you carry, the greater difficulty you will have to get through the "eye of the needle".

You cannot be caught up to the heavens to rule and reign with Christ when you are anchored to the earth. The man-child in the book of Revelation is caught up to the throne of God; but this will not happen unless every bond and every attachment is eliminated.

The demand in the spirit for some time has been to "come up higher", yet the baggage we have carried has hindered our ability to do just that. We have not really understood the impact that bonds and attachments have had upon our progress.

We know this walk with God is an unfolding experience; it goes from level to level, or as the word portrays - from glory to glory. With each new level comes a greater capacity to know or understand the truth. No matter how much we have learned, no matter how much we may "know", it is nothing compared to what is yet to be revealed within us. We still do not know, understand or see as we will. We have lived in the days of the partial, awaiting the day of open vision.

A word of the Lord came saying, "In your moments of greatest clarity you are still seeing only in part". It was not a put down, but it was an admonition to keep pushing - keep pressing forward. We may see more than we have seen in our life; we may have moved in the gifts of revelation, discernment, or wisdom - but it still has been only the partial.

There can be a tendency to be at-ease in Zion; to rest upon the laurels or achievements of yesterday. If we allow this then we fall into the snare of the flesh, and will find ourselves unchangeable and stuck in the ruts of yesterday. No matter how much it may hurt, you have to stay open, and teachable. You have to allow the Lord to put the searchlight deep and bring on-course correction to you. If you do not, then you will become another casualty along the path to sonship that we have seen with so many.

There will be no fulfillment of Romans 8 and the freedom of the glory of the sons of God without first the sons eliminate the bonds and attachments on every level within their heart. Everything which has hindered your ability to be connected to the Lord, without hindrance, must be removed. It is time for you to know, even as you are known.

In the book of Isaiah he speaks; "can a nation be born in a day"? Isaiah was referencing a quick work that God would do in the earth in bringing to maturity the sons of God. There is no such thing as Instant Sons, however this process of getting free will bring you to the point where <u>INSTANT</u> can happen. This word is a pivotal point in establishing the kingdom within our heart.

Guard your sight. Guard your vision. Guard your openness to the Lord - because this transference which works through bonds, is deadly.

This word is a warring directive.

You are in the battle of the ages, contending for the releases slated for this time. You are right at the front line, and the enemy will utilize any way possible to pull you off course. This word is a caution to us concerning what we face within the realm of bonds, and to what lengths the enemy will go to hinder the will and plan of God through you.

Come Out of Her

> "Therefore, COME OUT FROM THEIR MIDST AND BE SEPARATE," says the Lord. "AND DO NOT TOUCH WHAT IS UNCLEAN; And I will welcome you. **"And I will be a father to you, And you shall be sons and daughters to Me," Says the Lord Almighty.** - 2 Cor 6:17-18

There is a relationship awaiting God's sons; a relationship with the Father unlike anything they can imagine. There must be a severing, however, from that which has sought to defile them and take their life; *first*.

There are two aspects of this word we want to address; one is the deliverance of God's sons from Babylon, the other is cutting off the ability for the "whore" to sustain herself on the blood of the saints.

What God is doing during this season on the earth is not a sovereign act. He is responding to the groaning of your spirit for release. He is bringing a clarity and understanding that is empowering you to make the changes that need to be made - to break the cords and ties that have bound you.

We have labored under misconceptions and misperceptions as we have continued on our path of shedding the limited mentality and mindset of this age. God has been calling His people out. He is literally delivering themselves from themselves - *call it an extraction process.*

It's like going to the dentist; if you have a bad tooth, you pull it. Well, we have had an Adamic nature that has needed extracting, and with it the ties, bonds, attachments and mentality that has been associated with it.

God is bringing His people out of Babylon, and this process will continue to accelerate as these days ahead of us gain momentum.

What is Babylon and what are the tentacles that "Babylon" has had within the hearts and minds of God's people? These are a couple of good questions, because what appears, is not what is. What you may think of Babylon - what appears perhaps as the obvious - is only the tip of the iceberg of that which is more deeply entrenched within the sons of God.

> **And I heard another voice from heaven, saying, Come out of her, my people, that ye be not partakers of <u>her</u> sins, and that ye receive not of her plagues. - Rev 18:4**

God may have delivered you, physically, from the religious or Babylonian system that you were a part of, but He is going to deliver you to the uttermost. We are dealing with the internal removal of the whore, the tentacles of the "whore" that have created a conditioning deep within the minds of His people. It is one thing to come out of her, it is entirely something different for "her" to come out of you.

The bonds, the contacts, and the entanglements of the soul flesh that we still carry from our time of exposure to the whore are much more entwined and alive than we may have understood. It is one thing to physically step away from that which is an abomination to the Lord; in English, "the whore". However, it is something entirely different to see the attachments and the access of the whore thoroughly eliminated within your life.

We are dealing with so many facets as God delivers His people in this day. God is delivering His people out of Babylon; not the physical institution that they may have been a part of, but a removal of a paradigm of reality, or a way of thinking, that has come from their sojourn.

Let's define paradigm for a minute:

> **A set of assumptions; concepts, values, and practices that constitutes a way of viewing reality"** *Dictionary.com*

We still do not understand how many "learned restraints" and "religious conditionings" we still carry from walking in "old order".

Before we go any further, let's define the word "whore". We know the obvious definition, but let's take a look at a more literal definition:

Whore: A person considered as having compromised principles for personal gain.

We must understand that God is delivering His people from that which was of Him, but chose not to continue. What is the whore. In simplistic terms it was God's people, His bride, who chose not follow on after Him. In turn they began to consort with the world until you have this mixture of God, Satan, and the soul flesh of man.

It is nothing new, for if you are a student of the Old Testament you have read how time and again God's people would mix with the races and cultures of other people. They would take on the belief systems of a different culture, and God, in His anger, would bring judgment after judgment upon them.

The word is full of story after story of God's people rejecting the Lord and following other gods.

So what do we have during this end time, as the book of Revelation portrays? You have the whore, who has consorted with the kings of the earth; God's people, who have given themselves to another. They have given themselves to the world and the satanic powers that have governed this age. They walk as a whore, yet carrying the presentation and appearance as though they are God's people, God's worshippers, God's anointed. And they are not. They, and the religious institutions that are born of this unholy union, are the whore.

We are very concerned with the fact that God's people are still too heavily entrenched within the system; still too bonded and too given, with very little awareness. Until now there has not really been a deep enough understanding as to the dynamics of bonds and transference, and how very little it has taken to remain attached to that which God is judging in this day.

Therefore, COME OUT FROM THEIR MIDST AND BE SEPARATE," says the Lord. "AND DO

NOT TOUCH WHAT IS UNCLEAN; And I will welcome you. - 2Co 6:17

I think it is safe to assume that most of us feel we have done just that. We have separated ourselves from that which has defiled. The Lord has revealed the apostasy of the church, and we have stepped away from the religious order of this day. We have "come out of her". But it is far more involved than just the preliminary steps away from that which has become obvious to us.

To come out of her means that God removes "her" from within us. We are speaking about bonds, relationships and a deep conditioning within our own perception of truth and reality that remain within our heart. We can in "letter" leave behind the former things - step away from the whore - but the surgical knife must go deep to remove the conditioning that yet remains within our own hearts.

In many ways we have tied the Lord's hands through our inability to see the truth; through our inability to know ourselves as He knows us. But this is coming to an end. You are in the midst of these changes, for it is a deep deliverance that we are beginning to experience.

We still have not hated the Adamic, soul nature within us enough. We have not hated it with God's hatred. We have still allowed it to live, we have tolerated it, even if just a little – within our heart. We have allowed it to be fed. As long as there is the soul / flesh nature within us, un-crucified, then we really have not fully "come out of her". There are still the remnants of an attachment to the whore that must be removed.

What happens when bonds continue to exist? We have said this before - your capacity to see is hindered - your vision is progressively more and more impaired - and your connection to the Lord is only a measure of what it could be. You become the recipient of another's thoughts and issues and more critically, their judgments and dealings from God.

> **And I heard another voice from heaven, saying, Come out of her, my people, that ye be not partakers of her sins, and that ye receive not of her plagues. - Rev 18:4**

You must understand that you are factored into the judgment coming if you have not removed yourself; for God is not a respecter of persons. A jeopardy remains that as long as His sons are still in the "loop", God's hands are tied – that is until we really do "come out of her". The chords, the bonds, the sympathies and the misunderstandings must cease; for they create a <u>bridge</u> to your spirit.

What happens when a bond is created. A bridge is built. That is not too hard to visualize. A bond is a bridge, a bridge that becomes a conduit to your spirit. And we must eliminate every bridge if we are to fully come out of the "whore", or the system of this present age.

Study the signs in the spirit which come to you. At the base of the neck, or at the top of the head, both of these signs are "red warning flags". The top of the head is your openness to the Lord, and often you might feel a clamp come and sit on top of you. The base of the neck is where the soul or psychic bonds come that attach to you and feed off of your life force.

Study the signs, because until the physical eyesight is fully opened, we must use everything that the Lord has put at our disposal.

> **"But love your enemies, and do good, and lend, <u>expecting</u> nothing in return; and your reward will be great, and you will be sons of the Most High; for He Himself is kind to ungrateful and evil** *men.*
> **- Luke 6:35**

Expectation creates bonds as easily as sympathy. There was a deeper reason behind "expecting nothing in return", for with expectation you create a bond or contact. What is the saying....."no strings attached". You have heard that saying, well here is the meaning of it. We must get rid of the strings that have attached.

> **Or what harmony has Christ with Belial, or what has a believer in common with an unbeliever?**
> **- 2Co 6:15**

We need to re-define how we view an unbeliever. What did Christ say to Mary; woman behold your son, son behold your mother? (Jn 19:26) And the other scripture.... "who is your mother, father, brother..." (Mark 3:35)..... and the answer, "they that know the will of God and do it". There is not a lot of grey area here. Christ is speaking about the relationships of the kingdom.

Let us take a look at a scripture in Revelation, and I want to expound on this for a minute....

> **And there came one of the seven angels which had the seven vials, and talked with me, saying unto me, Come hither; I will show unto thee the judgment of the great whore that sits upon many waters: With whom the kings of the earth have committed fornication, and the inhabitants of the earth have been made drunk with the wine of her fornication.**
>
> **So he carried me away in the spirit into the wilderness: and I saw a woman sit upon a scarlet colored beast, full of names of blasphemy, having seven heads and ten horns.**
>
> **And the woman was arrayed in purple and scarlet color, and decked with gold and precious stones and pearls, having a golden cup in her hand full of abominations and filthiness of her fornication:**
>
> **And upon her forehead *was* a name written, MYSTERY, BABYLON THE GREAT, THE MOTHER OF HARLOTS AND ABOMINATIONS OF THE EARTH.**
>
> **And I saw the woman drunken with the blood of the saints, and with the blood of the martyrs of Jesus: and when I saw her, I wondered with great admiration. – Rev 17:1-6**

We are dealing with 2 timelines in this scripture; present and past. The whore, that which has been an abomination to the Lord, that which has "played the harlot" with the world, has been the <u>church</u>. This is not a new revelation. But the whore is drunk on the blood of the martyrs (past tense) and the blood of the saints (present tense).

Something is happening right now and I don't like what I have seen. For there has been a feeding going on. A feeding of the whore upon the blood of the saints.

The devil has power, but he has no authority. To get authority he must usurp it from a believer. In the same way, the whore has no life in herself, she must feed off of those who have life - God's sons. We are talking about the blood of the "saints", not the blood of the "religious world". There's not a lot of life in the Christian world - it's pretty dead. But to those who are pressing into a deeper walk with Him; yes, there is life.

The Scribes and Pharisees of Christ's time were the "religious order" of that day; that which crucified Christ. During this time it is once again the religious order of this day that has stood against what God is creating. I will not tender an opinion as to the fate of those who walk presenting a form of godliness and denying the power thereof. That is God's call. But the blood of the saints are those sons; destined, called and set apart, for this time of glorification and transformation. And that is a small, very small minority.

As long as His sons are still entrenched within the mentality or limited paradigm of the church – the whore – then the bonds and ties are feeding life to the whore. The church may be dead, but life is flowing into the whore from the remnant that are pressing on after the Lord. This is where the feeding is happening.

Why is there an urgency in the spirit to end bonds, to end attachments, and to get a hold of this impartation from the Lord that changes your paradigm 180 degrees? Because it is time for judgment; but judgment is constrained because God's sons are still entwined within the system and they do not even know it. They are still in the loop. This must end for the judgments are coming now.

This must stop but the only one that is going to be able to stop this will be you. Because this requires a very personal application.

You are the light of the world, and in you dwells the light, and the life. This is not rhetoric. You know that. You know how people are drawn to you. You are His bread to this dying age. You know how your presence evokes responses wherever you go. That is all a small microcosm to what is happening on a much larger scale.

These bonds and all that accompanies them has fed the whore and kept her alive. As far fetched as this may sound, you must understand how extensive the web of transference functions, and how little it takes to create a channel.

If you are an intercessor, then pray that the eyes of His sons get opened. We have seen in vision that as God's judgment flows forth that it will judge the righteous as quickly as the ungodly. The judgments coming will not be selective; if you are in the loop then you face a jeopardy of His judgment. As the word goes ... God is not a respecter of persons; the judgments will fall upon the just and unjust alike (Matt 5:45) - all by virtue of transference and "negative identification" if we want to call it that. I have seen the jeopardy of some, whom we love, and what they face if they are not able to remove themselves, within their heart.

> **For we which have believed do enter into rest, as he said, As I have sworn in my wrath, if they shall enter into my rest: although the works were finished from the foundation of the world. - Heb 4:3**

I have said before that we are writing the last chapters. We are mapping out the way into sonship. In many ways this is new ground, yet in many ways we are walking out a destiny that has already been completed. It is a mystical thing because we are trampling out the mighty winepress of God's wrath, yet, I know from the foundations of the earth that His works were completed. It is a fine line.

A number of times the spirit has come and said that we are walking out what has already been done. It may be done, yet I know we are also writing the last chapters. It is the destiny of His people to walk out this transition during this time. As it was said of Christ, and can now be said of the sons;

> **"Lo, in the volume of the book it is said, I come to do thy will Oh God". – Heb 10:7**

Breaking the Ties to Ancestry

As we enter this day of sonship we face many things. We are experiencing a deep work of transformation as God positions us to enter into resurrection life. We are starting to get free, a freedom that has only been possible through the deep working of the Spirit in our lives.

For some time now the Lord has continued to bring greater understanding concerning bonds - for one reason; it is the Lord's desire that you be free - totally free. <u>And you cannot be free until you understand the dynamics of that which has created the hindrances and restriction to that freedom</u>.

This word is born out of a vision which revealed another roadblock to our becoming. It deals with our ancestry as a people and the need we have to allow the Lord to strip away from us all of the heritage we still carry. We are carrying not only a connection to our own "personal" ancestry, but our connection as a people to the ancestry of the Adamic nature since the fall - and this goes very deep.

The Lord is requiring a complete stripping away of all that we are; for the door of entrance into sonship is narrow. In fact the door is only big enough for you to enter, without possessions; and without baggage.

The scripture ... "whom the Lord has set free, is free indeed" (John 8:36) .... is just another scripture unless this scripture can be applied and experienced. By faith we are free. Yes - but at some point the "by faith" must be realized. Why? Because you will not enter into the final releases of sonship unless you get free from the relationships and bonds that have fed off of your life.

A vision came recently which spoke of another type of bond that needed to be broken; a bond His sons have carried to the lineage of their Adamic nature.

As I walked down this path I could see a village; old, decrepit, and in great disarray. It was on the other side of the fence; but I was curious. What is this and what does the Spirit want to show? So I jumped over this fence and approached this filthy and decrepit village.

I found myself walking through this utterly abandoned city; all I could see was abject squalor and poverty. As I walked I began to realize that this was the last dwelling place of our ancestry; the ancestry of our Adamic nature. This was the dwelling place of those, after the flesh, that turned away from what God was doing in the earth. This ancestry was born of the Adamic nature, and it had rejected the word of the Lord from ages past. This place; remote, desolate and abandoned, is the dwelling place of those that are born of the seed of the Adamic nature. This is where "they" had lived out their days.

As I continued to walk through this forsaken town, I found that the squalor was staggering. There were only a few ragged children, children born of this lineage, still walking the streets. Poor, in rags, sick, and disease ridden; these were the children of this heritage - of this Adamic lineage. As I approached the entrance to a dwelling, I realized that this was the last dwelling place of our ancestry after the flesh.

And the word came... "<u>this bond must be broken, for you are not of this lineage.</u>"

The Spirit spoke; this is not your inheritance, this is not the inheritance of the Sons of Light, and we must separate ourselves that we might be free from all of that which was born of the flesh. And the vision ended.

As we continue to shed the bonds born of the flesh, the Lord is speaking that all of His sons must be delivered from the bonds or ties to their ancestry – specifically; the ancestry of the Adamic nature. We are not to know ourselves or be linked to the lineage of our ancestry, for we have been born into the order of Melchizedek. We are to be separated from that which our fathers were, and the fathers of our fathers before them.

As we step into this new day of the kingdom, we are to do so without baggage, for we will not be able to enter in through the door of access if we do so. We must let go of all of that which would seek to define us after the flesh. We must be delivered from our ancestry. Whether it is your personal lineage, or the lineage of the first Adam; it is the same.

The vision speaks of a level of transference that God is ending; for in Christ you are born into the order of Melchizedek. You have been rooted in Christ, a new branch, a new lineage, and thus you are created in Christ after the order of Melchizedek. You have neither a beginning, nor an ending - for as Melchizedek; you have always existed.

> **And having been made perfect, He became to all those who obey Him the source of eternal salvation, being designated by God as a high priest according to the order of Melchizedek. - Heb 5:9-10**

> **For this Melchizedek, king of Salem, priest of the Most High God, who met Abraham as he was returning from the slaughter of the kings and blessed him, to whom also Abraham apportioned a tenth part of all *the spoils*, was first of all, by the translation *of his name*, king of righteousness, and then also king of Salem, which is king of peace. Without father, without mother, <u>without genealogy</u>, having neither beginning of days nor end of life, but made like the Son of God, he abides a priest perpetually. - Heb 7:1-3**

We must break the ties and bonds to the ancestry we bear; to the lineage from which we have come. This is not what we are, nor will it define who we are. This is another level of the releasing of bonds.

The requirement is to let go; truly let go of all that would try to tie you to this world or to those who have not walked in the household of faith. Our lineage, our ancestry, is Christ. Nothing else.

This bond goes deep and this is one that we take a deliverance from once and for all. The next time you take communion, take it with us to see God completely erase the heritage or genealogy of the Adamic nature that we have carried.

Understand, I am not saying that you have to be "free" of what you consider your hang-ups; that is not the issue. The issue is what you are still bonded to. God can deal with the hang-ups, if that is even necessary, but at the root we let go of the heritage of that which has tried to attach itself to us. In truth it goes much deeper than just the ancestry within your family lines, this is dealing with the heritage that has come from the Adamic nature since the very beginning.

God is separating you from this world on a much deeper level of experience than you may have understood. We are admonished not to be a part of this age, <u>yet this can only be achieved when the link and tie at the root of the human race is severed from our past.</u>

> **But now Christ has been raised from the dead, the first fruits of those who are asleep. For since by a man *came* death, by a man also *came* the resurrection of the dead. For as in Adam all die, so also in Christ all shall be made alive.**
> **- 1 Co 14:20-22**

If we source this back far enough then we understand that we are breaking the links and ties with the Adamic nature when it first began. This deliverance goes deep; our father, our father's father, all the way back to the first Adam. This link, this tie - we declare - is broken. This bond is destroyed, and this we do in the name of the Lord.

> **But what does the Scripture say? "CAST OUT THE BONDWOMAN AND HER SON, FOR THE SON OF THE BONDWOMAN SHALL NOT BE AN HEIR WITH THE SON OF THE FREE WOMAN." So then,**

brethren, we are not children of a bondwoman, but of the free woman. – Gal 4:30-31

The son of the bondwoman cannot inherit; only the son born after the spirit. Our lineage is not that of the first Adam, our lineage is that of the 2nd Adam – Christ (1Co 15:45). This is your only lineage, and this deliverance, this change, is absolutely necessary as we step out of the limitations of what we have known - into the unlimitedness of Christ.

It is difficult at this stage to truly grasp that we are entering into the priesthood of Melchizedek where you have had no beginning and you will have no end. But you are here.

This transition of life; this release from every bond or tie we have known, is enabling us to link back in with who we have always been; since the dawning of creation.

God is bringing to mind those things concerning His sons. We are entering into the eternity of the Lord Jesus Christ, and as we enter through this portal we will discover that we have never had a beginning, nor will we ever have an end.

Section 9

To Know The Lord

- **Hunger**
- **To Know the Lord**
- **We Complete Him**
- **His Inheritance in the Sons of Light**

Hunger

This time period in the earth is plagued by a lukewarmness that exists within the church, and an indifference within the world as a whole. It doesn't take a great deal of perception to see that we are in a time that the Lord is allowing the iniquity to come to the full. How do the scriptures refer to this time frame? The love of many will wax cold; and as it was in the days of Sodom and Gomorrah, so it will be in the days of the Son of Man. We are not surprised with the scripture in Revelations 3; for this is the time that we are walking in.

> **14 "And to the angel of the church in Laodicea write: The Amen, the faithful and true Witness, the Beginning of the creation of God, says this: 15 'I know your deeds, that you are neither cold nor hot; I would that you were cold or hot. 16 'So because you are lukewarm, and neither hot nor cold, I will spit you out of My mouth. 17 'Because you say, "I am rich, and have become wealthy, and have need of nothing," and you do not know that you are wretched and miserable and poor and blind and naked Rev. 3:14-17**

We have spoken of the qualities of what God is looking for throughout this book within His sons. The qualities are an open heart and a teachable spirit. As well, we must let go of our concepts - we must truly "step outside the camp". We must live in what I would call a state of "emptying ourselves" that He might fill us.

This was the path of Christ, and it is our path as well. Christ emptied Himself out (Phil 2:7). And so must we.

> **So, let us go out to Him outside the camp, bearing His reproach. -Heb 13:13**

God has called you "outside the camp"; and so we walk.

What is interesting and equally challenging is that the state of heart spoken of in Revelation 3 is not obvious to those who walk accordingly. To those who are caught in this state of indifference; it is really not apparent to them. We might think that this scripture is quite obvious; but it really is not. This can be very subtle, and to a degree, we might all still be dealing with a measure of this within our own heart.

All of us have read these scriptures and assume - at face value - that we will recognize these scriptures as they are being fulfilled. But in a very real sense it takes revelation to see. It is not obvious to the eyes.

Perhaps you can think; "Well look at all those self-serving tele-evangelists; this must be obvious to many". But remember - *nothing is as it seems.*

God is moving forward. He is not in a static mode; He will not be defined and put in a box. If you are walking with God, then your life is in an ever-changing state of flux. You must understand that whatever revelation you had yesterday was only the partial. God is restoring more and more light to you, for He is bringing His people into what He has prepared for them.

If you have pre-determined just how far you will go, just how much of a price you will pay to walk with Him; then you are already on a fast track going backwards.

There are 2 modes of walking with God; either you are moving forward, or you are moving backward. There is no standing still and treading water. As God continues to move forward, if you are not moving forward with Him; then you are moving backward. It may not be entirely black and white, but this is a close semblance of what is at stake as God continues to move on.

In the book of Revelation, chapter 3, the word is:

> **Because you say, "I am rich, and have become wealthy, and have need of nothing," and you do not know that you are wretched and miserable and poor and blind and naked - Rev. 3:14-17**

This scripture is being fulfilled, albeit - *on a subliminal level*. As we have said before, most people are not aware of the choices they are making in their walk with God. They do not even realize that they have become poor, blind and naked.

How many of God's people are walking in this word of Revelation 3 and they don't even realize it. They have drawn their line - how far they will go. They may see themselves as being rich, having need of nothing. What a travesty. The only answer or safeguard we have in this day is that of truly hungering after the Lord.

What happens to people to cause them to miss out on God? Sometimes it can be as simple as just becoming too satisfied with what they have possessed, so that they fail to continue to drive on after the Lord.

There are many reasons people miss out on God; the cares of life, the position of a ministry - you could name many "leaves and branches" of the soul. For that is what they are; "leaves and branches" of a tree that must be uprooted. Of course they may have simply reached a point where the cost was too much - we are really saying the same thing.

To walk on with God demands a never-ending hunger fueled by the vision He continues to sear into your consciousness. You go so far, yet you are always aware that there is so much more.

In Romans 8 the word speaks of those who are led by the spirit. If you look more closely at the literal Greek for the word "led", you find that it actually depicts a state of being that is "driven". The sons of God are not passively led, they are driven by the spirit as they seek out to fulfill His will.

So what is it that is driving you on with almost an insatiable hunger that cannot be filled? It is that driving of the spirit within you. You are driven, and it is not something you can quantify. You can't measure it. And it is hard to separate it from within your own heart. You just know that there is within you this drive - that He has placed - that cannot be quenched. It is the drive of your spirit that knows and is groaning for the adoption of sonship.

When you stop to think about it, the feeling and sensation of hunger is ***not*** a comfortable one. To one who is at a point of starvation, hunger can be a very painful state. In many ways it is no different for any of us who truly desire to walk on the highest plane. What will it take? Your life will be lived always hungering after Him, always yearning for more of Him – this is what it will take.

The more you see of Him, the more you become, and the more your hunger is fueled to pursue after Him even more. We can never let the indifference of this age and society that we live in permeate our hearts to bring an indifference within us.

The church of Laodicea is a type and shadow of what exists in this day. Since you have a church that is neither hot or cold, but lukewarm, you find that God will spew those lukewarm believers out of His mouth. But you say, "they are believers". Not to God. To believe God does not mean you live your life in a state of détente; it means you live aggressively pursuing every promise and every word.

God is doing this, and as we mentioned at the beginning of this word, what is happening is that those who have chosen to go only so far and no further, will not be able to see what God is doing in this hour. Is God spewing these unbelieving "believers" out of His mouth? In a way, yes. But they are doing it to themselves, for their choices have put them in a state of the wise and foolish virgins, those that have eyes to see, and those, which do not.

How does the word go... "even what they had is being taken away" (Lu19:26). Will they recognize this? Probably not, because these changes are so imperceptible. It will all seem like peace and safety, and everything is just fine, but they will wist not that the glory of the Lord had departed from them (Judges 16:20).

There are great promises and realities hovering over each one of you at this point in time, just waiting to be ignited by your hunger. If you want a greater word of knowledge, hunger for it. If you want to really walk in the Spirit, hunger for it. You say, "I am being selfish by hungering for these things". No, you are not. Actually you are being anything but selfish, for until you move into the gifts and callings of the Spirit, you will not be able to impart to others, and bring them in.

Christ admonished us to desire earnestly the gifts. Covet them earnestly. God will not deny your hunger. If you desire earnestly to walk in His presence, to move with all of the gifts of the Spirit; He will not deny you. He may test you to see what metal you are made of, but if you earnestly seek Him, He will give you the desires of your heart.

How does the word go? ....

> **Then you will call upon Me and come and pray to Me, and I will listen to you. You will seek Me and find *Me* when you search for Me with all your heart. – Jer 29:12-13**

If you find that you are not driven after the Lord with an insatiable hunger for Him, then it is time to have another touch by Him. Perhaps you have seen men "as trees walking" (Matt 8:24), but now it is time to see clearly.

To Know The Lord

> "Come, let us return to the LORD. For He has torn *us,* but He will heal us; He has wounded *us,* but He will bandage us. He will revive us after two days; He will raise us up on the third day, That we may live before Him. So let us know, let us press on to know the LORD. His going forth is as certain as the dawn; And He will come to us like the rain, Like the spring rain watering the earth." Hosea 6:1-3

This prophecy in Hosea speaks of the path God's people have walked. It speaks of the promise of the 3rd day - that the Lord will raise His people up on the 3rd day that they might live before Him. His going forth is as certain as the dawn – the dawning revelation that He brings to His people as they come alive to this 3rd day of spirit. As surely as the Morningstar arising in your heart.

> ***So*** we have the prophetic word *made* more sure, to which you do well to pay attention as to a lamp shining in a dark place, until the day dawns and the morning star arises in your hearts. – 2Pe 1:19

> "I, Jesus, have sent My angel to testify to you these things for the churches. I am the root and the descendant of David, the bright morning star" – Rev 22:16

We have come to the third day as spoken of by Hosea. I don't know that we can exactly say "when" we entered this third day, but we are most certainly in this now. In the word it speaks that a day will be as a thousand years (2Pe 3:8).

So who knows? 1999? 2000? 2001? It doesn't really matter. We have entered the time of the "3rd" thousand year timeline since Christ. Even if we are wrong, we are not predicating what we feel upon this scripture. What continues to come in the spirit and what we have experienced, is a reality of Hosea 3.

It is in this season of the 3rd day that God brings to fulfillment all of the words and prophecies which have come through the mouths of His prophets from ages past. God will have a people that will live before Him - that will join Christ who is seated at the right hand of the Father.

There may be times when you have felt like Daniel who stood in the gap for his people. During his generation he became the instrument of intercession in reminding the Lord of His promise that He would bring His people back from captivity and into their inheritance. The prophecy went unfulfilled before Daniel came before the Lord to see the impasse and delay ended (Dan 9).

As a people, we too have seen a delay of the promises and the fulfillment slated for this 3rd day, the "day of spirit".

We are experiencing a deep drive in the spirit to see the fulfillment of His word and promises to this generation, and to see the establishing of His kingdom. There are times when it can be challenging to shake off the feeling – "What if we missed His timing?" "Perhaps the stewardship that we were given has been overlooked on our part?" "Possibly the unfolding of the kingdom in this hour was - and is - more predicated upon our initiative than we had previously understood?"

I am not sure just what would have happened had Daniel not stood in the gap during his tenure here on earth - or for that matter other great men of faith down through the ages. Martin Luther, Zwingli, John & Charles Wesley, and so many others who made a difference in their time are now standing with us as part of the "cloud of witnesses".

They ran the race, they carried the baton in their generation, they pursued after the Lord. They were driven to know Him and the power of His resurrection.

It has been written of Martin Luther that had he not prayed diligently, that the future of his timeline would probably have gone another direction. I don't know if we understand yet how great a mantle has been laid upon His sons <u>to bring to pass</u> the fulfillment of God's plan in this generation.

The very thought of it can break your heart, for you realize how much the Lord has limited Himself to move in the earth in this day. He has limited Himself to move through His sons; *but His sons must move.*

What is the admonition? That we press on to know the Lord.

In this day the outskirts of the camp are comprised of those who may have a measure of His power, a measure of His presence, but who do not really know Him. That is the jeopardy we face, for we cannot be caught up in the ministry, caught up in "working for God". Whatever our lives are, they must be an expression and outward manifestation of our constant and ongoing drive to know Him. We know the outcome for some may well be; "Depart from Me, for I never knew you." But that will not be the calling card for God's sons.

How can you put a price on knowing the Lord? You cannot. We know it will cost everything we have. Everything we are. Even your dreams must be surrendered to Him; for He must be everything to you. Everything.

There is no other path. We see the testimony of so many who have chosen other paths, because the demands of sonship were beyond what they were willing to pay.

How much do you love Him? How much do you really love Him? Because it is that love which will be the anchor that will carry you through the deep dealings He brings into your life. It has been the anchor which has carried you through the deep conflicts that you have faced, and it will be the anchor to carry you through that which you are yet to experience.

"Thou He slay me, yet will I serve Him" (Job 13:15). Can we have any other plumbline? This is not a platitude to His sons, this is the cry of our heart as we surrender everything to Him.

This is sonship. It is not about great and mighty works. It is not about signs and wonders. It is not about looking good and acceptable. It is about knowing Him. It is about entering into a spiritual oneness with the Lord, for He is everything.

There is no manifestation of sonship in this hour without a manifestation of the Lord. As the scripture goes ... when He is revealed, then we are also, for our lives are hidden in Him (Col 3:3-4).

Can you let go and let this happen? Because it will.

Sonship is not about rituals or religious acts. This is the real deal. Our relationship with Him cannot be at arms distance; we must know Him as intimately as Adam knew Eve. This was Paul's drive; to know the Lord and the power of His resurrection. This must be our plumbline.

> **More than that, I count all things to be loss in view of the surpassing value of knowing Christ Jesus my Lord, for whom I have suffered the loss of all things, and count them but rubbish so that I may gain Christ, and may be found in Him, not having a righteousness of my own derived from *the* Law, but that which is through faith in Christ, the righteousness which *comes* from God on the basis of faith, that I may know Him and the power of His resurrection and the fellowship of His sufferings, being conformed to His death; - Phil 3:8-10**

No matter what He may give us ... *it cannot preclude our drive to truly know Him.* There is no fulfillment of the prophecies and the promises in this day separate from a deep relationship with the Lord - <u>for to know Him is to experience Him.</u>

> **"Who is this coming up from the wilderness leaning on the arms of her beloved?" – Song of Solomon 8:5**

As the bride of Christ comes forth in this day - leaving the wilderness wanderings of God's dealings and deep preparation - they do so leaning upon the Lord in a relationship that He has wanted with each of them all along. It has taken many paths to perfect and bring this forth. Who are they which are coming forth in this day leaning upon the Lord's bosom? The lame, the halt and the blind.

The Lord has done what was necessary to create you and bring you forth as His son. If needed, He broke your leg, maybe He broke both of your legs. Whatever was needed, He has been faithful. This is your entrance into the kingdom. Like the prophecy in Hosea; He has torn you, but He will heal you, and He is raising you up (resurrection life), to live in this 3rd day, the day of spirit.

I wonder if we really understand that what the Lord is looking for are those who will truly enter into a relationship of knowing Him. This is what it is really all about.

It has never been about doing the greater works or moving in His authority to bind the nations and kingdoms of this age; the real intent and drive of the Spirit has been to bring many sons into a place of oneness with the Father. It is about the "Father's family".

> **But who can endure the day of His coming? And who can stand when He appears? For He is like a refiner's fire and like fullers' soap. He will sit as a smelter and purifier of silver, and He will purify the sons of Levi and refine them like gold and silver, so that they may present to the LORD offerings in righteousness. – Malachi 3:2-3**

Malachi speaks of His appearing; that He appears as a refiner's fire and that He will purify the sons of Levi. There must be a drive within His sons to stay in His presence until all of the dross of the flesh (soul nature) has been removed. What remains must be the mirror image of Christ Himself. The Father looks at His sons and sees Christ - the new creation - in each of them.

We cannot settle for anything less in this hour. We must come into the fulfillment of a relationship with the Lord on the highest level. As John spoke in John 3:30; "He must increase, but I must decrease".

There is no doubt that there has been a lot of "decreasing" and "increasing" over this past season of time within each of His sons, but we must realize that it all culminates in a relationship with the Lord that is absolute.

This is our fulfillment and this is the Father's fulfillment; you cannot lose sight of the true goal.

I know that each of you carries the scars and the wounds of the battle of this day and of His deep dealings that have been upon each of you. I also know the promise that He will heal His sons, without a scar remaining. What are the scars or wounds but part of the process of our path of coming to know Him – our ticket of entry.

So many over the years have withdrawn in bitterness to the path that was given them to walk. They did not have eyes to see or a heart to understand what God was truly doing in them. They did understand that He wanted to bring them into their inheritance, but first the work of the cross had to be complete. What happened? They became casualties. I have also seen those upon whom the hand of God rested; who went through so much, yet never complaining. Now they are rising into His presence with a thankfulness and joy as the Lord establishes a relationship with them that could never have come any other way.

Through the wisdom of the world we know this appears as folly. To His sons the path of righteousness has come at a great price; for they have sold everything to obtain this pearl of great price. Jesus emptied Himself out, and Paul was poured out as a drink offering unto the Lord through what he experienced. It will be no different for His sons.

> **For I am already being poured out as a drink offering, and the time of my departure has come. – 2Tim 4:6**
>
> **Have this attitude in yourselves which was also in Christ Jesus, who, although He existed in the form of God, did not regard equality with God a thing to be grasped, but emptied Himself, taking the form of a bond-servant, *and* being made in the likeness of men.**
>
> **Being found in appearance as a man, He humbled Himself by becoming obedient to the point of death, even death on a cross. – Phil 2:5-8**

Can God's sons in this hour traverse any different path? To each of you, upon whom the ends of the ages have come, has fallen a destiny to inherit the promises that so many died in the faith seeing, but never partaking of.

We Complete Him

I rejoice in my sufferings for your sake, and in my flesh I do my share on behalf of His body, which is the church, in filling up what is lacking in Christ's afflictions. - Col 1:24

This scripture has been a mystery in many ways because it speaks of the completion of the sufferings of Christ within and through His body; the mystical "body of Christ".

Every once in a while you get a glimpse of something - a moment in time when a larger picture unfolds before you – and pieces of the puzzle come together. This is one of those times, for we are completing an aspect of the ministry of Christ beyond what we have understood or seen. This is something that must be a revelation to your heart for it transcends our ability to really understand. It goes much deeper than what we can say.

We are at the culmination of the ages and you walk in many ways facing two fronts; God and the Satanic hosts. We face the Spirit of God which appears as a refiner's fire to His sons (Malachi 3), purging and purifying them; creating a bride that is spotless before Him. Yet you stand as the vehicle and channel of the authority of God in this age. You are bringing the final judgment upon an evil and hostile generation that has been set to destroy the man-child at every juncture in the road. An interesting dichotomy; God on one side, Satan on the other.

All of this is only one aspect of an even larger vision. The Lord has granted His people to partake of - *and to complete* – the sufferings of Christ. This is something which transcends our ability to really understand.

We know the scripture in Romans 8:17:

And if children, heirs also, heirs of God and fellow heirs with Christ, if indeed we suffer with *Him* so that we may also be glorified with *Him*. – Ro 8:17

We are only beginning to get a deeper understanding or glimpse into the high calling to which we have been called. It is so much more than what we have previously understood or perceived, for the Lord has granted His "body" to complete His sufferings. On the surface this seems like something so obvious to us, but I know that we are experiencing the reality of this, and in some ways it cannot be put into words.

The path of the purification of God's sons - the path of the cross that they have born - represents something beyond just "their release", or "their change". What is being experienced and walked out is a completion of the sufferings of Christ through His people.

At times it can appear as if it is all about "us"; what we are going through, the changes we are experiencing, the demands He is making. Yet what we are living and what we are experiencing has a much greater impact in the spirit realm than we have understood. We have touched on this in the word "The One World of Christ".

We are that "mystical body of Christ", and we are fulfilling the ministry of Christ in this hour. On every level.

You have been chosen - you have been graced - with the calling to complete every aspect of the ministry of Christ in the earth during this time. One very blessed aspect of this calling is fulfilling the "sufferings" of Christ.

We may not completely understand this. We may not yet understand the deep underlying significance of the work of the cross that we carry daily. But what we are living, what we are experiencing, and what we are going through, is having a dynamic effect upon the entire world of spirit.

It is not just about "you".

I know we understand that, but what we represent, the "leaven" in the earth, has a much greater meaning than what we have hitherto understood. We are destined to fulfill the mystical sufferings of Christ.

Your presence, and the path you have been given, transcends your release. God's sons are fulfilling the ministry of Christ more than they have understood.

I know the Lord will bring greater light concerning this aspect of His ministry in the earth within the sons, for we are only just scratching the surface.

God's people are the leaven in this age. They are the remnant - the handful of seed - which are creating changes across every level of life. In a very real, yet mystical way, we are completing the sufferings of Christ. Every breath you breathe, every step you take, every part of your being is partaking of and fulfilling His sufferings.

You are the Christ in the earth. The religious world will hate you as they hated Christ in His day. If you were looking to be popular, this would not be the path to take. If you are looking for social religion; this is not the path. I am being facetious; you would not be reading this book if your path followed that direction. But it is all part of the mystical sufferings of Christ that we have been honored to partake of.

Unto us, upon whom the ends of the ages have come;

His Inheritance - Within the Sons of Light

> "Therefore, COME OUT FROM THEIR MIDST AND BE SEPARATE," says the Lord. "AND DO NOT TOUCH WHAT IS UNCLEAN; And I will welcome you. **"And I will be a father to you, And you shall be sons and daughters to Me,"** Says the Lord Almighty.
> - 2 Cor. 6:17-18

The Lord earnestly desires an intimate relationship with us far greater than our own drive has been to know Him. In the word it speaks that the Lord earnestly desires the spirit He has caused to dwell within us (Ja 4:5). It can seem hard to fathom, but He desires this relationship even more than we do. The real reason we are driven to break the bonds and attachments of the soul level that we have carried is to enter into a spiritual oneness with the Lord. Without this step - *it cannot happen*.

God is delivering His sons out of Babylon in a way that perhaps we have not fully understood; for we are beginning to experience an absolute severing of everything that has tied or bound each of us to the limitations of this plane of existence.

What do you gain as you pursue a life without bonds, without attachments, without anything but a drive to know Him? What do you gain when you step out of the religious Babylon of this day? It can be very difficult perhaps for some, for this means leaving the relationships and leaving the comfort zone of friends that you have known. If you are driven to follow on to know the Lord, you will find that the sacrifices you must make will not compare to the glory and changes that will come to you.

To step out of Babylon, to truly rid yourself of the control and mindset that you have picked up during your sojourn with the whore, involves a greater work of the cross. Purity precedes perception. How does that scripture go? "Blessed are the pure in heart, for they shall see God". It takes this deep preparation within each one to bring them into the place of sight, and sight is what it will take to see every tentacle and every defilement that has attached itself to you, <u>removed</u>.

There is a level of His presence, during this time of His appearing, that is yet to be experienced by His people. It is an experience that will be embraced as His sons come through the completion of the deep work of the cross and the changes within them. What are we talking about? We are talking about living with an awareness of the Lord - 24/7.

I do not discount the level of experience any have had, or the level of the "partial" that you and I have walked in; but everything before this time has only been the "partial".

We are talking about entering into a relationship with the Lord that far transcends anything we could have imagined. This can only be done on the other side of a deep breaking of bonds, and a deep letting go of how we have seen the Lord. We are letting go of even our own "paradigm" of how we have "seen" the Lord. God is removing the filters through which we have viewed Him that we might truly come to "know the Lord".

> **then He said, "BEHOLD, I HAVE COME TO DO YOUR WILL." He takes away the first in order to establish the second. –Heb 10:9**

Sometimes it can be difficult when God requires that you let go of what He has given you. You may have walked in tremendous things, but if and when He requires that you lay all of it back at His feet; then you must be prepared to let it go. He will establish something within you so far greater. We must always hold things "lightly". So many have lost out with God for this very reason; they could not let go.

What we have seen has been through the lens of the partial; but God is taking away the first, that He might establish the second. He is establishing a new thing within your heart.

You must break the ties with the past, on every level, that He might create within you the capacity to see and hear as you have never experienced before. This can only be done as the Spirit brings clarity and deep revelation to you, for we are not talking about that which is apparent.

We are talking about what we have not seen. We are talking about an entire paradigm shift. We are talking about an impartation coming from the Lord to enable this change during this time. What awaits God's sons? The same experience that Elijah attained.

When the king's armies came before Elijah and asked who he was, his reply was simply, "I am Elijah, who stands in the presence of the Lord". This was Elijah's calling card, for Elijah lived in the presence of the Lord (1Kings 18:15). Elijah functioned from this level of awareness, and this will be your calling card, *now*.

Why do you break bonds? Why are you so determined that none of your relationships will be on the wrong level? So that you might enter into a oneness with Him. This is no small thing. We cannot walk in His presence during this time without which we have done our homework. This is the time of His parousia, the time of His presence in the earth, and it is to this door that we have come.

This growing awareness of His presence is living and tangible, and will become the perpetual abiding place of God's sons. We will truly begin to understand the "fear of the Lord".

> I pray that the eyes of your heart may be enlightened, so that you will know what is the hope of His calling, what are the riches of the glory of His inheritance in the saints... Eph 1:18

To understand the fear of the Lord is to realize that His inheritance is within each of us. You and I are the Father's inheritance.

> "And I will be a father to you, And you shall be sons and daughters to Me," says the Lord Almighty
> - 2 Cor 6:18

As we step out of the ties and bonds to the whore - to Babylon - to that which has defiled; there awaits an experience for us. We will experience the Father's family. We will be sons and daughters to

Him, and He will be our Father. We have experienced a token of this, but there is something far greater awaiting us.

What we see unfolding during this time is not so much about the releases we are experiencing - and will experience; it is about the Father's inheritance within the Sons of Light. He is finally getting a people that love Him, that are given to Him, and who will not serve another.

I cannot fathom how long the Father has waited for this day. I cannot fathom how deeply the Father has longed for a communion with His sons. It is time that the Father will receive His inheritance within the sons of Light.

The mystery of Christ within us, the mystery of all that we are, has been hidden from our eyes for a season; but the veils are being removed. The seals are being taken off the book; His living book. You and I. We are beginning to recognize and understand, at last, that the kingdom is within.

You reach a point, having seen beyond the veil, that you cannot settle for anything less than the full measure. The Lord has ruined you for anything less. You cannot return to old order, or even "new" order, for you have seen what He is making available, you have tasted as Hebrews speaks, of the powers of the age to come. The only difference is that this "age to come" has arrived.

The Father's inheritance is in the Sons of Light. This is almost too deep to understand, for His inheritance is WITHIN you. You are His reward. This may make you look at yourself differently. I know that within the humble vessels that God is raising up is His heritage. You are something far, far greater than you have understood. But you are starting to see.

We have walked before the Lord; we have limped, crawled or hobbled our way into this day of His kingdom. The Lord has given eyes to see, and He has ruined His sons for a level of fulfillment short of what they now understand. You are His fulfillment, and He is yours.

Section 10

Reality Or Illusion?

- **Is Your Reality An Illusion**

- **The Process of Sight**

- **The Veil And One Step Beyond**

- **When You Make the Inner As The Outer**

- **The End Of Illusion**

Is Your Reality An Illusion?

Our perception of reality is created through what we see, feel, hear, touch or smell. It is greatly influenced by the culture we are raised in along with the relationships and associations we have. It is over a lifetime of experience through these modes of perception that our lens of reality is created; or what I would call our personal paradigm.

All of these avenues of input mold, form and shape our views of reality and our belief system. The saying goes, "we are what we eat". Perhaps you have heard that saying. On a deeper level of consciousness this is even more true; for we are what we partake of – on every level. We become a physical expression of what we have accepted and assimilated.

This explains why there can be such a divergence of perceptions between cultures; good or bad, possible or impossible. Your perceptions are framed by the input that you have had as you have grown within this world system. This does not make it true or valid; these values are just one more bit of baggage we pick up on this sojourn.

We have said before that we actually "learn" unbelief. This is very true, for the programming or indoctrination we go through in this world system literally shapes our belief system. We learn unbelief. If your path has taken you through the church world, then you have a set of belief systems that are a unique challenge to you. If you have been in some other religion, the same applies. You will have to unlearn the restrictive conditioning that you assimilated.

To the eastern mystic the realm of spirit may seem commonplace; and to the western mind the realm of spirit may be perceived as being nonexistent. The problem each one faces is the inherent perception or belief system that must be unlearned.

Do you remember Smith Wigglesworth? He was a man of great faith who lived in the early part of the 20th century. Smith was uneducated; he could not even read. When the Spirit taught him how to read, he only read the Word of God. Nothing else. Whether or not he understood the dynamics of what he was doing; he had determined that the only truth or input he would receive would be from the Word of God.

Smith was determined that he would not allow any input into his heart but the truth of God's Word. Signs followed Smith as he walked before the Lord, for he was known to have raised the dead and perform many other miraculous works. His perception of reality was not tainted by the sterility of the culture he lived in. His paradigm of reality was deeply rooted in the word.

Paul speaks in the book of Romans about the renewing of the mind:

> **And do not be conformed to this world, but be transformed by the <u>renewing of your mind</u>, that you may prove what the will of God is, that which is good and acceptable and perfect. Romans 12:2**

As you continue to experience the renewing of your mind; a number of dynamics begin to change within you. You begin to hear and see on levels that you were unable to perceive before. The word begins to come alive to you in new ways. Whole new vistas of perception unfold; literally right before your eyes.

Over the years we have had different ones come to us in the spirit to deliver a message. The message that came numerous times was that what we sought was here; it was right in front of us. But there was always a caveat; *we needed to see through the eyes of the Lord.*

Those visions and appearings continued to goad us as we sought to understand just what the Lord was speaking of. Why couldn't we see it. It was spoken numerous times; "it is right here, it is right in front of you". I was baffled; why could I not see it?

The Cloud of Witnesses have expressed the same thing. "Why don't you see it. Why don't you realize who you are?" "It is right there in front of you". If I took one step left or one step right I would bump right into it. But we couldn't see it.

A lot of water had gone under the bridge - so to speak - before I began to understand why I couldn't see it – *yet*. I was in a process; the process of the renewing of the mind on a level that had not yet been completed. I may have been able to see many things; but I could not grasp what they were trying to tell me. I still wasn't seeing - not on that level.

What a learning curve, until I realized that we are experiencing an on-going renewal of the mind that is changing our capacity to see. Now I understood. Our capacity to "see" is in a constant state of flux. What we were not able to perceive or understand yesterday, is giving way as this process hastens to fulfillment. We are beginning to understand the dynamics of change that is going on within the renewing of our mind.

This should explain just a bit of the difficulty you may have had. To understand this experience of the renewing of your mind sheds further light on the difficulty we face as we speak to others. Unless the renewing of the mind is far enough along, unless the Holy Spirit has brought the work of change deep enough; you could talk all day long and no one will understand what you are talking about. They may say, "I understand", but they are really clueless.

You are literally experiencing a re-wiring of your mind and this is changing everything for you.

> **And be not conformed to this world: but be ye transformed by the renewing of your mind, that ye may prove what *is* that good, and acceptable, and perfect, will of God. – Rom 12:2**

Perhaps you are beginning to grasp the power and the intent of the Father behind Romans 12:2. It is nothing to take lightly, for this renewing of the mind is the pivotal point at which everything else changes.

One of the greatest struggles you face is recognizing just how much you have changed. There is no measuring barometer that will tell you the percentages; but you will know. Men will cease to be as "trees walking" (Mar 8:22). It is gradual, but like a constant drip of water; the work of the renewing of your mind is in a constant state of change.

One of the affects of this change or re-wiring within you, is that your understanding of reality makes a huge shift.

We have seen, as the scriptures speak; through a glass darkly. In our greatest moments of clarity we still have not seen clearly, but we are talking about something more than just a gift of perception or revelation. We are talking about a renewing at the core of our entire being.

The veil is coming off of the sons of God. It has been a veil that has existed because of the carnal mind we have lived with. We have not been able to see and grasp what is in our midst. We have said before that <u>Christ rent the veil</u>. The veil does not exist. Yet until we experience a deeper level of the renewing of the mind, we are still veiled in our understanding.

Delivered from the domain of Satan

The cry which comes from the Spirit in this day is, "*Come Out of Her My People*". God is delivering His sons from Babylon; on every level. The deliverance is going deeper and deeper within the framework of how we have thought, and how we have perceived.

We have addressed this issue before, but we want to take another look at it – from one more vantage point.

There is another plane of deliverance that should be considered as a deeper fulfillment; a deliverance from a dimension that we have known since birth – from the dimension of this world in which we have lived and perceived as "reality".

The scriptures state that we have been delivered from the domain of Satan into the domain of God's beloved son (Colossians 1:13). However there has remained a great deal of that scripture which needs to be appropriated; for we have only known a measure of that reality.

We believe that "we are in the world but not of it". That is the word. But there is a transformation, a deliverance of Romans 8 and Romans 12 that must be experienced for this reality to be "realized". When it comes to a level of experience and knowing, this scripture has not seen yet its fulfillment within a people.

The first step in learning to see

As God continues to bring you through this process of renewal, the demand comes from the spirit to "let go" of that which you have known; that which you have "learned". This renewing of the mind does not happen overnight, nor does it happen without your diligent drive to let go of your past perceptions.

The first step in learning to see involves the unlearning of what your lifetime of experience has taught you to perceive. I would question everything you see, everything your emotions dictate to you, everything your senses want to tell you. Question everything, and let the Lord reveal to you what is real, *and what is not.*

You can speak the very same word to a dozen different people and you will find a dozen different interpretations of what was conveyed. Why? Because each person exists within their own framework of reality, molded by their experience, and therefore, you get a dozen different perceptions.

In some ways you could say that you have literally been brainwashed into believing by what you have received from your senses. There is a great deal of conditioning that must be set aside if you are to perceive the truth, and in perceiving the truth, to change.

How do you change? You change by seeing Him. That is the scripture. You behold the Lord and you are changed from glory to glory into His likeness… (2Cor3:18). It is a process and that process is determined by your capability of really seeing the Lord.

The last hurdle we face is the conditioning of the mind

The last hurdle that faces the Sons of God in this hour is the re-conditioning of the mind, or the completion of the renewing of the mind. We know that by faith we have the "mind of Christ", but this reality or truth is yet awaiting a fulfillment within His people.

More than anyone would want to acknowledge, even as we stand here this moment, we possess within our grasp resurrection life. We possess the fullness of Christ. Yet, what has separated us from these realities? We know that answer; for it has been the deep conditioning of our mind in this present sojourn that has been a massive weight around our ankles.

We are letting go of our inaccurate perception of what is truly real, and what is not; for every word that God has spoken is reality. It is the illusion of this passing age and dimension that would scream out at you and say, "Give heed to me, for I am reality".

Science has proven that what we view as reality *(this physical plane)*, is actually less dense than we realize. They have shown that we are actually composed of loosely knit molecules, vibrating at varying frequencies. This physical plane, though appearing more solid to us, actually consists of fewer molecules (less dense), than the higher planes of spirit. Since we have our existence on the physical plane, even though it vibrates at a lower frequency than the higher spiritual planes, it actually appears to be more "solid" to us. Those which exist on higher, spiritual dimensions actually have greater mass or substance, but because their vibration is so much higher; they appear invisible to us.

Scientific studies have shown how newborn babies can swim, up to the age of about 4 to 6 months. At that point they begin to unlearn what they innately knew, as they become exposed to this dimension. Often times very young children can see angels, and it is only through interaction with their peers or parents, who may discourage such things, that the child loses that innate capability.

As we enter life on this level of existence, we actually come fully enabled to live and interact on many levels. It is through the interaction with our culture and peers, as we have said, that causes a rapid disintegration of those innate capabilities.

The mind, conditioned since inception and birth, has been trained to perceive this realm as reality, and for that reason the last stronghold to be overcome in the manifestation of the Sons of God is the carnal mind. The change that is now taking place within the hearts and minds of the sons is a paradigm shift in their view of reality.

We must see a severing of our existence from a dimension that we have been reared in since birth. This deliverance is happening. The man-child is being birthed, and according to the prophecy in Isaiah, "there will be strength to deliver". God will not shut the womb as the first sons come forth.

We must cease to respond to this dimension by what our eyes see and our senses dictate. That which has had mastery over us is destined to end now. When Christ sat at the right hand of the Father and said it was done; it was done. Our deliverance, our change, our glorification – *it is done*.

We are only now beginning to walk out this truth; a reality which truly exists only in the realm of spirit.

Faith must give way to living in a state of "knowing".

It is one thing to have faith for something - to believe for it. You have faith because you do not yet see it. But there awaits a deeper baptism as this renewal of the mind comes to completion. It is a transition from "believing to see", to "knowing" the reality of what you have believed for. So much of what we are believing for has been done. It is here. But we are still "having faith" because we have not yet seen it. But there will be a transition from faith to "knowing" as we experience this change within our minds.

> **All these died in faith, without receiving the promises, but having seen them and having welcomed them from a distance, and having confessed that they were strangers and exiles on the earth. - Heb 11:13**

This deliverance, this transformation, will give birth to a level of knowing which transcends what we have known as faith. For faith exists when you do not see the reality of the provision. The men of faith in Hebrews 11 and 12 were great men of faith. They saw from a distance. But in this time frame faith will transition to knowing, because you will no longer need to have faith for that which you now see.

This is the juncture that we are at. We are at the onset of the greater works and the manifestation of Christ's authority over this passing scene. The mind of Christ will cease to be an unrealized potential.

You will not move with control or dominion unless you are able to accurately perceive all realms. You will not subject every kingdom unto the Lord until you are able to rightly discern and know (2Tim 2:15).

The deeper the experience of knowing, the more you will be equipped to manifest all that He has put within you. You will manifest all that you are.

Nothing is impossible to His sons when you finally come to the understanding that <u>nothing is impossible to you</u>.

We have been given everything, yet until now we have spiritually lived in a semi-state of poverty. We have not known who we are. But the times are changing. You can feel it in the spirit; we are in the transition into sonship, the transition of something entirely new that God is doing. You may still see trees as men walking, but the time of change is here. Your reality may still be tainted with the illusion, but the illusion is passing away.

The call continues to go out to His sons, "Let go of everything you have held onto and follow Me".

This is the time of renewal.

The Process of Sight

In this word we want to address an issue that has greatly affected the ability of God's sons to truly see, and in seeing; change. At the crux of our capability to change lies the problem we have in seeing - without filters; truly seeing.

It is easy to take for granted our ability to see since this is an inherent capability that we have had since birth. Because sight comes naturally to us, we have made the assumption that what we see must be real, and is indeed valid.

Let's talk about this "process" of sight. What does it mean to see?

The mind is an interesting facet of our being. To "see" involves more than just the physical "act of sight". Seeing involves the entire cognitive process of the mind which in affect does the "seeing" and then renders the interpretation. What you see with your eyes is just scratching the surface in this process of sight.

The soul is the switchboard to your mind, and it is through a myriad of inputs, impressions, emotions and responses, that shape and form the process we call seeing.

Imagine being blind from birth; then being given eyesight for the first time. The natural assumption would be to think that you would immediately recognize and understand what you could now see, however, that would not be the case. The truth would be that the mind would have to begin a process of learning to comprehend the images that you would now be receiving through the physical act of sight. Additionally, there would be an entirely new set of dynamics because the emotions would also affect your reasoning process that once again would shape your comprehension of what you are seeing.

As you learn to see, you also learn your limitations and your belief patterns; in essence your entire view of reality. Talk about tying the Lord's hands. The process of seeing through this conditioned lens of the mind and soul can be exasperating to the Lord when He has said, "I have given you everything". And yet, we have not seen - we have not comprehended what was in our midst.

Your unbelief, whether you can accept this or not, <u>is learned</u>. Your limitations are <u>learned</u>. And we have been on a long sojourn to see a complete letting go of all of this conditioning.

It has been closely studied and documented that as an infant begins to age that it begins to lose the innate capacity to see and interact with the realm of spirit. The child begins to assimilate the oppressions of the culture in which it is being raised. As the child continues to age, the child's view of reality is constantly modified and channeled through the child's exposure to parents, siblings, and the society that it interacts with.

That child is a microcosm of what the human race has become since the fall of man.

Since birth we have really been blind. It is only now, through the progressive regeneration of our mind, that we are beginning to learn to see.

We know that the mind and senses can be very deceiving. What you see with your eyes, as interpreted by your mind, as real as it may seem to be, most often is not the reality you have assumed.

When the Christian is "born again", there is much more that happens than a general awakening. His spirit has come alive. He has begun the process of un-learning and learning which will enable him to move into the deeper things of God. It will be through the agency of his spirit in conjunction with the renewing of his mind, that he will begin to see.

> Behold, I was shapen in iniquity; and in sin did my mother conceive me. – Psa 51:5

We read in Psalms 51:5 how we have been born in iniquity and raised in iniquity, yet there remains a deliverance that will come forth and manifest in God's people, delivering them literally from this age. I know we would like to think that we are not a part of this age, but we have not understood the far-reaching ramifications of what God's people have lived under.

To come into greater spiritual sight we will have to allow the Lord to re-program the channels or avenues through which our mind has functioned. The truth is that what we see in this passing, temporal realm, is really not reality.

Although we have taken strides in freeing ourselves from the spirit of this age; we are still bonded to a belief system which has been propagated by the spirits of this age since the beginning. Until we step more deeply into this regeneration of the mind, we are still walking as a part of this age. Our thinking and paradigm of reality that this age represents must be fully replaced within us.

We are learning to see. Our mind is being regenerated and we are letting go of our past conditionings. We are understanding that to "see" involves more than just the physical act of sight. We are in a transition from seeing with our "eyes", to seeing through our "spirit". This is a hard one to explain, for this must be an experience. Our sight or perception of reality, cannot be dictated by our senses, our mind, or our soul. (These are one and the same essentially). Our sight must be dictated by our spirit, and this cannot be done without a transformation within us as we transition to a life in the spirit.

Have you ever experienced the joy of reading the scriptures when you find a nugget of truth that just comes alive for you? Then, months later, or years later, read the same scripture and see a truth you never saw before? That is but a small example to point out how we are in an ever-unfolding process of change. The truth or reality you perceived at one point, will yield to a deeper insight as time goes on. The more you experience a deeper renewing of your mind, the greater ability you will have to see and understand, and the more your mind will move out of the limitations and channels it has known.

> **And do not be conformed to this world, but be transformed by the renewing of your mind, so that you may prove what the will of God is, that which is good and acceptable and perfect. – Romans 12:2**

God is giving His people a new set of eyes and ears. Our greatest enemy has been our mind; which is always at enmity to God. How does the word go...

Because the carnal mind *is* enmity against God: for it is not subject to the law of God, neither indeed can be. – Rom 8:7

What our new set of eyes may see, or our new set of ears may hear, will be new to our mind. This is new ground, and the mind will want to be quick to judge. Be careful, for the mind is going through a process that will enable it, for the first time, to grasp what is truly a new thing that God is doing.

Much of what we seek is right here, in front of us. We see it, but we are not seeing it. We have not been able to recognize it. However, as the Lord brings the deeper deliverances of sonship, you will begin to discover an entire world of Spirit just awaiting you. Anxiously awaiting.

Everyone is focused on the coming "Armaggedon", but they are looking on the wrong level. The truth of what is happening is on a different dimension, but this takes eyes to see. We have tended to look for a manifestation of what we anticipate, and not really see what is happening. You can become discouraged fairly easily if you continue to look for a fulfillment of your concepts; for you will miss the unfolding of what God is really doing.

As this deep renewal of the mind continues to unfold, you will experience a level of sight that is entirely new. You will begin to see and hear with your spirit. This is a significant change, for you will cease to function from the soul; or the reasoning of your mind. This shift happens when you begin to function from your spirit; for you will see with the eyes of your spirit.

As we begin to see with the eyes of our spirit, what is seen will be translated down to every level of our being. It will be born of our spirit, and as our spiritual eyes open, what our physical senses perceive will have the correct spiritual interpretation.

This cannot happen without a deep renewing of the mind. This will become a living experience. It will become your reality, for sonship is not a theory; sonship is an experience.

Communication as we know it will transition as we walk more and more in the spirit. We will hear, and we will know, more as an assimilation of energy as it flows between us. We will probably hear, audibly, but those sounds will be on a level of vibration beyond this level of the senses.

It is a whole new world of seeing and hearing that we are entering into.

God's sons have been on a path of becoming and a path of changing as they have continued to "shed the weights and the sins which have so easily beset them" (Heb 12:1). Whether it has been the bonds and relationships that have fed on the wrong level, or the baggage of misperceptions and concepts of a lesser day, God's sons are pursuing after the deep changes necessary at this time. Perhaps what they have not understood is how deeply their views of reality have been hindered and colored by the controlling spirits of this present age.

The Veil
And One Step Beyond

> For our struggle is not against flesh and blood, but against the rulers, against the powers, against the world forces of this darkness, against the spiritual *forces* of wickedness in the heavenly places. –*Eph 6:12*

We have been talking about the renewing of the mind, a shift of paradigms, and a re-defining of what we believe. Another arena that has had a tremendous impact upon the ability of God's sons to see and to step out of the limitations of this age has been to understand that we have been living under a veil, or canopy.

We are not talking about the veil of our flesh, or what we perceive as the veil of separation that exists between us and God's kingdom. We are speaking of a veil - or more accurately - a canopy, that has existed over the face of the globe; regardless of religion, race, or culture - it doesn't matter. We are talking about a canopy that has been upon this age as wielded by the powers of the Satanic hosts.

The underlying spirit behind the operation of the satanic hosts in this hour is a religious spirit. This is the spirit of Lucifer or Satan, a religious spirit that seeks to be as God - to emulate God - to manifest a facsimile of holiness. This very spirit has functioned as a canopy that has spread over the human race since the fall of Adam.

We have seen the religious spirit in operation throughout the scriptures and through so much of Christianity today. The religious spirit has many tentacles. If you look closely you will see these tentacles in every aspect of life. The religious spirit is self-serving and judgmental. The religious spirit is the perfect channel for the un-regenerated soul nature. The religious spirit seeks to stand before God, righteous in its own acts, righteous in its own heart, proud and arrogant.

This religious spirit, which has rested as a blanket over mankind, is not relegated to just "religions"; this canopy has known no boundaries. This spirit has created a conditioning that operates through the soul of man; and it is in no way limited to churches or organizations.

This spirit is interwoven, like a tightly woven fabric, within the minds and hearts of all the people who live on the earth today. It is a veil or canopy that enshrouds what we know of reality on this dimension - creating a paradigm shared by all.

How in the world did we ever get here? And how do we get back to the place of freedom that is referred to in Romans...."the freedom of the glory of the sons of God?" Let's continue...

> **know that we are of God, and that the whole world lies in *the power of* the evil one. – 1st John 5:19**

What power is this?

Look around you. There does not seem to be any way to equate the difference between the oppressed from the richly endowed. How does the entire world exist under the power of the evil one, when you see such a dichotomy exist? Understand, this control and leverage is not limited to governments, monies, or any other tangible thing. The control that is wielded exists on another plane entirely. We are speaking about that which has controlled and conditioned the way people think - regardless of race, color, religion, or country. All have existed under this control. All have existed under this canopy.

This veil over mankind has been created, fostered and nurtured for thousands of years by this satanic, religious spirit. There is not one who has escaped its manipulations. There is not one who is free from the entrenchment of the god of this age. That is why we are admonished not to be a part of this age, and to step out of the restrictions and limitations of this age.

People may believe they are free. Perhaps they are fortunate enough to live in a country that may afford them some level of liberty. But they are in no way free from this canopy that has existed over the earth which has created a conditioning or view of reality that no one has escaped.

The problem the sons of God face in becoming concerns their ability to see and rightly discern. As long as we are bonded or hemmed into a modality of thought or a paradigm of reality that is colored by the religious spirit, we will never see the truth, and we will never change.

To see truth one must step out of that which has hindered the ability for truth to be seen.

We must walk free from this age. To do so we must walk free from the conditioning of our mind that has been created while living under the canopy of this religious spirit.

The influence and conditioning of this spirit has, up to this point, successfully hindered and hamstrung the people of God from walking into the deep things of the Lord. We see it time and again as we speak to different ones. It has been difficult for many to shed the deep conditioning of the religious spirit.

As long as our view of reality is seen through the lens of the conditioning of this religious spirit; we will never come to the place of knowing. Nor will we come to the place of seeing. Always seeing, but not quite understanding; men appearing as trees walking (Mark 8:24). Because of the inability to rightly discern the word of truth, change will always be illusive, and unattainable.

Until man is delivered out of the soul realm; until we fully see the regeneration of the mind, as spoken of in Romans 8, there will exist some level of this oppression and limitation upon the believer. It is born by the conditioning of the religious spirit; for this religious spirit operates through the soul.

Let's talk briefly about the flood of deception that is flowing out of the mouth of the dragon during this season of time.

> **And the serpent poured water like a river out of his mouth after the woman, so that he might cause her to be swept away with the flood. - Rev 12:15**

We understand that God is bringing His sons into the plane of spirit. You are leaving a walk in the soul, and you are coming up higher into a walk in the spirit. As you transition from a walk born of your soul to a walk in the spirit, you will become less and less prone to the rampant deception that has filled (and is filling) the earth.

> **for false Christs and false prophets will arise, and will show signs and wonders, in order to lead astray, if possible – Mar 13:22**

How is deception fostered and propagated? We are told in the scriptures that we have come to a time of deep darkness (2Tim3:13), a time where even the elect could be deceived.

How does deception work?

> ***This* I say then, Walk in the Spirit, and ye shall not fulfil the lust of the flesh. – Gal 5:16**

Deception operates through the realm of the soul. If you walk in the spirit, you will not be deceived. Deception is created in the sensory realm of the soul by manipulation, and this is a jeopardy that God's people face.

With a violence of faith there is a demand rising from the sons to see the end of the reign of the soul flesh nature. It is time for judgment on the gods of this age and a subsequent releasing of God's sons. It is time for us to have a new set of eyes and a new set of ears; a total re-programming of our mind. It is time to see differently.

We are stepping outside of this canopy that has existed over the human race since the fall of Adam. The world may exist in darkness, but the sons of God will not.

For many this day is a day of great darkness, for they are living beneath this canopy of illusion. But for the sons of God it is a time of great light.

When You Make The Inner As the Outer

I am reminded of an appearing some years ago which follows the train of thought in the Book of Thomas. The vision concerned a merging together of what we are, the "inner" with the "outer".

> **"when you make the inner as the outer and the outer as the inner, then you will have come into the kingdom - Logos 22**
>
> **"If two make peace with each other in this one house, they shall say to the mountain, Be Moved, and it shall be moved. - Logos 48**

What these passages address concerns a level of agreement or oneness within yourself. We are speaking of coming to a level in God where you cease to live with the conflicting signals of the soul; a point where you no longer walk with the duplicity of the soul.

> **But let him ask in faith, nothing wavering. For he that wavereth is like a wave of the sea driven with the wind and tossed. For let not that man think that he shall receive any thing of the Lord. A double minded man *is* unstable in all his ways. – James 1:6-8**

We are talking about a level where you cease to walk with the conflicting signals of faith and unbelief - within you.

There are two aspects of the mind that co-exist simultaneously; the conscious and the sub-conscious. It is said that man uses upwards of maybe 5% to 8% of his mind. Where is the other 92%? Buried deep within the sub-conscious.

When Adam sinned and was cast out of the Garden, a veil came down and separated him from his relationship to the Father. His ability to live in the spiritual world came to an abrupt change. Leaving the garden and the advent of a veil-of-separation had far greater consequence than most realize. It was at this point that the sub-conscious mind was really created. Before this time, Adam was able to use his mind with his spirit. Every faculty that was given to him by God was at his disposal. Every faculty.

It must have been incredible. With the manifestation of sin, man's separation from God was more involved than merely a walk in the Garden. Ever since then man has been subject to the power of his subconscious, never understanding fully who or what was pulling his chain.

It is time to understand that since birth you have been subliminally conditioned. Your subconscious has been conditioned to the realities (or illusions would be better stated) of this world. Your belief system has incorporated all of the limitations of this age, and the sterility of deadness that exists in the earth today.

It has been proven that if you do a certain thing for 21 consecutive days, this repetitive act will ingrain tracks within your subconscious that will create what we call "habits". This can also be called "patterns"; something we do without thinking, because it has become an act of the subconscious mind.

Stop and think for a moment; how many things do you do habitually which are part of your normal, day in and day routine. You would be surprised just how much of your actual functioning is a product of subconscious conditioning. When you take that force into account, you will see just how challenging it can become to be freely led by the spirit.

We can either continue to be creatures of habit; people that are governed by the subliminal suggestions of the media and every other force pervading this world system today, or we can stop this train dead in its tracks. How did Paul reference this...

> **wherein the good that I wish to do I do not do, but I practice the very thing I would not do. – Ro. 7:19**

To break the tape, to finish the course we have been given, there must be a reconditioning of your subconscious mind. You must come to the place where you function in a oneness within yourself; spirit, soul and body - conscious and subconscious. You have the power to create whatever you ask or think. What we are concerned with is the duality that has still existed, a duality or "double-mindedness", that has hindered the changes within you every step of the way. There must no longer be the dark recesses of unbelief and negative conditioning within the subconscious.

This involves, without question, the renewing of the mind as Paul speaks of in Romans 8. We have been looking at one more aspect of what was created because of the fall. Now we realize, perhaps even more clearly, the magnitude of what God has promised to restore to His sons as He delivers them; spirit, soul and body.

The limitations you have known have primarily existed only within your mind. We are talking about your perception; your personal paradigm, and how you have seen reality. You have been given everything pertaining to life and godliness (2Pe1:3), yet we have walked as paupers. The jail cell that we have accepted has never existed - except within the mind.

God is bringing a level in which we are beginning to see the merging of both the conscious and the subconscious. We will not walk as Paul, who found himself doing those things he would not (Rom. 7:15). Not at this time. The provision is for a total release, and that means both the conscious and subconscious aspects of the mind.

God's plan is for a complete renewing, a complete deliverance; spirit, soul and body. How does the word go.... "saved to the uttermost".

Do you believe in gravity? Yes?

Because you experience the reality of it everyday of your life, you know it exists. It will be the same thing with sonship and with what God has spoken over this age. We will transition from what we have known of "faith", into what I would call a state of "knowing". You could call it a level of consciousness. You cease laboring to believe, and you enter into the <u>rest</u> of the Lord that "knows". This will come more and more out of your levels of experience.

There is a rest in the Lord which is spoken of in Hebrews. It is time we enter that rest, it is time we stop walking in a state of duality, for we are in the time of the restoration of <u>all things</u>.

One of the first items on the docket is the restoration of all the innate capacities within us, lost since the time of the fall.

It is with great joy that we welcome this new day, a day of light, which has come to expose the dark and hidden recesses of illusion.

The End of Illusion

In some Eastern religions or philosophies they refer to this present existence as "maya", or illusion. They believe that this temporal realm as viewed through our eyes is but a passing illusion. That the "real" world exists in the spirit. It is interesting, because this is true. This passing age is an illusion. Why is that? Because the god of this age has at his fingertips the ability to manipulate what you see around you. That is actually an understatement; for everything around you is in a constant state of flux.

For the sons of God, however, there is only one reality; His word. That is and will always be - our plumbline.

In this section we have continued to probe deeply into what is behind the scenes as God brings forth a renewing of the mind. Our responses to this passing "illusion" must give way. We cannot continue to react to the appearance of things, to the emotions and stimuli that continue to be generated toward us. We must come up higher, because in the realm of soul is illusion and deception. We just need to fly up above the clouds where the sun is shining.

The word speaks of this present age which exists under the power of the evil one as enveloping the earth, like a canopy (1st Ja 5:19). It is a veil woven by the spirits of this age creating illusion after illusion. This illusion has had deep inroads into the conditioning of God's people, for the illusion that is created is designed to make you feel as though what you are searching for is still a great distance away.

This same illusion is that which has separated God's people from the fulfillment of His word; fostering within the hearts and minds of His people the "feeling" that fulfillment is not yet in their grasp. "Always reaching, but never destined to attain."

> **Hope deferred makes the heart sick, But desire fulfilled is a tree of life. – Prov 13:12**

The operation of the spirit of illusion has woven the appearances of delay and separation; creating in many almost a heart-sickness for the lack of fulfillment and release.

Unless you are walking in the spirit it will be very difficult to rightly discern the truth; for nothing is as it appears outwardly. That alone can be a difficult transition because we are so prone to believe in what our eyes tell us, and what our senses perceive. Yet so much of it is illusion. We know that if you walk according to the soul, that you will be susceptible to the illusion of this passing age. We have said this before.

So often our battles are against "paper dragons", that which has no substance, no reality; fabricated by the spirit of illusion. An illusion created within your mind - just waiting for you to give it credence.

It is absolutely necessary that we wait before Him. As each day unfolds situations may come crashing down; but we must realize that what we see and what is focused towards us is being created by a spirit world that seeks to destroy the man-child - *You*. Rather than dealing with the problem on this apparent level of reality, we need to take it up a notch or two and deal with it from our leverage in the spirit.

We will not react, nor will we respond, to the illusion that is being constantly generated. It is created to move you off of your positioning in the Lord. I know there are times when this "illusion" can be rather overwhelming; especially if you don't have any food on the table or money in your pocket. Yet it is still an illusion. The real answer will not be found on the level of the senses; the real answer is in the spirit. The answer will be found as you move into the authority of the Kings and Priests of God, and the mantle of Christ's authority through you that begins to stop this train dead in its tracks.

How often words have come to us to stop fighting the battle from this physical level, for it is in the realm of spirit that we exercise the real control. If finances have been a battle, then we need to discern what is working in the spirit, rather than believing the answer can be resolved on this physical level. That is just one example.

It is like sickness. Science has researched and come to the

conclusion that over 90% of sickness is in the mind. You are what you believe. How often in the word we saw Christ rebuke an infirmity, and the spirit immediately left. We are dealing with a spirit world; a spirit world that seeks to work in darkness – a spirit world that seeks to keep you unaware of their existence - a spirit world that wants to keep you beating your head against the wall trying to get answers and solutions on this physical level. All along they have been pulling the strings.

What is the answer?

We must get out of seeing with our eyes.

Since birth we have drawn the conclusion that what we see is "real"; but I believe we are beginning to recognize that this is not the truth.

Let's talk about "quantum physics" for a moment.

The theory of "quantum physics" stipulates that reality is in an ever changing state of flux, depending upon your personal viewpoint. In essence, how you view the reality around you molds and shapes that reality which then becomes your truth. In other-words, you determine your own reality and in your perception you literally create a physical manifestation of it. Whether something was true or not at the onset, your personal perception creates it to be so.

As we change our view of reality - our view of what we are seeing - quantum physics has theorized that our reality shifts to mold to our internal view.

Interesting.

We have been talking all along about the power we have to create and that we are co-creators with God. This is part of our destiny. Whether the theory of quantum physics is correct or not; we know that as His sons we have the power to create.

We are in a time of deliverance right now. This deliverance has to do with our thinking - how we see and how we perceive. It is time to stop counter-creating and crossing out what God is doing in the earth by virtue of how we have seen everything around us. We have given substance and credence to what has been a lie, an illusion, and in so doing we have countered the very thing God is creating.

Many years ago a number of things came through in the spirit as we began to gain momentum in moving down this path of sonship. One statement was that we should "question everything that we see". Another was to understand the power the mind has - our mind has - to create illusion based upon our own reaction to the stimuli that we encounter.

The more we respond to the illusion, the more we create it - <u>and we are not even addressing what is being created on a global scale right now.</u>

On a global level there has been a lot spoken about "global consciousness". About what can be done if people are in a like minded state of belief. What we haven't seen is the incredible power that has been wielded by the governments and the media of this age. They can so easily create what they want the public to believe by the illusion they present. That illusion is then fostered and propagated through every medium available. In so doing they can create a global consciousness almost overnight - and thereby create a substantive reality. It may have been pure illusion at the onset, but by the time they are finished, this "global consciousness" has created a living reality.

This is what is happening every day - right now. There is so much mis-information that is being generated, and it is creating a common paradigm within people, <u>globally</u> - a consciousness that in itself begins to take on a life force.

The more the Lord begins to expose the deception and evil at the highest levels, the more you understand how much misinformation and illusion is constantly being propagated. The only truth in this hour about anything that is presently going on in the world, will be the truth which the Spirit reveals. I would not trust what I see, what I feel or what I sense. There is only 1 anchor, and that is what the Lord is revealing.

If the Lord has not spoken concerning an issue, then in my opinion, the jury is still out. We must refuse to look at anything based on the appearance of things, whether it concerns what is unfolding in the earth right now, or even how you may see yourself.

We have still seen "men as trees walking", but it is time for a deeper baptism that releases His sons into the reality of the mind of Christ. We have lived under both the lie and the truth and this co-existence is coming to an end.

Concepts that people have held onto have hindered their ability to change, because these concepts acts as a filter through which you see. You cannot hear if your mind is so clogged with concepts. We must let go and hold onto one thing - the Lordship of Jesus Christ.

The ability to see during this time will determine the capacity for people to move more deeply into this time of the wise virgins.

How do the scriptures speak about illusion; "they will call evil – good, and good – evil" (Isa 5:20). You could say that it is also the operation of the spirit of deception, for they tend to go hand in hand. You must be able to walk on a plane of spirit where you are able to discern and know the truth, and see the lie for what it is. Once you see something for what it truly is, and not what you have been led to believe, then the power it had over you is gone.

When the spirit of illusion is removed, we will be left with an ability to know and experience the truth on a level that we have not known. A greater clarity and vision will begin to unfold for each of God's sons, as they will be able to rightly discern and know the truth.

With the end of illusion I believe we will see a breaking of the back of the spirit of delay. The spirit of delay, as referenced in the book of Revelation, is kept alive and well by the acceptance of illusion. But with the end of illusion will come the end of delay.

> **Then the angel whom I saw standing on the sea and on the land lifted up his right hand to heaven, and swore by Him who lives forever and ever, WHO CREATED HEAVEN AND THE THINGS IN IT, AND THE EARTH AND THE THINGS IN IT, AND THE SEA AND THE THINGS IN IT, that there will be delay no longer.. Rev. 10:5-6**

With the removal of the operation of the spirit of illusion within the hearts and minds of God's people will come fulfillment on a level we have never known or experienced before. Eye has not seen, nor has ear heard... (1Co 2:9).

I believe that resurrection life is attainable, right now - yet it has continued to remain an unfulfilled potential.

We are not talking about a trickle of release. We are talking about a torrent of fulfillment, for what we will see will be the creation of a domino effect of fulfillment upon fulfillment.

Section 11

The Warfare

Of

The Saints

- **The War Is Over His Word**

- **You Are The Fuse**

- **The Warrior Priest/Kings**

The War Is Over His Word

From the beginning, God's people have lived by the word that God gave them. No matter how often the barrage from the spirit world would come saying, "Hath God said", the response has been to stand fast to the word that was revealed deep within their heart.

The conflict the sons of God have lived with daily is not so related to their circumstances or even the assault of demon power in their life as it has been to the internal conflict over the word which God has spoken over them. It's a war over the word, and to be specific, it's a war over the word implanted within you. Will you hold fast to that word, or will you relinquish it in a moment of testing?

Our battle is truly a fight of faith; a faith that believes, appropriates and manifests the word ... *unto us, upon whom the ends of the ages have come.* (1 Cor 10:11)

In many ways we have been in a race; not a race between the manifestation of the sons of darkness and the sons of Light, although that could be one perception. Rather, it has been a race to become.

> **"Unless those days had been cut short, no life would have been saved, but for the sake of the elect those days will be cut short." Matthew 24:22**

There is a dual timetable involved. We know the intent of the satanic hosts; "if the days are not cut short – no flesh would be saved alive". There is another timetable, however, which concerns the completion of the work within God's sons - truly a "mystery". That timing concerns the "date set by the Father" for His sons to enter into their final changes.

> **Now I say, as long as the heir is a child, he does not differ at all from a slave although he is owner of**

everything, but he is under guardians and managers until the date set by the father. – Gal 4:1-2

When Christ walked the earth the demons shuddered and said, "Have you come to torment us before the time"? They knew there would be a time - a culmination in the affairs of men - of their judgment. The time had not yet come when Christ first appeared. That "time" was reserved for now; as Christ appears fully within the sons of God.

Now is the time, and God is cutting these days short.

When Christ stood up in the synagogue He quoted the scripture in the book of Isaiah;

The Spirit of the Lord GOD is upon me, Because the LORD has anointed me To bring good news to the afflicted; He has sent me to bind up the brokenhearted, To proclaim liberty to captives And freedom to prisoners; To proclaim the favorable year of the LORD – Isa 61:1-2a (Luke 4:19)

Christ did not complete the 2nd half of the prophecy in Isaiah because the time of judgment had not yet come. The fulfillment of this prophecy has awaited this day in which Christ's ministry would be fulfilled through His people.

"And the day of vengeance of our God" – Isa 61:2b

This prophecy has awaited the time when the sons of God would walk out the 2nd half of the ministry of Christ in the earth; and it is to this time that you have come.

We have read in the scripture that "the prince of this world has been judged" (John 16:11), yet this has remained an un-applied truth until the time of the completion of the maturing of God's people.

Praise the LORD! Sing to the LORD a new song, *And* His praise in the congregation of the godly ones.

> Let Israel be glad in his Maker; Let the sons of Zion rejoice in their King.
> Let them praise His name with dancing; Let them sing praises to Him with timbrel and lyre.
>
> For the LORD takes pleasure in His people; He will beautify the afflicted ones with salvation.
>
> Let the godly ones exult in glory; Let them sing for joy on their beds.
>
> *Let* the high praises of God *be* in their mouth, And a two-edged sword in their hand,
>
> To execute vengeance on the nations And punishment on the peoples,
>
> To bind their kings with chains And their nobles with fetters of iron,
>
> To execute on them the judgment written; This is an honor for all His godly ones. Praise the LORD!
> – Psalms 149

The Psalmist in the 149th Psalm speaks of the honor that is given to His godly ones to execute the judgments which have been written from before the foundations of the earth. This is one aspect of the ministry of the sons of God; those destined to carry the mantle of Christ's authority in the wrap-up of this age. What an incredible time to be living; for we are living at the conclusion of one age and the beginning of the age of His kingdom.

The culmination of God's agenda during this time is directly related to the maturing and subsequent manifestation of the sons of God.

<u>There will be no kingdom unless there are the sons who rule and reign within that kingdom.</u> There is no manifestation of the sons without the manifestation of Christ, the Son. This is the Lord's agenda; it is not ours. We may be the vessels of honor He has chosen, but He is the rod of iron through us.

God has never been about programs; He is about transforming a people that will move and function from the realm of the spirit - the realm of His presence. All of this helps us to understand, perhaps more clearly, the war over the word that we face day in and day out. We are groaning and travailing within our spirits to bring forth the word; to make it flesh - once again.

Those who are marked for this hour will enter into their inheritance to rule and reign with Christ as they overcome the assault of the enemy from without; and their own fears and weaknesses from within. We have come to the time that we will see the completion of the purifying work of the spirit in the life of each of His sons.

When do the sons of God enter into this period of what we would call the "ruling and reigning of Christ" - the last 3 ½ year period of the ministry of Christ? I believe we are in these days now; but we have yet to grasp or fully understand just where He has positioned us. We are still playing a little catch up right now.

How often the Cloud of Witnesses and other "brethren" have come inquiring as to our progress. They know that at this juncture in time that the ministry of Christ - on the level of spirit - has already begun. How often they have come asking for help in the conflict, yet we have not fully grasped what we have become or where God has positioned us. We have not understood what we are capable of doing. The ministry of Christ over the realm of spirit has begun. It has really begun.

The warfare we experience is being experienced as well by our brethren in the realm of spirit. It is a strange duality of existence that we are beginning to live; for we are entering into an aspect of the Godhead that is beginning to leave behind the limitations we have known that are part of the natural plane.

So much of the warfare against the saints pivots around the darkness and deception that pervades the earth. The existence of bonds and attachments have continued to ensnare His people, and this has been the greatest conduit for this darkness and deception to be disseminated.

The leverage for judgment, the leverage to complete His will, is tied very closely to your ability to see. We must stop fighting the paper dragons and the illusions; we must move into the deep anointing of the seer in this day.

This has been challenging at times because what our eyes see and what we believe are often 2 different things. As it is referenced in the Book of Thomas....what we seek is here, but it has been hidden from the eyes of men.

To quote the book of Joel...

> Blow a trumpet in Zion, and sound an alarm on My holy mountain! Let all the inhabitants of the land tremble, for the day of the Lord is coming; surely it is near. A day of darkness and gloom, a day of clouds and thick darkness. As the dawn is spread over the mountains, so there is a great and mighty people; There has never been anything like it, nor will there be again after it to the years of many generations.
>
> A fire consumes before them, and behind them a flame burns. The land is like the garden of Eden before them, but a desolate wilderness behind them, and nothing at all escapes them. – Joel 2:1-3

You can go on and read thru verse 11 and see even more clearly what is presented concerning this time frame that we are now in. What do these scriptures speak of? They speak of you, the Christ company, moving with all dominion, power, and authority - as the Lord directs.

This is why the warfare against you has been so focused to keep you from believing who you are. Every word of God that is over your life can no longer remain a static potential; it must become your reality today. If you say, "I don't have any words over me". My response is; "Yes, you do". Every promise in the word of God is a word over you.

The Word is our <u>Book of Realities.</u>

We have mentioned this before, but it bears repeating. The Word of God can no longer be a Book of Promises to us - the Word must become our **"Book of Realities"**.

It is much easier to live the life of complacent Christianity; acknowledging the truth, but never contending until that word has its full manifestation within you. The word was never meant to tickle ears and make you feel good for another week, the word was meant to become rooted and have complete expression within you.

The word of God is not another nicely bound book with a lot of printed pages, it is a **Book of Realities**; the realities of how the Father sees His sons and what He has made available to them to become.

These realities have one end purpose; to be manifested <u>without measure</u> within the sons. It was spoken of Christ that the Spirit "was given without measure". Is that too much to believe for? – that God wants to endow upon you the fullness of Christ? What is the fullness of Christ? *The Spirit without measure.* Everything. All of it. Isn't this the word? Everything pertaining to life and godliness has been ..... *given to you* (2Pe1:3). That is the bottom line.

Who says we have to have a thimble full. Let's take it all. Let's believe for it all. Let's manifest the victory that has already been won. That victory is not getting through the day without conflict, the victory is that we manifest the word - made flesh - within us, as a perpetual state of living.

This is the "travail of the sons of God" in this hour. The word has come and has struck a deep chord within your heart. In turn this has brought you into the travail and birth-pangs of sonship. This is not some strange thing happening as Peter has spoken of (1Pe 4:12); this is the travail of the sons.

If this is what you are experiencing, then you are right on course. This groaning is too deep for words. The war over the word might be raging within you, but it doesn't matter. We know that if we do not abandon the word, then it will have its manifestation and release - with all power and authority - through you and in you. There is no other path. His word must have free course and must become flesh once again.

==To see Christ is to see the Father. To see you - on this level - is no different. The spirit realm has known who you were all along; but it is time that you are to know "as you have been known"== (1Co 13:12).

It is the time of the unveiling of the sons of God, and that unveiling first happens within you. You truly discover, perhaps for the first time, who you are and what you have become.

Hold fast to that word, no matter how deep the work within you may go. Hold fast. Let that word have its effectual working within you until you become all that the word is.

You Are The Fuse

We have been playing catch up during this last season of time because we have not been that aware of the conflict in the heavenly realm. This is beginning to change for the Lord is bringing His sons into a plane of judgment and the absolute implementation of His victory over the realm of darkness.

We are going to talk about what turns the power loose. What ignites the authority you have been given? How does it work?

To move into a functional relationship in the spirit - a term we have used many times - means that God is bringing you alive to the world of spirit. Every aspect of your being; spirit, soul and body, is beginning to come alive. As this process continues to unfold within you, you will find that you will be drawn more and more into the conflict of the ages on a level you never knew existed.

> **henceforth expecting till his enemies be made his footstool – Heb 10:13**
>
> **then *comes* the end, when He hands over the kingdom to the God and Father, when He has abolished all rule and all authority and power. For He must reign until He has put all His enemies under His feet. – 1 Co 15:24-25**

This can seem like a rather negative topic to talk about, "the conflict of the ages" - but it really isn't. What is the destiny of the Sons of God? - **to implement the authority of Christ over the gods of this present age**. Every dominion, every throne, every principality, and every kingdom must be brought down and made a footstool under His feet. We have been anointed to complete the ministry of Christ in this hour. We have been anointed to bring down everything which has withstood the Lord.

The more these changes continue to come within each of His sons, the more they find themselves beginning to track on a level that before now was unknown to them.

What does it mean to enter into the conflict of the ages? And how do you enter into it?

Some of you may not be that aware yet of the spiritual warfare that is taking place, but the more you come alive, the more you will enter into this conflict.

Your ability to be effective in the realm of the ministry of judgment is predicated upon your ability to see. We have spoken of this over and over within this book; but this is the plumbline.

In times past I would have thought that the greatest gift we could be given would be "faith", but I am more convinced that the greatest endowment at this time is the ability to see. It is the seer anointing we have spoken of so often. We are no longer in the days of the "church age", where the "gifts" of the spirit may have functioned. We are in the days of "spirit", and in this age of spirit you no longer function with "gifts", for you function out of what you have become. The gifts may be given or taken away; but the sons that become is a different thing altogether.

> **Everyone who competes in the games exercises self-control in all things. They then *do it* to receive a perishable wreath, but we an imperishable.**
>
> **Therefore I run in such a way, as not without aim; I box in such a way, as not beating the air; - 1Co 9:25-26**

More than ever this scripture must be our reality if we are to be effective in the realm of spirit. We can no longer "beat the air".

To effectively help the Cloud of Witnesses - to effectively bring judgment and deliverance in the realm of spirit - evolves around your ability to really see what is happening. It is the same principle as with moving in personal ministry. If you are able to see and discern the need then the power and authority you have will be targeted and effective. Without that element, it is like shooting with a shotgun. You must have the ability to be highly focused and targeted in that which you do. Your authority is ignited or "turned loose" through your ability to discern or see.

Let me address a very specific dynamic concerning this issue of entering into the conflict of the ages.

We have spoken at different times within this book about the ability to grasp a revelation from the Lord. We have spoken about having a catalyst that can ignite the word - *bring it to pass*. That catalyst is your ability to see.

What ignites the fuse? What turns loose the power of God? Your ability to see; to rightly discern. I don't know how to explain this any other way except to say that your spirit has a certain vibration to it when you grasp the truth; and that "vibration", that "God essence" is the trigger that turns everything loose. We are not talking about anything mental. This is not about how much you "know". This is not about scriptures you can recite. This is about getting a hold of a revelation at the core of your being; and when you really see it, then there is a vibration your spirit has that is literally the blasting cap.

When you have experienced the word, a "revelation", at the core of your being; then you have been transformed into the blasting cap that can turn that reality loose.

I hope I have conveyed this; because this is at the root of what we are going to talk about concerning the conflict that is unfolding right now.

Let's look at this from another vantage point. This goes back to an experience we had some 10 years ago.

We were praying for an individual, one that we were close to, even though he was on the other side of the veil. We had been having regular appearances from him and we were deeply concerned about being more effective in helping him.

We were in a field, and the fight was against a few evil entities and their physical channels (call them witches or whatever they were). As in so many visions, the realms were separated by a fence. The fence always has a gate; a gate of access. I knew we were dealing with both realms, an interaction of the physical and the spiritual realms, but I did not know what to do about it. As the conflict came to an end, it ended almost in a stalemate, because our effectiveness was just not that great.

Before coming back through the gate in the fence our friend made it very clear, that to truly be effective in helping him, (and others in the realm of spirit), that we must be able to see. If we can rightly discern the battle, then we will be empowered to make a difference.

What was being conveyed is the same principle we have been speaking of throughout this book; **if you can see, then you become the catalyst to make it happen.** How do we enter into the effective ministry of the judgment of Christ during this time? **We must see.**

This is why the word keeps coming on bonds and transference. <u>The minute you break through into deeper perception - everything changes. At that instance you enter into a much deeper participation in that which is unfolding in the realm of spirit, and equally, you have become much more effective as a channel of Christ's authority.</u>

We have spoken throughout this book that God is bringing a convergence of realms. The sons of God - whether on this side of the veil - or the other - are being brought into a participation together as we see the transition of ages come to the fullness of times.

We are in no way alone in this conflict, for we have many that are standing shoulder to shoulder with us in this battle. There are many vested interests in the outcome of this conflict and the subsequent manifestation of God's sons. There is much at stake, and all of creation, as Romans 8 says, is patiently waiting. We are seeing more and more participation from the Cloud of Witnesses in the spirit as we "link hands" in the ministry of Christ during this time.

We have spoken before that we are a triune being; spirit, soul and body. It is the "whole man" - all that we are - that is being drawn into this level of functioning. Every aspect of your being is becoming more and more alive; your spirit, your soul and your physical body. We are beginning to live with one foot in the heavens, and one foot in the earth planes. This is your reality. This is part of the functioning of the sons of God.

As you continue to come alive you will find that you are driven to possess what the Lord is pouring out in this hour. You are coming alive, and you are ceasing to evaluate what you see on a linear level - or what I would call the level of the mind - which tends to see things black and white.

Your life is becoming more and more spiritually attuned and you are beginning to understand that you are living in 2 realms simultaneously. You are spirit more than you are anything else in this present incarnation; our awareness is just catching up.

Do we have the victory? Absolutely. It is our destiny to walk out this victory and to administer His authority and complete the judgments written. It is our destiny in this last generation upon the earth to send the myriads of demonic spirits and satanic spiritual hierarchy into the abyss. We will walk in His victory and we will be His channels to complete these works. Furthermore, we will move into the glorification of our bodies, for this is the word.

Why have we seen so much teaching coming on bonds? Because we must become well versed in moving in the realm of spirit, and we must get free.

It has been the drive of God's sons to experience and manifest the word. To de-mystify the word in many ways. To take the scripture and manifest it. As Christ said, "today this word is fulfilled in your hearing". We are taking the scriptures and we are living them. They are not theory or concept. No book has been written that can explain what it means to live these words, for we are charting a new course. The word is no longer just print on a page, the word is finding a living expression and experience within His sons.

I know the Lord is opening the eyes of His sons right now. We are dropping our concepts and we are dropping our personal paradigms. Everything is being made new. And we must be very careful not to draw conclusions, create concepts, or base what we see through an understanding of God's past moving.

Now more than ever we realize what it will take to move into a level of deep effectiveness in this warfare in the heavens.

The Warrior Priest/Kings

> "I kept looking, and that horn was waging war with the saints and overpowering them until the Ancient of Days came, and judgment was passed in favor of the saints of the Highest One, and the time arrived when the saints took possession of the kingdom. Dan 7:21-22

You can read the entire book of Daniel 7 and get a very clear picture as to the conflict of the latter times and the resultant judgment and finality on the spirits of this age.

We have entered for some time now the warfare that earmarks this day in which we walk, yet, we have been slow to recognize this. Unfortunately, most people still think in terms of "future tense"; because that is the general conditioning within our society. Within Christian circles most of God's moving is either relegated to the past, or put into the future. It takes very little faith to believe in the past or the future. It takes a great deal to believe that now is the acceptable time of His appearing and His fulfillment. As we have said before; this is the front line.

This ingraining of what I call a "future tense" mentality has deep roots within the hearts and minds of people - always in the future, always believing, but never really attaining. It is the proverbial carrot syndrome. The truth is that now is the acceptable time; the time of the fulfillment of all things is here - now.

Maybe we should put a piece of tape on our foreheads labeled, **IT IS NOW,** because it is not that difficult to get lulled back into a future tense mentality. If we do not walk with a consciousness of "right now", then we are either living in the past or in the future.

We are in the conflict of the ages, and the authority of the Kingdom is resting upon you. The judgments of God are in the earth, and like the "domino effect", they are beginning to fall in sequence.

When you read Daniel 7 the scripture can be difficult to relate to for at some point judgment is passed and the saints possess the kingdom. What does that mean in English? At what point does this happen? Or has it happened and we have been asleep at the wheel? Is it yet to happen at some distant time in the future, probably not in our generation?

I don't believe so for every signpost we have seen along the way of this present journey has pointed to the reality that we are living this time right now. We are dropping our concepts or theories of what we have felt the experience of this scripture might be. We need to let it come forth, because we are in this time now.

What kingdom are we possessing? The kingdom within. Not an external kingdom - *it is the kingdom within*.

You may say "it doesn't feel like I thought it was going to feel". Perhaps everything just doesn't seem to line up with your concepts or personal revelation of what you thought it would really be like as these days of the kingdom unfold, but I will tell you this - this is the time.

Judgment has been decreed but it absolutely MUST be enacted by YOU. Judgment flows no other way. I don't believe the process of bringing down principalities and powers happens coincidentally; it happens because you specifically know what you are doing and you do it. The Lord directs His army; they hear Him - and they get the job done. Yes Sir, Lord!

What does it mean to possess the Kingdom. First of all, the mentality of future tense must be dropped. Secondly; we must realize that we are possessing the kingdom right now. Right now. It doesn't matter to me how "finished" you think you are, you are here, you have been prepared, and it is happening now.

Do not judge by what you feel, and do not judge by what would appear; for the god of this present age is able to control and manipulate this natural plane. We know that we war - and that we stand - by the word of God. As God decrees, that is how we see it.

When Christ came the disciples expected Him to set up His kingdom - right then, right there. Yet His response was that His kingdom was not of this world.

> **Jesus answered, "My kingdom is not of this world. If My kingdom were of this world, then My servants would be fighting so that I would not be handed over to the Jews; but as it is, My kingdom is not of this realm." – John 18:36**

There is so much happening right now but it is not happening on the level that you may have expected. How about Armaggedon? At this moment, Armaggedon is in full swing, but it is a spirit realm reality. Does this mean it will not translate down to this plane of the earth? No. Not at all.

None of us have been intense enough yet in our drive before the Lord to see His kingdom fully established. What does it say in Revelation....they loved not their lives unto death. Is that your truth? It must be. You must not love your life unto death.

We haven't known yet what it means to walk before the Lord on the level of intensity that He is demanding, but we are beginning to get glimpses. This intensity before Him is imperative, because the spirit world is not going to lay down and take this smelling daisies.

If you haven't lived this yet, then lay hold of your calling, because the army of the Lord is here. As Jesus said, "today in your hearing these words have been fulfilled".

We must drop our concepts of fulfillment. Yes, but you say.... "I had all these concepts about what it was really going to be like, and this is nothing like I imagined.

Well Dorothy, you are not in Kansas any longer. This is a wake up call.

Do not let the enemy keep you in a holding mode; and he is slicker than you think. You are prepared, you are ready, and it is now. The battle in the heavens is raging, for it is time that judgment will flow from the house of the Lord.

The sons of God are ordained not only to loose futility from all of creation, but to kick down the strongholds of evil and darkness that have withstood His kingdom.

> **and to bring to light what is the administration of the mystery which for ages has been hidden in God who created all things; so that the manifold wisdom of God might now be made known through the church to the rulers and the authorities in the heavenly** *places.* **– Eph 3:9-10**

What is this manifold wisdom? That God has sent His sons, in Christ, to kick down their strong holds and usher them into the pit. It's a done deal.

We have spoken about that imperceptible change that is going on within you; daily. You are changing and that change is exponential. We have spoken of this. And your change is going to continue to increase more quickly. We have also spoken of breaking your bonds with how you see yourself. You must do this - for we cannot tie the Lord's hands.

Change how you see yourself in the mirror, <u>or throw the mirror away</u>. The Lord has need of you, but you must do this.

You have entered into the battle of the ages; the end time conflict. This is really what Paul in Ephesians spoke of concerning "an administration suitable to the fullness of times". This battle is already won, but as we have said, you are ordained to give "legs" to it. You are implementing the victory and the judgment which has already been done. It has been finished - you are in the mop-up operation.

Step up and say "Lord, count me in". Bring on the high country, with all the Nephilim and men of renown. We'll take a prey, by the grace of God, we will take a prey and possess the kingdom for the Lord.

> **"Now then, give me this hill country about which the LORD spoke on that day, for you heard on that day that Anakim** *were* **there, with great fortified cities; perhaps the LORD will be with me, and I**

shall drive them out as the LORD has spoken." So Joshua blessed him, and gave Hebron to Caleb the son of Jephunneh for an inheritance. – Joshua 14:12-13

May we all possess the spirit of Caleb, for although he was advanced in years, he was ready to take on the high country. We too have been ordained to drive out the Anakim and the evil of this day from the land which belongs to the sons.

And this we will do in the name of the Lord.

Section 12

In Pursuit Of Resurrection Life

- **Put On the Imperishable**
- **Resurrection Life**

Put On
The Imperishable

> "....flesh and blood cannot inherit the kingdom of God; nor does the perishable inherit the imperishable" - 1st Cor. 15:50

The kingdom that we seek, a city made without hands, will not be possessed by that which is mortal, according to Paul in the book of Corinthians. Paul speaks further in the scriptures about the change that will take place which we have spoken of earlier.

Man, in his lowly estate, has been the vehicle God has chosen to confound the mighty. We have seen reference made to this new creation when Paul speaks of Christ in you, the hope of glory - the mystery of the ages. What is this mystery; is it the recognition of Christ within us? Or is it something greater, far greater. Did not Christ Himself speak that greater things than these shall ye do.

In 1st Corinthians 15 Paul is speaking about a change that must take place within the believer; a change from the basic flesh and blood physical structure that now comprises our physical bodies. A change that will bring us into the full manifestation of resurrection life – our "seal" of sonship. According to Paul, flesh and blood will not inherit the kingdom, but a new creation will.

> But someone will say, "How are the dead raised? And with what kind of body do they come?" You fool! That which you sow does not come to life unless it dies; and that which you sow, you do not sow the body which is to be, but a bare grain, perhaps of wheat or of something else. But God gives it a body just as He wished, and to each of the seeds a body of its own. - 1 Cor 15:35
>
> All flesh is not the same flesh, but there is one flesh of men, and another flesh of beasts, and another flesh of birds, and another of fish. There

> are also heavenly bodies and earthly bodies, but the glory of the heavenly is one, and the glory of the earthly is another.
>
> There is one glory of the sun, and another glory of the moon, and another glory of the stars; for star differs from star in glory. So also is the resurrection of the dead. It is sown a perishable body, it is raised an imperishable body; it is sown in dishonor, it is raised in glory; it is sown in weakness, it is raised in power; it is sown a natural body, it is raised a spiritual body. If there is a natural body, there is also a spiritual body. - 1 Cor 15:39-44

When a seed is planted, part of it dies as the next level of transformation takes place. When a chicken is hatched, the shell is no longer needed for it has become useless. It has served its purpose. Your present physical incarnation has been the "shell", the housing of your spirit and present consciousness. It is time that this shell is giving way to the birthing of something entirely different – a new creation with each of His sons.

In this transition of the spirit and soul; I believe we enter into another existence, body or form. We have a heavenly temple awaiting us. Paul speaks of the body of the flesh, and the body of the heavenly. He says there will be a metamorphosis; a change in the twinkling of an eye. We have spoken of this; a transformation that will be the creation of a new order.

According to 1 Corinthians, inherent within each of us is the expression or blueprint of what we shall be. As we enter into the resurrection of Jesus Christ our body will no longer respond to the soul, as it has in this present state, but our body will respond to our spirit. A whole new creation. There has been a body that has responded to the soul, but in this time of metamorphosis, the body you will have will respond to your spirit.

There is a great deal of conjecture going around as people try to identify or "explain" this process that we are in. I hear a lot of stories and some have merit. But I cannot say for certain exactly how this process will be completed, or exactly what this experience will be. We have not yet entered it. Some say there is a changing of the DNA structure. Others say our blood is changing into something different.

To me, it doesn't really matter. We can go back after the resurrection and say, "Yep, it was a DNA change. Or nope, "it had absolutely nothing to do with it". Same with the blood. Technically the scriptures say that "flesh and blood" will not inherit the kingdom, so it would seem the discussion about the change of the blood doesn't seem to hold a lot of water.

In any event, it is not really the issue. The issue is getting it. The issue is positioning ourselves where we can experience the breakthrough and walk into the deeper things God has for His people.

I could share visions we have had about these changes but it still doesn't matter. What matters is that we get free, and we see the cords and ties that have fed off of the life of Christ removed.

The kingdom of God is coming, yet it is already here. The kingdom has been here for centuries, yet men have not seen it. Even as it is written in the Gospel according to Thomas from the Dead Sea scrolls; Logos 108-113: "His disciples said to Him, 'When will the Kingdom come? Jesus said, "It will not come by expectation; they will not say: See, here, or See, there. But the Kingdom of the Father is spread upon the earth and men do not see it."'

Also in Logos 48-51; His disciples said to Him: "When will the repose of the dead come and when will the new world come?" He said to them: "What you expect has come, but you know it not."

Before you will see the possessing of the kingdom of God on every level or plane of existence, you will see the manifestation of the sons of God. The kingdom must first be fully established within His sons before you will see it fully established within this earth. And it will never be established until His sons change from the flesh and blood structure of their being and possess the incorruptible body of His resurrection.

Throughout this book we have been talking about the fact that we are breaking through to walk in 2 different worlds, simultaneously.

If we are still believing that a physical death is necessary, then we are still buying the illusion.

One of the first things the Lord did was to show that He had the power over the spirit of death. He only had to speak a word and Lazarus was resurrected. Why have we not contended for this breakthrough before now? Because we have still believed in the process of death. But Christ, the resurrection, has already abolished all death and all rule. This has been a dormant potential awaiting a faith and drive on the part of God's sons to reach in and take it; to throw off the lie and the illusion and realize that this is the acceptable time.

We are realizing more and more that the judgment upon the spirits of this age are more intrinsically tied to this release of resurrection life; for the whore - as John saw in the book of Revelation - has fed off the life force of the sons. This will end and with this will come the deeper breakthrough of resurrection life.

We have spoken throughout this book about the issue of bonds. The effectual working of judgment and the breaking of bonds are tied together. As we enter into this deep ministry of judgment we will find that God will break off of you those who have been ministering death to you. And as that which has taken away your life force is judged, you will see the release of the ministry of Christ through you unto the principalities and powers of this age.

We have spoken of the administration of the kingdom; and we have spoken of the ministry of judgment that has rested upon His sons as a mantle. There is no difference between breaking through to resurrection life and the ministry of judgment. They go hand in hand.

We have spent too much energy trying to get out of something that we thought was us instead of rejecting it. Too often we have been fighting an illusion and those vipers are going to fall off into the fire so that you can rise into what God has for you." –(Acts 28:3-9).

We have been going through a renewal of the mind (Ro. 8) for a long season. We should be anticipating many changes now, for this is the time. This renewal is something that has never been seen, yet it is the very thing that is enabling us to see, to hear, to perceive - and consequently - to change.

The breakthrough of resurrection life will unfold as we see this process of the renewing of the mind completed. Hand-in-hand the judgments issue forth upon that which has taken the life of the sons, while God simultaneously completes the work of the renewing of the mind within each of us.

Whether or not you can perceive the almost imperceptible molecular change that is beginning to happen within you is not the issue. But understand this - a shift is on - and God's intent is that there will be a people who will put on the incorruptible.

This will not lie dormant for another 100 years as another promise which has been rejected by man in his unbelief, for the spirit that raised Christ from the dead has begun to quicken your mortal body (Romans 8).

Resurrection Life

I believe we are at the threshold of the deeper appearings of the Lord at this time; appearings that will result in the final transformation of resurrection life and sonship.

As we went to press the title of this book became clear one early morning, around 3:00 am; what we call "channel" time. The only real change was the addition of a timeline, 2010 to 2012. Why the Lord gave that I can only surmise because we are in the season right now of change.

We have sensed this for many months now. For the last 18 to 24 months the visions have been coming about this time of complete change that we have come to.

Does this have anything to do with the Mayan prophecies, Nostradamus, or anything else? None. There is so much misinformation floating out there. People can probably find a prophecy to substantiate whatever their "belief system" might be; the hosts of wickedness have done a thorough job in propagating so much confusion and deception.

During the 40 days between Passover and Pentecost Christ appeared to many of His followers. These were appearings to those who had been prepared. During this time, once again, Christ is appearing to complete the work within the sons. He is appearing or manifesting Himself to those whom He has prepared for this time to walk as the Kings and Priests of God. This appearing of the Lord is part of the end-time events and it is what has begun to unfold now.

If you follow the word closely you notice that it says; "in like manner", or in the way that He left, is the way that He will return. The Lord did not leave in glory and the Lord's return in these days presently, what we would call the "secret coming"; will not be with the trumpet or with the voice of an archangel.

We know that in our pursuit of resurrection life that the last element of transformation will be completed by His individual appearing to His sons. But don't misunderstand; I am not putting sonship on the shelf or at arms distance, for we are pressing through the veil of limitations. What the Lord has begun will be completed.

We have touched on various points throughout this book dealing with the transformation of our bodies. I know that we would like to understand this further; to grasp the depth of what is happening within us. But this we know - we are changing. How did we address it earlier in this book....*metamorphosis; a* change from one order to another. It is happening even if we cannot quantify it at this point.

> **Just as we have borne the image of the earthy, we will also bear the image of the heavenly. Now I say this, brethren, that flesh and blood cannot inherit the kingdom of God; nor does the perishable inherit the imperishable. – 1Co 15:49-50**

> **For this perishable must put on the imperishable, and this mortal must put on immortality. – 1Co 15:53**

We have spoken of our DNA, that there is a change happening at the core of our being. We know that the scripture speaks that flesh and blood will not inherit the kingdom, and we sense changes on levels that we don't yet understand. We cannot put our finger on it, but we know that a change is slated to be completed within God's sons.

> **who will transform the body of our humble state into conformity with the body of His glory, by the exertion of the power that He has even to subject all things to Himself. - Php 3:21**

We know the power that the Father exerted towards Christ in transforming Him is being focused towards us (Phil 3:21). This is scripture. This is nothing new, except that for the first time in history we are in the season of its fulfillment.

We have seen the elementals approach His sons and say that they "knew who we were". That when we existed as spirit, that we were as gods over them.

We know that we have come to the company of the spirits of just men made perfect (Heb 11). We also know that many have been sent back into the earth at this time, including Daniel (Dan. 12,) to receive their allotted inheritance.

We walk in the company of a great host of witnesses; those that walk with us in the cloud, and those whom the Lord has chosen to send back during this time. If this sounds a bit strange, it is no different than when Christ spoke to the disciples about John the Baptist. You recall the words. Christ told them that John the Baptist was Elijah, if they could accept it.

We are talking about resurrection life, but we are also talking about the prophets, the faithful, whom God has sent back into the earth during this time to receive their inheritance. And what would that inheritance be?

Resurrection life; the completion of all that they are to be.

From the dawning of creation we were with the Lord. We were with Him when He created all things; we just haven't remembered – yet. But the Lord is bringing to mind all of those things which He has freely given us; all of those things which He has created within us. He is bringing to remembrance a relationship with Him that we have always had, since time began. We may have lost track along the way for a short season because of the veil, but even the veil is but an illusion.

Are you ready? It will cost you everything you have. You will have to let go of everything. Can we do that? Not without His grace, but His grace is with us, so we will finish the course, we will complete this race.

We are spiraling up into His presence. As the weights of the Adamic nature are being shed we will continue to soar upwards into all that He has prepared for us.

The first wave of the breakthrough of the sons of God will set the stage for subsequent releases. Once we see the first beachhead established, many of His sons will follow – wave after wave as the process is completed within each of them uniquely. And the promise for this hour can be found in Isaiah, for God "will not close the womb". There will be successive companies of sons that will break through, one after the other, into resurrection life and glorification.

According to Bible prophecy, once these changes begin, everything will move very quickly. This is the beachhead that has been committed to us to take. Others have run the race in their generation, but to us has fallen the responsibility to break the tape; to break this tape, *now*.

Section 13

The Quickening

Of The Mortal Body

- **Come Alive!**
- **The Integration Of Your Spirit, Soul & Body**
- **Tracking In The Realm of Spirit**

Come Alive!

Over the past several generations we have watched as the Holy Spirit has deepened the work of redemption in the believer; <u>spirit, soul and body.</u>

What began back on Azusa street at the turn of the century was the beginning of a deep redemptive work of the Spirit that would see a completion or fulfillment during this time. It was the beginning of a new baptism, as God's people began to come alive to God and to their own spirit.

Now may the God of peace Himself sanctify you entirely; and may your spirit and soul and body be preserved complete, without blame at the <u>coming</u> of our Lord Jesus Christ. - *1Th 5:23*

This is an interesting scripture because it points to a timeline in the heart of the Father, a timeline that will see the completion within the believer of the mystery which Paul in Colossians speaks of.

Of *this church* I was made a minister according to the stewardship from God bestowed on me for your benefit, that I might fully carry out the *preaching of* the word of God, *that is,* the mystery which has been hidden from the *past* ages and generations; but has now been manifested to His saints, to whom God willed to make known what is the riches of the glory of this mystery among the Gentiles, which is Christ in you, the hope of glory.
– Col 1:25-27

In looking at both of these scriptural references, we understand that there is a plan in the heart of God for His sons, a plan that involves a complete and total redemption - spirit, soul, and body.

When will we see this completion? …. *at the coming of the Lord.* And when is this "coming of the Lord"? As we have spoken – *we are in these days now.*

People generally understand that they have a physical body and a soul, but very few have understood that they have a spirit as well. A spirit that is as real, as unique, and as individually separate as every other facet of their being.

People have tended to combine spirit and soul together; some call it spirit - some call it soul. Some refer to it as their "higher self". But we understand that we are dealing with something much more than this.

We are a triune being - which means we have a spirit, soul, and body. We are just beginning to understand this and only now beginning to learn about our spirit. We are speaking of another level of awareness within yourself; for you are much more than just a physical and soul manifestation, you have a spirit begotten of God which is coming alive.

We have come to the days of spirit, and these are the days of the kingdom. We are coming into the knowledge of our spirit, and we are beginning to understand the difference between soul and spirit. We are learning what it means to track in the spirit, and we are learning how to see with our spirit, and how to hear with our spirit.

This is a whole new consciousness; a whole new way of life.

As we have said before, you cannot take this new day of spirit, and force it into the theology or concepts of the day of the soul. The dynamics are entirely different. The rules are different. The principles that govern the realm of spirit are different. And we are being required to learn and come to a functional relationship with our spirits - within the realm of spirit.

How do you explain this experience? I am not sure you can, for sonship is not a liturgy. Sonship is an experience.

It is becoming increasingly more important that we become aware of what is being made available to us during this time. When the doors are open, someone needs to go and shout; "the door is open!". The door is open to a whole new level of experience. Reach for it - <u>Expect it</u> - <u>Look for it.</u>

As you track in the spirit and God brings visions, dreams, appearings, and further enlightenment; to whom does this come? To you, of course. But to what facet of "you"? These experiences come to your spirit. Your spirit will filter these things down to your soul or physical consciousness, but it first starts in your spirit. We must realize that our spirit is not some esoteric theory. Our spirit is a living reality and very much a part of who and what we are.

We are coming alive to our spirit. It is like shaking hands; "Hello spirit, this is me". And Spirit says back; "Hello me, I am your spirit".

Visualize that for a minute. Introduce yourself to your spirit. Open up and make a connection. During times of deep meditation or prayer you are merging together all that you are. You are coming into a place of oneness; where the "outer" is becoming as the "inner", and the "inner as the outer". You are becoming integrated within yourself. That perhaps is one of the greatest benefits of waiting upon the Lord, or meditating upon Him. For you are only successful if you are able to integrate your whole being; spirit, soul and body, during those times.

One of the greatest transitions that will come to you as God establishes the seer/son/prophet anointing within you, is that the Lord will bring a merging of your spirit and soul. God bridges your soul and spirit, where the lapse of time between the Lord speaking to your spirit, and your consciousness receiving it, is virtually removed.

We must understand that our spirit is that aspect of us that functions within the realm of spirit. We have a soul which is a function of the mind and of all the emotional aspects that comprise our consciousness, and we have a physical body.

When God speaks that He will save you to the uttermost (Heb 7:25), He is talking about the redemption of all that you are; your spirit, soul and body, preserved blameless unto the coming of the Lord.

We have spoken of the timeline of His presence in the earth - the time of the manifestation of Christ within His people - but the questions are: How soon can we get it? and Where are we in this unfolding scenario?

For the last 100 years we have seen the progressive work of redemption within the believer taking place. The signs which have begun to follow this work of redemption have been an increase in the manifestations of visions and dreams (as Joel prophesied), the increase of the appearings of the Lord and what we would call a gradual quickening of the mortal body. We are not limited to just these manifestations, but the by-product of this quickening of the mortal body is a level of experience and abiding in God that we have not seen before now.

Where are we in this timeline and scenario? With the quickening of the mortal body and the level of awareness that is coming to God's people I would say that we are right at the door - knocking. More than knocking, I believe we might have placed our foot through the door. There is a drive and demand born of the Spirit of God within His people that is demanding the completion, now.

When I speak of "the quickening of the mortal body" this may sound a bit foreign. In fact so much of what we are experiencing in this day leaves us lacking for words to describe just what it is that is happening within us, and to us. What we are talking about is the absolute takeover of the Spirit of Christ within the sons – this is the true quickening of the mortal body.

As this interpenetration of all that Christ and the Father are comes forth within each of His sons, we are finding that our bodies are coming alive to a world of spirit that we had not previously been that aware of.

This quickening of the mortal body, in affect, is a vibrational shift that is happening within you. Your capacity to see, to hear, and to perceive into the unseen realm of the spirit, becomes more and more tenable and ever more a part of your present reality.

At what time in the scope of God's moving and God's involvement with man do these realities come forth? And, are there any signposts along the way that give us an indication as to the times and seasons of this completed work in Christ?

These "signposts" have been coming for the past 100 years, but they have been gradually accelerating more and more over the past 3 to

4 decades as we have entered into the times of the parousia, or "presence" of the Lord.

I realize I have tossed several scriptures at you already, but here are a few more. The Greek literal translation for "at his coming" is translated "parousia", or "presence", which indicates a time; a select time of the appearings of Christ. It is this parousia or presence of the Lord that we have seen unfolding progressively over the past 30 years.

> **But each in his own order: Christ the first fruits, after that those who are Christ's <u>at His coming.</u> - 1Co 15:23**
>
> **so that He may establish your hearts unblamable in holiness before our God and Father <u>at the coming</u> of our Lord Jesus with all His saints. - 1Th 3:13**
>
> **For who is our hope or joy or crown of exultation? Is it not even you, in the presence of our Lord Jesus <u>at His coming</u> – 2Thess 2:19**
>
> **And now, little children, abide in Him, so that when He appears, we may have confidence and not shrink away from Him in shame <u>at His coming</u>. - 1Jn 2:28**

The unfolding of the Parousia or the Presence of the Lord in the earth, and I do not mean the physical earth - but in the "earth" of you and I – are bringing many telltale signs indicating that we have come further into the days of the Kingdom and into this time of change than we have realized.

We have spoken of the unique signs and manifestations coming within our bodies as we continue to experience this vibrational shift. These manifestations are just another signpost to the quickening of the body, which is coming alive and becoming more sensitive to the unseen world than ever before.

> **And if Christ is in you, though the body is dead because of sin, yet the spirit is alive because of righteousness. But if the Spirit of Him who raised Jesus from the dead dwells in you, He who raised**

Christ Jesus from the dead will also <u>give life to your mortal bodies</u> through His Spirit who indwells you. – Romans 8:10-11

There is a strong tendency to put fulfillment into the future, because this is the general mindset of the religious community. They always have concepts which keep the reality of fulfillment at arm's distance, but what we must understand is that this is happening now.

Romans 8 is in the process. Stop and take a close look inward; changes are happening.

We have not been sent into the earth to see these promises from afar, as if living in a distant land. We live here, now, in this present incarnation, for a purpose. This word, this revelation, this reality, is coming alive within God's sons for a very good reason. God has set aside His sons during this time to step through the veil of what I would call, "mortality". We are stepping into the realities of sonship, immortality and life; beyond what anyone has been able to imagine. "Eye hath not seen, nor hath ear heard of those things which God hath prepared for His sons" (1Co2:9).

There is a direct correlation to the appearing of the Lord within you and the change that you are experiencing These are the days of His appearing within each of you, and it is this appearing that is bringing about the quickening of your body. It is this appearing that is "catching up" the sons of God onto a level of dwelling far above all rule and dominion. How does Christ put it....

"In My Father's house are many dwelling places; if it were not so, I would have told you; for I go to prepare a place for you. "And if I go and prepare a place for you, <u>I will come again</u>, and receive you to Myself; that where I am, *<u>there you may be also</u>*. – *John 14:2-3*

What is happening? The book of Revelation calls it "being caught up to rule and reign.....

> And she gave birth to a son, a male *child*, who is to rule all the nations with a rod of iron; and her child was caught up to God and to His throne. **Rev 12:5**

Those who embrace the rapture theory are looking to be caught away from the judgments coming, rather than understand that the change that is happening within the sons of God is the very thing that is bringing forth the judgments in the earth at this time.

We are facing a timeline before us that is seeing a shift in the level of life we have known. This change, born out of His appearings and His presence, is bringing the sons to a level of abiding that has been prepared for them.

> **For we know that the whole creation groans and suffers the pains of childbirth together until now. And not only this, but also we ourselves, having the first fruits of the Spirit, even we ourselves groan within ourselves, waiting eagerly for *our* adoption as sons, the <u>redemption</u> of our body. – Romans 8: 22-23**

During this time the soul is being redeemed, the spirit is coming alive, and the body is beginning to change. We are beginning to sense, to see, to hear, and to interact with a world that before now was, by and large, unseen to us.

We have entered a timeline that is beginning to see dramatic changes; and the changes we are experiencing on the physical, soul, and spiritual level are but indicators in the road of what is coming. It is here now.

> **For we know that if the earthly tent which is our house is torn down, we have a building from God, a house not made with hands, eternal in the heavens. For indeed in this *house* we groan, longing to be clothed with our dwelling from heaven; inasmuch as we, having put it on, shall not be found naked. For indeed while we are in this tent, we groan, being burdened, because we do not want to be unclothed, but to be clothed, in order**

> **that what is mortal may be swallowed up by life.** –
> **2 Cor 5:1-4**

We are coming alive to all that has awaited God's sons from the beginning of time. This is the time.

We can say this both to the devils that tremble and to a spirit world that has awaited our manifestation; this is the time of Christ's parousia. It is the time.

> **...who will transform the body of our humble state into conformity with the body of His glory, by the exertion of the power that He has even to subject all things to Himself.** – *Phil 3:21*

I don't believe that we will attain resurrection life through a progressive change as we have seen at work over the past 3 to 4 decades, rather, these changes are positioning us to be empowered to reach in and touch God. As God touches us, we will see the final transformation.

It really is the scripture in the beatitudes....blessed are the pure in heart for they shall see God (Matt 5:8). This deep work that has been hidden from the eyes of men has been at work deep within you; and it is coming to fruition. You are being positioned for what I believe will be one of the last elements of change necessary as God glorifies His sons.

We know that there will be great changes at the last trump; but I am speaking of that silent, hidden coming, (Rev 16:15).

It is upon us now.

The Integration of your Spirit, Soul and Body

The Lord is doing something which has not been visited upon the earth before this time. There is a shift happening; a change so great, that even the Angels look on in awe (1Pe 1:12). What is it? The creation of a new race of people - the sons of God.

Paul speaks in 1st Thessalonians that your spirit, soul and body are to be preserved blameless unto the coming of the Lord.

> **Now may the God of peace Himself sanctify you entirely; and may your spirit and soul and body be preserved complete, without blame at the coming of our Lord Jesus Christ. 1Th 5:23**

Paul is talking about a change that would happen in the latter days; a change that would happen within a people whom the Lord had prepared and set aside.

This change involves the redemption of every aspect of who and what you are; your spirit, your soul and your body. Paul is talking about the complete salvation and redemption of all that you are.

Where do we fall within the timeline of this fulfillment? Are we at the beginning of this season of His presence in the earth, or have we yet to enter this season?

These changes we speak of have been happening and progressively unfolding over the past several decades, so I would have to say we are in the middle of this season of His appearing; His parousia. We should be expecting deep changes for this is the season of the Lord's appearing to each of those believers whom He has prepared for this time.

When we speak of the coming of the Lord, it may seem to be a bit confusing, because the scriptures speak of 2 unique scenarios. The first describes Christ coming as a thief in the night (a silent coming). The second concerns Christ's coming in glory, when every eye will see Him and all the nations will mourn because of Him (Rev 1:7). Where are we? This season of His presence that is unfolding now to those whom Christ has prepared is the time of His silent coming. It is also the time of the "wise and foolish" virgins.

This season of His appearing will only be for those who have eyes to see. It is not apparent, and you will not perceive it, unless you heart has been prepared for this time.

This spiritual coming that precedes the physical coming where every eye sees Him is the prelude for all of the major end-time events that have yet to come. Why? Because these end-time events are predicated upon the manifestation of the sons of God, who are the agency through which these major events and judgments will be brought forth. Like the experience which happened to the disciples on their way to Emmaus (Luke 24:13-31); we are in the season of His individual appearing.

During this time of His silent coming, the Lord is completing His handiwork; *you*. He is completing His living temple. Zechariah the prophet foresaw this day when he spoke …

> **Then he answered and said to me, "This is the word of the LORD to Zerubbabel saying, 'Not by might nor by power, but by My Spirit,' says the LORD of hosts. 'What are you, O great mountain? Before Zerubbabel *you will become* a plain; and he will bring forth the top stone with shouts of "Grace, grace to it!"' Also the word of the LORD came to me saying, "The hands of Zerubbabel have laid the foundation of this house, and his hands will finish *it*. Then you will know that the LORD of hosts has sent me to you. Zech 4:6-9**

Zechariah saw that the completion of this work of sonship would be by grace and grace alone.

God has a plan. That plan involves your entrance into resurrection life - on this side of the veil. (Phi. 3:10-11, Ro 6:5, Rev 20:6) As you enter into the fullness of sonship, you will do so from this level of existence. You will not have to transition to the other side before partaking of your inheritance. It is your destiny to break the tape on this side of the "veil". You are destined to enter into the transformation of sonship and become complete in Him – the integration of your spirit, soul and body. Now.

It has never been about inheriting the promises and becoming "on the other side of the veil"; it has always been about having a people who would transition from life into life, from this side of the veil.

The death you bear daily by the work of the cross in your life is the only death you are truly ordained to partake of. It is not the will of God that His sons experience a physical death at this time. The provision is available for you to move from this life, into the newness of life (resurrection), on this side of the veil. The provision is available, yet it remains for the sons to press into it.

From the beginning the Father has sought to create a family; a family of sons and daughters within whom His spirit dwelled. The Father has sought this indwelling of His Spirit, in His sons, more than we have understood. It is the heart of the Father that we enter into an absolute oneness with Him; experiencing the complete indwelling of the Godhead. This is what the Father is seeking. To truly please the Lord we must come into this level of oneness, or "abiding". This experience is far beyond what we can imagine; but it is on the table. And this change and transition will happen within a people who have been prepared.

Even though we are a triune being, we still see ourselves primarily from the "soul/physical" perspective. We tend to see and hear through the agency of this body/soul connection. This is how we assimilate our reality. As we continue to grow and mature in Christ we begin to realize that we are not as limited as we thought we were. We actually begin to enter into the unlimited-ness of Christ as we take on more and more of His attributes.

You are changing into something entirely new, as we have said before; a different order of creation. God is doing something new in the earth, He is creating a new thing within you.

> **Behold, I shew you a mystery; We shall not all sleep, but we shall all be changed, In a moment, in**

> **the twinkling of an eye, at the last trump: for the trumpet shall sound, and the dead shall be raised incorruptible, and we shall be changed. For this corruptible must put on incorruption, and this mortal *must* put on immortality. 1 Co 15:51-53**

The Greek word for "changed" seen in both 1 Co. 15:52 and 2nd Cor. 3:18 is metamorphoo, which literally means transfigure or transform. Similar to a worm being changed into a butterfly - it becomes a new order of creation. We are not dressing up the old - God is doing something new.

And you are right in the middle of this change.

The deep work of the cross and the complete identification with Christ is leading us to one conclusion; an integration of our spirit, soul and body before Him. We will cease to function as 3 separate entities. The function of our soul, the function of our physical body, and the function of our spirit, will all merge together as we become one before Him.

> **Jesus said to them: "When you make the two one, and when you make the inner as the outer and the outer as the inner.....then shall ye enter the kingdom." Logos 22 the Book of Thomas**

The book of Thomas is quite a mystical writing. There is much to be gleaned from this small manuscript. What is recounted here has been shown to us a number of times over the years. This deals with the integration of all that we are. We cease to be a separate spirit, off doing the will of God, encumbered by a soul and physical that is unaware and struggling through the daily rigors of life. Rather, we come into an integration of all that we are, all that is within and without.

Many people we have ministered to over the years are what I would call a "free spirit". This means their spirit is "free", not bound or tied to their physical or soul - thus it is free to go and minister and do the Lord's bidding. As great as that may sound, having a "free spirit" brings with it many sets of issues. Because you become aware of so much, both in the spirit, and in the soul, you end up tuning into other people's problems and you can easily take them on as your own. So, to be a "free spirit" can be challenging for the Christian believer as he begins to mature in the Lord. This, in part, is why we must know our spirits, (as we mentioned in the word just prior to this).

The point I want to make is not to define the "free spirit", but to convey the concept that you are literally 3 beings; all rolled up into one. Each aspect of your being can have influence or sway over the other until the work of the cross has been completed in your life.

In the final analysis, what you are in your spirit is truly who and what you are. The more the work of the cross is completed within your life, the more you will come into a oneness with Christ. And, the more your spirit will have total and free access to move in you and through you. You will stop walking as a soulish Christian, and you will begin to walk as a spiritual Christian; able to hear, see, and function within the realm of the spirit.

This is the goal. Get out of the soul and psychic. Stop living as a carnal Christian. Stop walking a fleshly life. Begin to walk in the spirit.

We are in a transition; a transition that is seeing people begin to live in the spirit. This is where your life, your abiding, your reality and your consciousness are anchored in Him. This is a reality that has begun to unfold within a people; a people not limited to race, country, origin or group affiliation.

God is doing this; one here and one there. An awakening is happening; not an awakening like the new age people speak of that is open to anything out there, but an awakening to God on the deepest planes of your being.

Everything which is happening in this hour is created first in the realm of the spirit. What you see unfolding on this natural plane is a distillation of what has been first created - and is unfolding - in the spirit realm. This is how it works. When God speaks, it is created first as a spirit realm reality; then it filters to the natural plane.

You are walking out a reality that has already been created. Do you understand? It has already been created. By the time you begin to embrace the changes, the experiences and the realities within your own being; know and understand that it has already happened. You are living that which is filtering down from the plane of spirit; that which God has already created and has already released.

When Christ speaks of the greater works, He is speaking of spirit realm realities. The evangelism of the kingdom is a spirit realm reality. Does this mean that they will not have a physical manifestation? No, but the real substance is not what you see on this plane; it is that which is happening in the spirit realm. This is where it must first happen. As it is created on the spiritual plane, then it really becomes a "mop up" operation on this physical level, for it has already been done.

If you look closely at the scripture you see that when Christ went to sit at the right hand of the Father it was because it was all done. Christ said, "It is Finished".

A great deal has been done already, including Christ's victory over death, for death is defeated if we can believe this. We are walking out a reality that has already been completed in the realm of spirit.

In the church age we functioned from the soul level. In the kingdom age, we function from the spirit, and unless you have eyes to see; you will not see it.

This experience of sonship will see the absolute ascendancy of the spirit over every aspect of your being. Your physical body and soul will come under the authority and ascendancy of your spirit. You will cease to live in limitation; for in the realm of spirit there is absolute and total freedom. This is the scripture; for where the spirit of the Lord is, there is liberty (2Co 3:17). This is not doctrine, this is an incredible experience that is associated with sonship and the total and absolute redemption of all that you are. This is a whole new life.

As the spirit moves into ascension over the soul, our physical bodies will have to change to reflect this. The physical body has been a reflection of the soul, but the resurrected body will be a reflection of our spirit (1Cor 15).

Tracking
In The Realm of Spirit

The Spirit that raised Christ Jesus from the dead is coursing through you, as your body undergoes the changes of sonship.

This age of Spirit, or what we could call the 3rd day (Hosea 6:3), has been in the process of unfolding for the last several generations. We are living at the threshold of the manifestation of the sons of God; as God has been moving to prepare His people for a higher spiritual level.

It is time for the experience of resurrection life and the glorification of the believer's body. We are at the door; for these experiences have begun.

Since the turn of the 20th century we have seen God gradually releasing more and more of His spirit. Joel foresaw this period as an outpouring of God's spirit upon all of mankind.

> **"It will come about after this That I will pour out My Spirit on all mankind; And your sons and daughters will prophesy, Your old men will dream dreams, Your young men will see visions. – Joel 2:28**

We have been living and walking in an extended season of the fulfillment of this prophecy; as we have seen the rise of a great deal of spiritual awareness - globally.

The world is coming alive. They sense the changes. For the sons whom God has prepared, there is a tremendous shift happening. It is the day that we are seeing the heavens opened, and a great deal of awareness of the whole spirit age unfolding before us. We are seeing the conjunction of the natural realm and the spirit realm - a conjunction of 2 ages as we have spoken of.

This is a time of restoration; and the Spirit that raised up Jesus from the dead is beginning to give life to our mortal body. Your body.

The Spirit that raised up Jesus from the dead is quickening our mortal bodies by His Spirit that dwells in us. - Romans 8:11

Resurrection life is not a theory. It is not a platitude. It is a progressive experience that God has been bringing to the sons that He has prepared for this hour. The Spirit that raised Christ Jesus from the dead is flowing through your mortal bodies, and changes are happening.

Christ is the resurrection, and the experience of Christ, "the resurrection", is unfolding within you. God's sons are beginning to enter into a spiritual oneness with Christ and the Father.

Your eyes are being anointed to see beyond the veil. Your ears are being anointed to hear beyond the veil. Your bodies are beginning to respond to a spirit world that has been unseen to you; for you are coming into the day of His kingdom. This is a day of reality.

What does this mean? It means the Spirit is giving life to your mortal bodies, because these mortal bodies have been dead.

As the Spirit within you continues to come alive to the realm of God's kingdom, you will find that your body begins to respond to the realm of spirit. Your body is becoming a switchboard that is tracking in the realm of spirit. As your body "comes alive", you begin to feel and sense the realm of spirit. We call these "signs".

As these signs come you will need the revelation of the Holy Spirit to understand specifically what the signs mean for you. We rejoice that we have come to the threshold of a wonderful new day, for it is time to fully enter in and receive our inheritance.

Don't underestimate these initial stages of the redemption of your body, for this is a sign that God is quickening your mortal body.

Look to the scriptures to interpret or shed light on the signs that you are receiving; for they often manifest differently for each person. Many of the signs you will develop from experience. Ask questions, and always keep track as a faithful scribe; for the Lord will bring clarity and understanding just when you need it.

The Lord has brought you into the realm of the spirit, a realm that affects all other levels. As we have said, it is the time that the sons of God effectively war in the spirit and effectively minister and bring forth the kingdom. This cannot be done without deep spiritual perception.

These signs come to you from the Holy Spirit to illuminate and reveal to you what is unfolding in the realm just beyond sight. These signs in the body are but one avenue of perception. They are a type of "seeing eye dog" until the time of "open vision" is fully established.

We do not take lightly the day of small beginnings, but we also understand that the day of "open vision" is quickly overtaking us. The sons of God are coming into a functional relationship in the realm of Spirit; for the kingdom must be administered. The judgments have been set aside to be completed, and there is much work yet to be done. It will not happen unless God's people make this transition into a life in the spirit.

You are coming alive on every level. Anticipate it, expect it, and reach in for it; for this is the time of the final equipping of the saints.

The signs which come to you as you experience the progressive renewal of your body, are a way that the Holy Spirit uses to alert you to what is happening in the realm of the spirit. Not only will you experience physical symptoms within your body - what we call signs - but you will experience a heightened level of hearing and seeing. As you progressively come up higher in your vibration and state of presence; that which was hidden to you before will become visible.

The promise in the scripture is that the Lord will expose that which is being done behind closed doors (Eph 5:3, 1Co 4:5). I believe a great deal of this "exposing" is done through the perceptive qualities of the sons as they enter into these deeper states of renewal.

When Christ died, He eliminated the veil. We have spoken of this. It is gone. It is done. Yet it has remained because we have still believed in the veil and the illusion of limitation and separation; all of which are passing away.

In the spirit world there is no such thing as time or distance. What we know of time does not exist in the realm of the spirit; only on the physical level. The same applies for distance; for you can think on a location and be there instantly.

We have not realized just how limited we have really been in this natural plane. We have been running this race with lead weights. It may have strengthened us within, but at some point you toss off those weights!

The signs which have been coming in the physical body, and the simultaneous enlightenment that is coming to the eyes, is pulling down the shroud or barrier that has existed within us. We are beginning to track in the spirit world.

Do you know what makes spiritual warfare against the saints so effective?

<u>A lack of awareness.</u>

It is crucial that you are able to track in the spirit realm because your authority is only as effective as your ability to see. If you cannot discern the hand of the enemy you will not be able to judge him.

These physical signs in the body might seem strange to you, yet we must understand that the Spirit that gave life to Christ is quickening our mortal bodies. This is just one part of the experience that is happening. There is much more than this awaiting you.

The lack of vision, sight and perception that exists today is the norm, and it should not be. The enemy has been highly effective in creating a level of sterility within the cultures of this world system. Most people, by and large, live their lives completely unaware of the world of spirit that is constantly controlling, manipulating and directing them.

As you break into the realm of sight you will find that everything changes. The enemy is nailed at the gate because your God given authority, Christ in You, becomes effective. Without it; your effectiveness is only "partial".

Do not take these words on perception lightly for this means the enemies absolute downfall.

How will the kingdom be administered unless it is administered by the sons who see; and in seeing are able to effectively judge? It is your destiny to walk out the judgments written (Ps 149); that which is waiting to be enacted by the sons of God. Right Here. Right Now.

Having said all of this, let's talk about some of the specific signs that we have been tracking on over the past 30 years.

The signs which come to you may have unique and special significance only to you, and may reflect that unique aspect of ministry that you are to have.

This is a topic that could be exhaustive in discussion, but we will keep it focused and to the point.

Most of the signs or symptoms you receive in your body fall in the category of sympathetic or symptomatic. Often in personal ministry the signs we would get represented that which another was going through. Those are sympathetic signs. The symptomatic signs are those signs you receive that indicate what is directly affecting you. If you get heart pains, unless you have a physical issue, chances are that sign is a symptomatic sign indicating that you are under direct assault.

These signs come for you to implement Christ's victory and authority through you. The victory has already been won. It is finished. However we know that we are walking out that victory. These signs come as you enter into the manifestation of Christ's release and authority and become the instrument of God's judgment in this age.

The Holy Spirit, is alerting you to something that is transpiring in the spirit realm. Your bodies are becoming like a switchboard, for these signs come for present application and appropriation.

First of all let us tell you what we know concerning how the signs manifest for the male versus the female, and what they represent:

For Males:
Your left side represents that which is coming from a female contact, or it represents the physical level, or it can represent the false. It can mean any of these. The right side represents that which is coming from a male contact, or it can represent the spiritual, or the true.

For Females:
The opposite is true; your left side represents a male contact or the spiritual, or the true; your right side a contact from a female or the physical or the false.

You must realize that all signs need to be discerned in the spirit to know what they mean and what they represent; this is just a summary of what we have experienced and have studied and learned.

How does the proverb go...."it is the glory of God to conceal a matter, but the glory of kings to seek it out" (Proverbs 25:2) . When these signs and symptoms come to you, search out the scriptures for you will find pearls hidden within the scriptures that will give illumination to that which the Spirit is showing you.

We will best address these signs by identifying different parts of the body and what the signs have meant to us. As we have said, this will be a unique experience for each of you as you study and monitor the changes happening within you.

The Head: All of your relationships are represented in the back of your head down to the neck area.

The Upper head area: Is for marital relationships or it could represent your pastoral covering.

The Middle area of the back of the head: Represents your family or natural relationships. From the back of the head moving forward towards the ear is for children. A little further forward could represent other close familial relationships.

The Back of the Neck: This area does not represent any of your spiritual relationships, rather it represents contacts that are born of the soul and psychic. When the enemy lies to us, he does it through the emotions. These contacts work in controlling your emotions.

Much of the assault that comes against you in this day you will pick up in the back of your neck. This is something which you need to study closely when these contacts come through, for they represent a level of psychic warfare that you are facing, and this is usually coming or being channeled through someone you know, a relationship or bond you have that is on the wrong level.

The problem these contacts present is that they are generally born of the soul, and thus they are very prone to becoming a channel of devil power. When the enemy finds an individual who is hostile towards you, one with whom you have a soul or psychic type of bond or contact, then the enemy is able to jump on the energy of that person so that what comes through to you is greatly magnified in power against you.

When you begin to get these signs in the neck stop what you are doing and study closely where this could be coming from. Study your thoughts, anything that might give you an inclination as to who or what this could be that the Holy Spirit is pointing out. Once again, realize that the enemy seeks to oppress and hinder you through the emotional realm.

The first step in getting free is rightly discerning what is going on in the spirit realm. Once you see it for what it is, then the power that this contact or channel had over you is gone. But you must first see.

The Front of Neck: This sign could represent a spirit of fear hitting you.

The Top of the Head, the Crown: The crown area represents your openness to the Lord. Often times you will feel an anointing on the top of your head for the Lord is bringing a great openness to Him.

If you feel an oppressive sign on the top of your head, then something is coming through to block your openness and connection with the Lord.

A Band around Head: This is a sign of an intercessor. When you receive this sign it represents a depth of intercession that your spirit is into.

The Ridgeline area between top of forehead and top of head: This is a great sign which means that God is bridging the gap between your soul and spirit and bringing you into a level where He is eliminating the gap between the time He speaks to you and when you finally hear. This bridging of the gap is so crucial as God brings His sons into a functional relationship in the realm of spirit.

The time is coming and I believe is upon us that there will no longer be a gap between the time the Lord speaks to you and the time that you hear. He will speak and you will instantly hear.

The Ear: The ear is an area that represents a great deal of spiritual activity.

A sharp pain in the ear: Or the bone behind the ear which represents a lying spirit hitting you.

Around the Ear: From time to time you may pickup a fluttering sound around your ears which represents the presence of Angels with you.

The Mouth: Represents Prophesy & Speaking. Anointing on mouth is a sign that you are to prophesy.

The Nose: Signs in the nose can often mean that you are coming into a deeper level of discernment. However, if your nose itches then that is a sign of witchcraft coming against you.

If you see this in the spirit, it will look like lightening, only colored in red.

The signs are so vast, that what you see with your eyes is an entirely different perception than the physical signs in your body; but both are equally important for your vision and perception that is opening up.

We will stay focused on the signs you receive physically within your body, but realize that as you continue to come more and more alive to His spirit and the realm of the Spirit, every faculty that you have will come alive more and more.

The Eyes & Forehead: An anointed sign across the eyes may come for wisdom and knowledge, however if you get a sharp prick in the eye it represents a fairly high level of demonic assault.

> **But if you do not drive out the inhabitants of the land from before you, then it shall come about that those whom you let remain of them *will become* as pricks in your eyes and as thorns in your sides, and they will trouble you in the land in which you live.**
> **– Numbers 33:55**

In this scripture it both speaks of the prick in the eye and the thorn in the side. Both of these signs manifest as you come under more intense assault.

The forehead is a marvelous area, for in the book of Revelations it speaks of the enemy that seals His people upon their forehead with 666. (Rev 13:6, 14:9, 17:5, 20:4) The scripture in Revelations also speaks of how the Lord will seal those unto Himself on their forehead.

> **"Do not harm the earth or the sea or the trees until we have sealed the bond-servants of our God on their foreheads." - Rev. 7:3**

The anointing or burning sensation on the forehead represents deeper perception and insight that is coming.

The Teeth: That you are beginning to break down the word and understanding is coming.

The Jaw: A sign in the jaw means that you are assimilating the word

The CheekBone: Signs in the cheekbone represent spiritual attack that you are under. You recall the story of the widow and the unjust judge as she hit him under the eye. (Luke 18:5 Literal)

The Temples: Signs in the temples are dealing with your thought processes. An anointing or burning sensation in your temples is a great sign which is dealing with the redemptive work of the renewing of your mind.

A light pressure means you are absorbing the teaching and impartation that is coming to you.

A sharp jabbing in the temples is a sign of direct assault, that the satanic hosts are trying to gain access to your mind.

The ARM: Signs in the arm represent the exaltation of the Lord. For the Lord's arm is being made bare in your behalf.

> **The Lord has bared His holy arm in the sight of all the nations, that all the ends of the earth may see the salvation of our God. – Isa 52:10**

The anointing in the arm is always related to a sign of victory. You can read throughout the book of Isaiah which constantly speaks of the mighty arm of the Lord.

The Forearm: Deliverance. God is going to bring miracle deliverance through His judgments. The forearm down to the hand represent more of a deliverance or healing that God is bringing.

The Upper Arm: From the upper arm up to the tip of your shoulder; God is bringing victory and if you get the sign at the tip of your shoulder or joint where the arm meets, then this is a sign that you are moving in authority over Principalities and Powers. The upper arm is related to spiritual warfare and your victory.

The Elbow: The elbow is a great sign because the Spirit is indicating that a judgment, release or deliverance is in the process. It is being executed as you receive that sign.

The Feet: <u>The sole of your foot</u> means that wherever you move you possess. Go in and possess the land. (Joshua 1:3) <u>The heel of your foot</u> represents a bruising of the enemy. You are bruising the head of the enemy. (Genesis 3:15)

The Knee: Sign in the knee is a sign of submission. (Isa 45:23)

The Upper Shoulder: Signs in the shoulder concern the administration of the kingdom, Christ's authority over principalities and powers.

> **For unto us a child is born, unto us a son is given: and the government shall be upon his shoulder: and his name shall be called Wonderful, Counsellor, The mighty God, The everlasting Father, The Prince of Peace. – Isa 9:6**

The sign at the tip of the shoulder with the arm indicates that the victory of the Lord over principalities and powers is in operation.

If you get a pinching in your shoulder this signs means the enemy is trying to get through, usually through your mind or thinking.

The Hand:
The hand represents the Outreach Ministry of Christ. (Eph 4:8) We have found the fingers of the hand most often relate to the following:
Apostle - The Thumb
Prophet - Forefinger
Evangelist - Middle Finger
Pastor - Ring Finger
Teacher - Little Finger

The Joint of a finger: If the sign appears in the joint it means there is another related sign in execution. The sign in the joint means that the authority over principalities and powers is being executed.

The Thumb & Toe: Authority/Kingship. Signs in the thumb usually represent the kingship ministry of Christ in you, and that you are coming into the authority of the Kings and Priests of the Lord.

Often when you are under direct assault your left or right toe will feel as though someone is cutting it off. You may awake in the morning and your toe is almost numb. Just know that you have been in spiritual conflict, oftentimes through the night, and when you arise, you are just that more alert to what is transpiring in the spirit realm.

In the Old Testament when the marauding army would defeat a kingdom, they would cut off the thumbs and big toe of the king of the land they defeated. It represented an elimination of the ruling monarch's power. The toe can also represent an anointing of the king ministry. (Judges 1:7, Ex 29:20)

The Palms: Receiving and Giving - If there is a burning anointing it means you are to minister and lay on of hands, for with the palms we give.

The Palms: Digging - If you have a feeling of wanting to dig at your palms, this is an oppressive sign and is often representative of witchcraft coming against you.

The Back of Hand: A crawling sensation is a sign of the spirit of confusion, a confusion coming to hinder your ability to receive of the Lord. It means the door of reception is closed and it also represents a level of demonic power coming against you, oftentimes witchcraft.

The Wrist: Indicates someone is being cut off, if it is sympathetic, or that the spirit realm is trying to cut you off, if it is symptomatic.

The Stomach: This concerns the area of nerve centers and emotions.

The Pit of your Stomach: Generally means a spirit of lust is hitting you. This sign can be so strong as to make you think that you are truly sick. Once you break the transference it is amazing how quickly that sign will vanish.

As a point of mention, when we speak of a spirit of lust I know the common thread of thought is that which is sexually perverse. But a spirit of lust may or may not have any direct relation to this, for a spirit of lust can be manifested in many ways.

The Bowels: Pressure in emotions. (John 7:38)

The Heart: Signs or a pain in the heart indicate there is direct assault coming against you

The Lower Back: Along the ridge of lower back this sign is dealing with the breaking the back of rebellion.

The Upper Back and Spine: A pain in the upper back can indicate that you are spiritually depleted.

A sharp jab in the back is what we call a knife in the back, and is usually concerning transference and assault that is coming against you.

The 5th Rib: This sign is a sign of treachery that is coming against you. (this relates back to the sign in Numbers 33:55).

The Hips: A sign in the hip is a very positive sign that you have or are wrestling with God and that God is prevailing. (Gen 32:25)

Crawling & Itching (especially the nose): Any type of sensation like this has to do with witchcraft.

Cold: If you shiver in the presence of someone it is usually a sign of devil power or enemy.

Inner Nervousness: Demonic presence.

Heaviness: Is a sign of resentment hitting you. As well, if you are in the presence of satan, the heaviness can be almost mesmerizing.

In summary these are but some of the signs that are coming as our bodies are coming alive to the world of spirit. You will most likely experience signs that will be unique just to you, as your body continues to come alive.

Seek the Lord for clarity and understanding and He will give you understanding. Until we come to the place of complete and open vision, these signs will be with us to help us on our journey into the complete manifestation of sonship and the glorification of our bodies.

How to Break Restraints and Oppression

We have not dedicated much of this book to handling the spiritual conflict that comes through in the spirit, so we wanted to add just a few notes.

One of the easiest ways to break an oppression is to change your vibration. If you can change the dial, you can drop the assault and oppression in a moment. To do that just change what you are doing, for example: take a cold shower, get something to eat, go to a movie if that works for you, go jogging, worship, whatever you find that works for you, but change your vibration. And often that means break the bridge that you have created mentally as well.

In spiritual conflict we have seen the ability entities have to shift their vibration and literally disappear in a moment. Learn to shift your vibration.

Notes

Section 14

A Workshop

For Seers

- **A Workshop for Seers**
- **Breathing Techniques**
- **Diet & Your Spiritual Awareness**
- **Visualization & Imagination**
- **Simplicity**
- **Auras**
- **Journaling**
- **Worship**

A Workshop for Seers

> "But solid food is for the mature, who because of practice have their senses trained to discern good and evil." And..."therefore, leaving the elementary teaching about the Christ, let us press on to maturity.." - Heb 5:14-6:1

People who have believed in God have typically been afraid of a walk in the spirit. The reproach that has been created over the past 100 years through the growth of the "spiritualist movement", has given it an "aura" of the occult. To some a walk in the spirit may even seem like an off-shot of the occult. Yet if you are to walk into the deeper things of the Lord, you will have to become a mystic.

So here is *our* definition of a "mystic":

One who has become aware and sensitive to the realm of spirit and who pursues after a deeper experience of knowing the Lord.

If you are to move into the dominion of Christ and the administration of His authority, then you must become mystics. <u>You must be able to see and to hear in the spirit.</u> The realm of spirit must be as real, if not more, than the natural plane you have lived on. To do this you must let go of the traditions you have been brought up with. And this we have spoken of throughout this book; letting go of your concepts, unlearning your learned belief systems, and staying pliable and teachable.

The world of evil has known what is coming and what God has planned to bring His people into. As much as they have known, they have not understood nor have they perceived to what extent the changes will be that will manifest within His sons.

They have fought it by bringing the false manifestations before the time. This has brought about a tremendous amount of conditioning that God's people have had to let go of. They have had to let go of their fearfulness and the conditioning within their mind that would cause them to draw back from a deeper walk in the spirit.

Earlier in the introduction we briefly touched upon the history of the restoration of God's moving in the earth from the 1300's to present day. One thing that we must realize is that in the days of the medieval world, the belief in "superstitions" was no more restrictive than the limited religious thinking that exists in the world today. Back then it was obvious, blatant if you will. But now, it is very subliminal and hidden.

If there is one principle we have addressed throughout this book it is the fact that we are moving into another world; a world of spirit. When you enter the realm of spirit, nothing works the same and nothing functions according to the principles of the natural plane,

The more we change and let go of the weights of this Adamic nature, the more sensitive we become. What may have had no affect on our awareness or spiritual vibration yesterday, can be an anchor of 1,000 tons today.

We have come to the age where God, in the spirit, is beginning to teach and impart to His sons the changes of this new day.

God is bringing the keys that are opening the doors that have been closed. This journey into God's presence is becoming more and more brilliantly lit, for we know that the path of the righteous grows stronger as each day passes.

There are many dynamics that affect our ability to see, to hear and to track in the world of spirit. Throughout this book we have touched on many of these. As much as we need to understand the elements that can have a negative effect upon our spiritual awareness; (eg: bonds and transference), we need to implement the little keys that can bring us into a greater sensitivity. We will briefly touch on some of these.

The drive of the Spirit is to see the sons truly get free. As the book of Revelations states; "to come up higher".

We have not walked this way before, so we must be careful not to "lock ourselves in". It doesn't matter what you were yesterday, whether you saw auras or you did not. It does not matter what level of the "partial" you may have walked in. Just understand that this is a new day and God is bringing you into a life that is completely new. You are in a time of change and what you were, the "cocoon" of your present incarnation, will not be a limitation to all that you are to be. Do not relegate the deeper things of God and the seer anointing to another, for every son will walk as a seer, a priest, and a king.

What is the seer, the priest, the king, or the prophet but Christ in you. We are seeing the release of "the Christ" through you; and as Christ knows no limitation; neither will you.

God is enlarging the place of your dwelling; He is stretching out thy tent pegs. He is giving His sons a new land to embrace and experience. (Isa. 54:2)

There is a great deal at stake because there must be a people that will rise in the Spirit to walk with God. More than ever I believe we are beginning to recognize that there rests upon His sons a measure of responsibility or "accountability". The kingdom is not going to "just happen". What God is doing during this time is linked to you.

We know the time is being cut short, and the mantle of transformation that is resting upon His sons must be embraced and walked out.

> **"Who has heard such a thing? Who has seen such things? Can a land be born in one day? Can a nation be brought forth all at once? As soon as Zion travailed, she also brought forth her sons.**
> **- Isa 66:8**

His sons are being born running. No matter how far we have come, we have not yet arrived; **but we are so very close.**

In this brief workshop our intention is to introduce you to some basic keys and principles that have been shown to us and have helped us on our personal sojourn into His presence. There is much that could be discussed concerning these issues, but for now our main goal is to give you a cursory overview. These are some of the keys that are part of our personal discipline. I know that we have not begun to tap the depth of either the Word or the keys that God is yet to release during this time.

Before we start, these are the first few steps you need to take are:

1. Break your bonds

2. Repent and forgive

We must clear the deck within our heart. We must let go, for we cannot harbor anything toward another. We must break the ties, the cords and the bonds. And we must forgive.

So, let's talk just a bit about the following areas:

1. **Breathing Techniques**
2. **Diet and Your Spiritual Vibration**
3. **Visualization & Imagination**
4. **Simplicity**
5. **Auras**
6. **Journaling**
7. **Worship**

Deep Breathing Techniques

The use of Deep Breathing Techniques
During times of Meditation and Prayer

It has been found that people can reach a deeper level of concentration in prayer and eliminate the influences that distract their mind through the application of rhythmic breathing. You can shift the level of your awareness and your state of mind through changing the rhythm of your breathing.

All that we know of life is built upon an understanding that every item of matter has its own frequency of vibration. Through controlled breathing you can virtually control certain aspects of your own vibration. Anyone who wishes to obtain any degree of control, whether it is concerning his spiritual or physical health, can do so through properly approaching his breathing during times of meditation or waiting upon the Lord.

Do not underestimate the significance of the speed and rhythm of your breathing; because the alteration of your breathing can produce some amazing effects. Proper breathing can help you in waiting on the Lord; and it bring to you physical releases that you might need as well.

While breathing, your mind should be focused upon what you want from the Lord. In conjunction with your controlled, rhythmic breathing, you need to visualize what it is that you are seeking to accomplish. Hold that visualization, and do not doubt that you will have what you have set your spirit upon. We will talk in a moment more about visualizing; for every day that we live we are constantly visualizing - we just haven't been aware that this is how we function as human beings.

Any doubt or conflicting signals will greatly deter what I would call the "manifestation process". You know the scripture...a double minded man will receive nothing of the Lord.

> **But if any of you lacks wisdom, let him ask of God, who gives to all generously and without reproach, and it will be given to him.**
>
> **But he must ask in faith without any doubting, for the one who doubts is like the surf of the sea, driven and tossed by the wind.**
>
> **For that man ought not to expect that he will receive anything from the Lord, *being* a double-minded man, unstable in all his ways. – Jas1:5-8**

The application of controlled, slow breathing, coupled with visualization, can give you great immunity in almost any spiritual battle.

See yourself clothed in His presence, because the truth is, you are. The more you set your spirit upon the truths conveyed to you in the scriptures, the more their reality or truth will displace the lie and illusion you may have previously accepted.

Your Rate of Breathing

We normally breathe from 16 to 18 breathes per minute, however as you slow down the rate of your breathing you will begin to see dynamic changes. At 10 to 12 breaths per minute you will find that it will become very hard to feel excited, irritable, or nervous. If you can keep your breathing to a steady rhythm of 10 breathes per minute, for five minutes, then you will find that your brain will become very clear and focused.

Many of the conflicting vibrations and thoughts you experience will be canceled out by slow and rhythmic. Through this very simple process you will also be able to eliminate the distractions and wanderings of your mind, which is something we all struggle with during times of waiting upon the Lord.

The most effective application of deep breathing should be done by breathing through your nose, on the inhale, and out through your mouth, on the exhale. Steadily, quietly and regularly without strain, and preferably, in a quiet place. We would also suggest not entering into a period of waiting on the Lord or meditation right after eating.

Once again, it is important to remember to visualize as you enter into this level of meditation and waiting on God. He is more close to you than your breath, and as you enter into a state of deep meditation, know that you are aligning yourself with His omnipotence, His power, His protection and His divinity. As you breathe in, you are drawing these realities into you.

To Attain Greater Perception

The slower the rate of your breathing the greater the control you will have over the vibratory activities of every aspect of your being.

If you are able to reduce the rate of your breathing to 3 or 4 breathes per minute, then you will experience a much clearer and heightened level of awareness. You will find a subduing of all of your bodily vibrations to such an extent that they will cease to cause "clutter" or conflicting signals.

In addition to bringing all of your bodily vibrations in sync, this slower rhythmic breathing has a broadening affect upon the 6th chakra or "third eye" as some cultures refer to it. You will find that your very subtle and delicate spiritual perception will begin to open up.

Diet
& Your Spiritual Walk

As we continue on our path to know the Lord, we are becoming more and more aware of what affects our spiritual sensitivity. This age that we walk in is an age of over-stimulation. Because of this we are quickly becoming a sterile society - void of perception.

This over-stimulation of our "senses" comes from many different directions; television and the movie industry, the media and print industry, billboard ads, radio, fast food chains, and the list could go on. We have truly not realized just how over-stimulated we have become within this culture that we live. This explains why our perception can get so easily clouded.

The scriptures speak that *"if the time was not cut short, that there would be no flesh saved alive" (Mark 13:20).* We may think of that scripture in terms of the occurrence of a nuclear war, but I will say this, the path that the earth is on right now is one of imminent destruction.

> **But the two wings of the great eagle were given to the woman, so that she could fly into the wilderness to her place, where she *was nourished for a time and times and half a time, from the presence of the serpent.**
>
> **And the serpent poured water like a river out of his mouth after the woman, so that he might cause her to be swept away with the flood. But the earth helped the woman, and the earth opened its mouth and drank up the river which the dragon poured out of his mouth. Rev 12:14-16**

There is a satanic plot which has set mankind on a course of destruction, even without a nuclear holocaust. You ask what this is? It is the process of the destruction of the earth and the earth's resources. The growing pollution of the earth and the earth's atmosphere, and the decreasing quality of the food that can be harvested from the "nutrient depleted" soil that exists today, is creating a domino effect that is gradually effecting every level of life. We are talking about more than just pollution, the lack of water, and enough crops capable of sustaining this planet, we are talking about the rise of disease on a monumental scale.

If you are wondering; do we ascribe to the "green movement?" Are we on some fanfare to save the planet? No, that is not our focus. The approach being taken today will not bring enough change quick enough, and for the most part most of it is politically generated anyway. No, the real answer are the sons of God. That is the only answer.

Some of the keys which have come to us over the years have been simple ones; eliminate the distractions, simplify your lifestyle, take control, watch what you eat, and what is eating on you. Most important; be aware, for it is difficult to take control of your life and atmosphere if you are not aware that you have lost control in the first place.

Daniel is known as one of the great mystics in the Old Testament. From Daniel an excellent lesson can be learned. Perhaps you remember the story of Daniel (Dan.1:8). After Daniel was taken captive by Nebuchadnezzar, he was brought along with other young men to serve the King. In preparation for that service, the King commanded that these young men be well fed from the King's table. What the King considered "well fed" and what Daniel considered "well fed" were two different things. As the servants brought the young men the portions of wine, and rich foods, Daniel had asked to be allowed to eat only raw vegetables and water. Nothing more.

As the story unfolds, Daniel looked healthier among the lot of them. More than that, he began to be known as one who could interpret dreams, and understand "mysteries". Daniel walked on a spiritual level that was unparalleled at his time. He had many visions and appearings from the Lord and of His bondservants. I would not attribute all of that to his diet, but there is no doubt in my mind that it was instrumental in Daniel's ability to be more aware and sensitive.

You also have the story of John the Baptist, who lived on locusts and wild honey as his diet. Both of these men of God were tapping into keys and principles that enabled them to be more alert and sensitive; "even if they did not fully understand the dynamic of it at the time".

On a scientific level you must understand that everything within creation is composed of vibration. As you appear physically, you consist of matter which is vibrating at a much lower frequency than the angelic beings who live on higher planes. As your own vibration lifts, so will your perception and awareness of those who dwell on those higher dimensions.

The greatest cleanser and "vibration lifter" of all is the ongoing process of purification that the believer is experiencing in this day. Daniel's prophecy in chapter 12 speaks of those who will be "purged, purified and refined", and who will offer up acceptable sacrifices unto the Lord. Given that benchmark, what other keys are there that would help us in our ability to be more aware of the Lord?

Our diet.

The carefulness of our diet only serves to assist us in creating more of an atmosphere for our entire being to be more sensitive before the Lord.

From our years of experimenting with our diet, I would say that we have gradually progressed towards vegan-vegetarianism, which is a vegetarian diet that has also eliminated dairy as well. Not for a fad, but because our bodies felt a great deal better; the sickness that we were so prone to left, and we found that we were more sensitive to the moving of the spirit.

If any of you have ever done a "fast", one of the benefits of a fast is that you gradually become more and more clear. Part of that is attributed to the cleansing and removal of toxins from the body, and the other aspect deals with the removal of heavy, overly processed foods in the diet which promote *lethargy and heaviness.*

There are many parallels that exist between the physical functions of our organs, and their spiritual counterpart. Take for example the liver. The liver functions to eliminate poisons in the body. As those poisons are disseminated, the natural cause and affect is a healthier body on a physical level, and a greater clarity and sensitivity on a spiritual level.

The acidic based fruits, like oranges, pineapples, and dark leafy greens, stimulate the function of the liver, and thus help promote clarity within your being.

Any food item that is of a stimulant nature, like coffee, caffeine and sugar, will tend to "cloud" your perception or better put, "dull" your senses. Why? Because they over-stimulate your senses.

I would recommend that you consider eating foods that are less processed, more raw, and foods which are higher in water content. The higher the water content, the more that food will have a higher vibration to it. The more dense the food, like red meat, the lower the vibration of that food, and the more adverse the affect it will have on your system.

The scientific community has actually been able to measure the energy of various foods in what is called "megahertz". Some foods have no energetic worth, while others actually complement your body and give you energy, rather than take it.

To quote an article we read recently from the book; "Transition to an All Natural, High Energy Lifestyle" by Rebekah Winquest;

"Simply put, your vibration is the amount of electrical energy that your body puts out and needs throughout the day. For example, science has documented that every plant, food, animal, person, organ, cell, thought, color, etc., has its own vibration, which can be measured in megahertz (MHz). The body's main organs (heart, brain, lungs, etc.) should vibrate at about 70 MHz, when it is healthy. Chocolate cake only provides 1-3 MHz of energy. Most of the fried burgers at fast food outlets give a whopping -5 to 3 MHz – pretty sad for a "complete meal". Those happy meals aren't so happy! There are "high-vibration" foods, which can add high amounts of energy to our own. For example, raw almonds have 40-50 MHz; green vegetables and wheat grass have 70-90 MHz...it appears that natural, plant-based foods give off an incredible amount of energy, where processed (sugary, starchy and fried) and

fast foods give little to no energy. There are many common fast foods and candies that actually give off a negative amount of energy!"

What we are talking about is creating an atmosphere - your personal atmosphere - for your own clarity and perception. Nothing more.

A spiritual life, or "living on the highest plane", is created by the choices we make. If we are headed towards a more spiritual lifestyle, then we need to make those choices which will assist us in that direction. It is all a matter of choices, and sometimes we must give up the lesser to obtain the greater.

There have been so many books written on diet that they could probably fill many libraries, however I think in the end, each one has to find out what works for them. Much of this will be a learning curve for you, so be prepared!

Sometimes the bonds we have with food and diet are stronger than the bonds we have in relationships. It really comes down to how driven you are to live in His presence, and whether a change in your diet will better help you to achieve that process. You are the judge of that.

Visualization
& Imagination

Not enough can be said about the importance and power of these two words; visualization and imagination.

Your imagination is one of the most powerful tools you have at your disposal. Your imagination is literally that which gives "legs" to the authority and power you have in Christ.

What you see (imagine or visualize), you can create.

Let's talk just about the power of visualization.

Visualization is the process of creating images within your mind of what you seek. Your are envisioning yourself in a certain set of dynamics. You are envisioning a result. When a martial artist breaks through a series of blocks or wood, he "sees" himself on the other side of this experience. This is nothing new; with the rise of the "new age" movement we have seen a great deal of interest in visualizing.

The truth is that there is a great deal of power behind visualizing. It can be used, in God, to create release and fulfillment. You can take the scriptures and "visualize" yourself walking in them. As the Lord gives you insight into what He is doing, you can visualize the releases, the changes, even the implementation of His judgments, through visualization or the use of "imagery".

Whether we are actively "visualizing" or not; what many do not understand is that we actually live in a semi-state of "visualizing". How is that, you wonder? It is because the process of how we think flows along these channels. Whether we are thinking about the present or the future, or about the past, we see ourselves in certain ways. If we are planning ahead for an event, we often "picture" the resultant outcome - you are "visualizing". We function this way far more than we know. It is almost a default how we process our thoughts, always picturing a situation ... scenario A or scenario B, and so on.

Once you understand that you live in and out of a state of visualizing, then you can take a more focused stance and determine what it is you want. You begin to guard how you think, or what you are "visualizing". It is an expression of the scripture in Proverbs;

For as he thinketh in his heart, so *is* he. – Prov 23:7

Or as Paul has caution;

> ***We are* destroying speculations and every lofty thing raised up against the knowledge of God, and *we are* taking <u>every thought captive to the obedience</u> of Christ, - 2Co 10:5**

Visualizing is powerful, because it is tied into our thought processes. The enemy has understood this, which is why we are cautioned to guard our thoughts and to guard our heart.

One of the most powerful aspects of prayer and meditation is the act of visualizing while you wait upon the Lord. So many scriptures speak of "meditating" day and night on the Lord; meditating on His precepts, on His word. This is not something passive. You are aggressively visualizing the fulfillment of those words; of those prophecies. For the sons, the act of visualization is an aggressive, focused, and intense stance to reach in and embody His word.

There is a tremendous power behind visualizing when you are in a state of meditation before the Lord. You have the power to create life or death. You create what you see in God. What He shows you in the spirit, you have the ability to create. Be careful, you can also create your own mire or "slough of despond".

Because you have the indwelling of the Spirit of God within you, you already are functioning as a co-creator with God. You may not be aware of what you are creating, but your actions, your thoughts, and your inner visualizations are creating every moment you breathe.

The Lord is only now beginning to bring His people to a point where they can effectively harness the power that He is releasing within them. The power of life, or death, the power to create or to destroy.

In this hour God's sons, the channels through which God is moving, are working in concert with the Lord to create what He wants done in the earth. You are co-creators with the Lord, and the power of visualization is of paramount importance; especially when utilized during times of prayer and fasting.

I believe the visions and dreams that God brings to His people is one way that He shares with you His intent. God is giving you insight that you might see what He is doing and what He is yet to bring to pass. As His son, you reach in through your prayer and meditation and help to create that reality - both in the natural and the spiritual planes.

You are visionaries.
All of God's sons are visionaries.

Let's touch on the power of the imagination. As much as visualizing and imagination are similar, there is a distinct difference by what we have seen in operation in the spirit realm.

On the natural level, imagination and visualization overlap quite a bit. But in the realm of the spirit it is your sanctified imagination that directs your spirit.

Understand that everything we are speaking of is still only the partial.

When you break through into a state of abiding in the spirit you will notice that everything operates from your intent. You will what you need. You will where you need to be. I am using the word "will", but in this context our will or imagination are the same. You see what you need, and you have it. You see where you need to go, and you are there.

Call it imagination, call it intent, call it your will. As you move more and more into a functional relationship in the spirit, with the Lord, you will find that your imagination will be the engine that directs your movements.

The world of evil has understood these principles, for they constantly barrage the sons in an attempt to get them to believe in the lie, to believe in limitation, or oppression.

Ephesians is a good book to review over and over; for Paul gives some very basic keys concerning the spiritual warfare or assault that comes on the mental level towards God's sons. (Eph 6:13-18)

You have the power to create. The power of your imagination and your visualization cannot be emphasized enough.

From a purely scientific perspective, let me share with you how the mind functions.

When you enter deeper levels of meditation, or "waiting on God', (whichever term you want to use), and you begin to really rest and practice the prayer of listening; what happens? You go inside, or within yourself. You are listening acutely for His voice.

As you delve more deeply within, you move from the beta state (normal mental alertness) to the alpha state and eventually to the theta state (prior to sleep). It is in the brain state of the "theta" where magic happens within the crucible of your own neurological activity.

In this theta state your brain waves range from 4-7 hz. It is also known as the "twilight" state which we normally only experience fleetingly as we rise up out of the depths of sleep, or just prior to falling into sleep. It is in this theta state that you "see". Imagery, inspiration, visions and more. Combined with your breathing, as we spoke, if you can take your times of meditation or waiting upon God into this level, you will find a tremendous level of vision and hearing open up.

As you practice visualizing or focusing on the word, it is within this level that the cerebral cortex becomes a vital channel for what is called the mind/body connection. The brain literally cannot tell the difference between what is real and what is realistically imagined.

It is powerful. You may find your body reacting to stimuli you are visualizing or "seeing" within the theta state, even though it doesn't really exist in the natural world. Interesting.

This is why visualizing can be so powerful.

Simplicity

We have addressed aspects of this topic, simplicity, throughout this book. We will now focus on this briefly because herein lies a key to a greater level of awareness and sensitivity.

To walk in a state of freedom one needs to understand the bindings which have previously tied them. In this age of television, the print media & radio, in short "our culture as a whole", we live in a state of constant bombardment.

People in the "free world" are anything but free. If they could see the energy that surrounds them and is constantly hammering them; it would be a rude awakening.

If you were to picture this energy in the spirit it would appear almost like mass confusion; so much input constantly going on. There are so many constantly vying for some control of you; how you think, what you perceive, your standards etc. Many of you can attest to the spirits and energy that emanate from television and movies.

This is why it is so important to simplify your life. Simplify the inputs into your life; whether it is the books you read, the television you watch, the food you eat, or the relationships you have.

Earlier in the book we mentioned Smith Wigglesworth, who lived in England and died in the late 40's. As a young plumber he could neither read nor write, but he loved God. When the Spirit eventually taught him to read it was only the word of God that he learned. He had no interest in assimilating anything else; he only wanted to fill his mind and heart with one thing - the Word of God. Smith was known widely for moving in the resurrecting power of God, as he healed and raised people from the dead. Is there a connection? I would say so.

I reflect back so often to the life of the early shepherds tending their flock. Life wasn't simple for them, I am sure, and it had its complexities, but life was much more simplified than the life we have today. There were not the overt forces seeking to sway, control and manipulate that we have now.

With the rise of the computerization of our society, people have in themselves become like computers. Very mental. Full of knowledge, and full of clutter. Knowing everything about nothing.

To simplify our lives means that we need to let go of so much of what we have fed on in the past. Let Him be our feeding, our life and our sustenance.

As we first began making this transition from the church into the "beginnings of this new day" we were constantly admonished to "let go".

So often we would go back to the Lord and ask, "Let go of what?" Or, "are we done yet?" Often the response was, "Not yet; you need to let go – <u>more</u>". The more we were able to simplify our lives and let go of the trappings of this age; the greater became our capacity to see. But before you go on a "witch hunt", just realize that the Lord must even reveal to you what He wants you to let go of.

You may think that it is pretty obvious what you need to work on. That may be true, but I know that until the Lord reveals to you in the spirit expressly what you need to do, you will only be able to achieve a measure. This process of simplification can really only be done when you work in concert with the Lord and allow Him to show you. He will tell you what needs to go; whether attachments, concepts, bonds etc. When He shows you, then you are able to shed it; as the weight that it has been to you.

We are cutting the last ties, as a people, to this world system. We are cutting the moorings that are holding the ship back. You were never a part of this age, so why do you hold anything dear. Just let it go, it was never a part of you anyway.

This step in the simplification of your life and "letting go" is one of the "simplest" yet one of the most powerful keys that we have seen.

Auras

This is a topic that we do not want to dwell much upon here; but it is important for you to understand that <u>everyone</u> can see auras.

I know, you say that is not possible. I have never seen an aura in my life. But I would disagree. You are seeing, you have just not yet recognized it.

The easiest way to see an aura is to have someone stand silhouetted against a white wall. Then relax your eyes, and do not look directly at that person. Look with what I would call a "soft focus".

Relax and do your breathing exercises.

Let go in your mind. Stop trying. Breathe, and relax.

<u>Allow yourself to see</u>, and you will see. It may not at first be the quality of what you are hoping for, but you will begin to see, because you must understand <u>it is your spirit that sees</u>. You may at first see just from the periphery of your eyes, but take heart, you are beginning to see.

More than we understand, this transition into the seer anointing is a function of learning your spirit and beginning to see and to hear through the faculties of your spirit. You are laying aside the limitations of your physical being. You are beginning to connect with your spirit. This is a major step forward into the manifestation of sonship.

You can all see, but like we spoke of earlier in visualizing, "you must see yourself doing this". Do not visualize the opposite. Do not think of yourself as one who is not a seer; who cannot see.

Perhaps this is easier said then done for many. You must break your own concepts of yourself. That's right! You are not allowed to lock yourself in. Not when God has said that He has given you EVERYTHING pertaining to life and godliness.

Just for the record let's quote this. This should be the foundation of your meditation - every day.

> **...seeing that His divine power has granted to us everything pertaining to life and godliness, through the true knowledge of Him who called us by His own glory and excellence. – 2 Peter 1:3**

This promise is not just for your brother or your sister, this promise is for you. You have been given everything. You are equipped. You may not have gone to the bank yet and cashed the check, <u>but God has made the deposit.</u>

OK. Now that we have this established, what do you do with what you see. Like everything that comes to you from the Lord, you make notes. Study what comes to you. Study what you begin to see. Your sight and your vision is a unique expression of who you are in Christ. You must realize that it will be different for everyone; for each of you are a unique handiwork or creation of God.

If you have a gift of "seeing auras", then that is another challenge. You cannot fall back on what you have known. Everything must be spiritually appraised. We cannot get into a mode of assuming that what you knew yesterday, born of the soul or the "partial", will be the same today.

It is an exciting time in which we walk. As every aspect of your being continues to come alive, you will see and you will hear and you will experience God on levels you never dreamed of before. How does the word go? "Eye has not seen, nor has ear heard of those things which God has prepared for those that love Him." (1 Cor 2:9). We cannot imagine enough. But we can sure give it "the good 'ol college try".

This is not the time to dive more deeply into talking about the colors of the aura or other manifestations you will see. Whatever comes to you must be interpreted in the spirit; and often what you see will be tailored just for you. As this opens up for you, write to Anne and myself. Perhaps we can be a voice of confirmation to what the Lord is showing you.

Journaling

Perhaps one of the most important aspects to developing your spiritual sensitivity and perception is what we call "journaling"; basically "making notes". You have probably heard the term.

I am surprised at how many people of God do not take exhaustive notes of what the Lord is speaking to them or showing them. It is crucial. As the word goes…if you are faithful in a little He will make you ruler over 10 cities.

> **"And he said to him, 'Well done, good slave, because you have been faithful in a very little thing, you are to be in authority over ten cities.' – Luke 19:17**

That scripture sounds like a mouthful, but the principle is faithfulness. Take what He gives you and walk in it faithfully; according to what He is showing you.

Do you want more visions and more dreams? Do you want Him to speak to you more frequently? Then a simple and important step is to keep a journal.

What was Joshua commanded? To meditate both night and day upon His word (Joshua 1:8). This must be our command. As we wait before Him, we meditate upon His word, (which includes the dreams, the visions and the personal directives or words that He has given us).

Often what we receive from the Lord comes in fragmented pieces. A little here, a little there. "Line upon line", as Isaiah spoke. We have found that as we have continued to make notes and track on what the Lord is speaking, that sometimes years will pass before we really get a clear understanding or picture of what He was revealing to us. We have noticed that sometimes the pieces of the puzzle come together gradually, but the understanding and clarity does eventually come.

Had we not faithfully recorded every word, every vision, every dream, we would not have been able to "connect the dots" and understand. Sometimes the truths spanned many years or events unfolding in the earth, and without an ongoing record, we would not have been able to perceive the thread of what the Lord was speaking.

We cannot encourage you enough to write everything down that He shows you. Track on it. Study it, and gradually the Lord will fit the pieces of the puzzle together. In this process He is training your spirit and your soul, and you are becoming. It is fascinating how the Lord moves. While He seems to be doing one thing, He accomplishes a dozen things.

As you track with the Lord in the spirit, you are constantly changing. You are hearing more and more as your vibration continues to come up higher. You are learning to recognize His voice more clearly. You are seeing the threads and patterns. You are connecting it all together as you see Him unfold His plan in the earth. In the process, He is training you to "see", and He is training you to "hear".

People have asked us how to learn the voice of the Lord. It is more simple than you know. Keep a record and monitor what He shows you. If you are faithful with a little, He will give you more; much, much more.

You will find that you will begin to see more and hear more if you are diligent. If you want to see in the spirit more, you just need to monitor everything that comes to you; even the faintest glimpses. The more you monitor and track on everything, the more it will open up for you.

You are His sons; you are the sons of Light. As we see the darkness continuing to spread upon the earth, we know there is a light coming to dispel it; and that light is within you. You are the Sons of Light - the Sons of God.

Worship

Worship is at the heart of our lives. Worship is at the root of all that we are. Our lives are truly a worship unto the Lord. We will only touch on this briefly because worship is already an integral part of your life.

First of all we must realize that everything we do, visualize, imagine, breathe, journal, see auras, it doesn't matter what, it all emanates from a heart that is full of worship for the Lord. We love Him more deeply than life itself.

Worship is a wonderful way to lift your vibration. It bypasses the mind or soul. Worship doesn't need to be in words that we know, worship can be in tongues, or worship can be just standing before Him quietly; speechless.

If you tune in closely enough, you can hear the worship that is going on day and night in the spirit.

I know the word speaks that our lives are a living worship before Him. As Paul speaks in Romans; we present to the Lord our lives as a living and acceptable mode of worship.

> **Therefore I urge you, brethren, by the mercies of God, to present your bodies a living and holy sacrifice, acceptable to God, *which is* your spiritual service of worship. – Romans 12:1**

Yes, our lives are a worship to Him. And the more we let go of this world in every way within our being, the more we are that living worship to Him.

There are not enough pages created that can underscore what worship means to His sons. Since we are talking about modes of perception in this brief workshop, we must understand that all roads lead to His presence. Everything we do, and in every aspect of our being and walk before Him, it all leads to one place; His Presence.

For with thee *is* the fountain of life: in thy light shall we see light. –Psa 36:9

but if we walk in the Light as He Himself is in the Light, we have fellowship with one another, and the blood of Jesus His Son cleanses us from all sin. – 1 Jn 1:7

You must realize that in His presence we see everything; for in His light, we shall see light. In His light we experience a oneness with all of God's kingdom, and a true fellowship and worship in the spirit.

What is worship but our standing in His presence; and in His presence, we see everything.

In Conclusion

There is no real conclusion that we can add to this book except to say that the only conclusion is the full embodiment of Christ within His people. This is the time for the true Manifestation of the Sons of God, and the experience of the resurrection within a people.

You may contact us at **www.SonsOfGod.com** for any questions you may have.

At our website you can sign up for our email notification system and we will gladly notify you when we post at our site; which is on-going, or when our next publication is available.

We will continue to develop what we have presented within the pages of this book. You will find additional postings of our writing in the unique section (www.SonsofGod.com/furtherteaching) we have created to provide supplemental teaching to this book.

For over 35 years we have walked before the Lord, in pursuit of resurrection life. As Paul speaks in Phil 3; to lay hold of that for which also we have been laid hold of by Christ Jesus.

Anne and I have ministered in new testament, non-denominational churches for many of those years until He called us outside the camp, some 12 years ago. God was getting ready to do something new, and as new wineskins, a much deeper work and preparation was needed within our hearts.

For the past 12 years He has taught us many things; as He exposed us to many trains of thought. All of it has led us to this time, the time He is completing His work within His people.

Edward & Anne

Topical Index

A

abandonment 41, 51, 159
abiding 68, 74, 116, 174-5, 282, 286, 290, 292, 324
  spiritual 126
ability 14, 41, 44-6, 48, 51-2, 112, 115, 161, 163, 179-82, 186, 188-90, 216, 239, 248, 259-60
  greater 234
abominations 191, 195
Abraham 200
Absolute Surrender 155
acceleration 150
accomplishes 331
accountability 156, 312
accusations 161
act
  religious 212
  repetitive 242
  sovereign 190
activity 88
  spiritual 301
Adam 8, 14, 28, 38, 201-2, 212, 237, 240-2
Adamic 193, 199
Adamic lineage 199
Adamic nature 20, 63, 74, 190, 198-9, 201, 277, 311
administration 6, 14, 84, 98, 106, 133-7, 139, 141, 143, 145, 147, 149-51, 266, 273, 304, 310
  new 135
Administration Suitable 6, 133-4
admonition 19, 188, 211
age to come 222
agency 35, 76, 110, 145, 163, 167, 290
agendas, hidden 111
ages 13-14, 16, 20, 36-7, 54-5, 71-5, 81-7, 91-3, 101-2, 108-10, 166-7, 233-4, 237-40, 242-4, 258-9, 326-7
  apostate 108
  the conflict of the 258
  new 12-13, 18, 37, 53, 65, 92, 94
  passing 229, 244-5
  present 135, 157-8, 194, 236, 244, 258, 264
agreement 142, 161, 180-1, 241
  soulish 143
Anakim 266-7
ancestry 6, 171, 198-201
  personal 198
anchors 19, 181, 211, 247, 311
Ancient of Days 149, 263
angelic beings 319
angels 11, 18, 35, 37, 43, 45, 55, 114, 137, 195, 204, 209, 229, 248, 288, 302
  fallen 114, 147-8
anger 52, 178, 192
anguish 61, 101
ankles 159, 164, 185, 229
anoint 41, 46
anointed cloth 112
anointing 41, 53-5, 61, 112, 116, 135, 158, 186, 212, 301, 303-5
  burning 306
  deep 255
  great 55

seer 106, 118, 259, 311, 328
apostasy 192
Apostle Paul 17
apostles 23, 100, 305
appropriation 299
area
  crown 301
ark 6, 63, 97, 130
arm 212, 303-5
  holy 304
  upper 304
Armaggedon 235, 265
army 21, 36, 39, 57, 69, 100-1, 264-5
  great 169
army of god 37
ascend 103
ascendancy 31-2, 293
  absolute 293
ascension 67, 93, 293
assault 252, 255, 300, 307-8, 325
  direct 298, 303, 305-6
  intense 302
assimilate 233, 290
assimilating 303, 326
atmosphere 130, 143, 318-20
  earths 318
  personal 320
  right 51
attachments 127, 176-7, 183, 185-6, 188-91, 193, 196, 219, 255, 327
attributes 290, 318
auras 7, 106, 309-11, 313, 328-9, 332
authority 24, 32-3, 35, 39, 54, 62, 92-3, 134-7, 140, 156-60, 195, 256-9, 262-3, 297-8, 304-5, 322
  given 161, 298
Authority/Kingship 305
awakening 109-10, 115, 233, 292
awareness 73-5, 93, 102-3, 105, 116, 120, 127, 158, 162, 174, 176, 182, 220-1, 262, 281, 283
  great 106
  growing 180, 221
  spiritual 7, 294, 309, 311
Azusa Street 42, 69, 282
Azusa street experience 23, 103-4

B

baby 60-2
Babylon 190-1, 195, 219, 221, 227
  religious 219
Babylonian system 191
backwards 205
baggage 17, 103, 181-2, 188, 198, 200, 224, 236
  persons 182
balance 83, 91, 93, 160, 167
banking institutions 145
banking system 145
baptism 42, 68-9, 103-4, 143
  deeper 230, 247
  new 17
baptism experience 42
barriers 55, 137, 158, 176, 297
  creating 17
basic keys 312
baton 5, 15-16, 19, 185, 210

INDEX - 333

334 – INDEX

battle 21, 38, 101, 189, 214, 245, 252, 260-1, 265-6
  spiritual 315
battle array 37, 39
battlefield 21
beachhead 21-3, 278
  great 22
  last 21
beast 41, 43-5, 47, 270
  the 172
beat 136, 168
  powerful 315
beatitudes 42, 287
to become 181
beholding 28, 76
being changed 183
beings, energetic 115
Belial 180-1, 185, 194
belief 12, 247, 310
belief systems 14, 42, 111, 160, 192, 224, 234, 242, 275
believer 18, 23, 35, 41-2, 49, 65, 67-9, 73, 98, 103-5, 110, 126, 157, 180-1, 194-5, 280
  lukewarm 207
believing 34, 120, 228, 230, 245, 256, 263, 273
believing to *see* 230
Bible prophecy 278
bibles 22, 151
birth 13, 60-6, 102, 121, 148, 227, 229-30, 232-3, 242, 246, 285
  given 60
birth-pangs 91, 257
birthing 8, 47, 60, 62, 76, 101, 129, 149, 156, 271
birthing process 61, 64
bitter 45, 50
bitterness 52, 214
blameless 14
  preserved 31, 282, 288
blatant 62, 100
blessings 31, 102, 113, 124, 177-8, 185
blind 187, 204-6, 212, 232-3
blindness 44, 136, 150, 186-7
blocks 35, 85, 182, 301, 322
blood 154, 179, 190, 195-6, 237, 270, 272, 276, 333
blood structure 272
body 8-10, 31-2, 44, 50-1, 106, 163, 216-17, 243, 270-1, 276, 280-6, 288-9, 294-9, 302, 307, 319-20
  believer"s 294
  healthier 319
  imperishable 271
  incorruptible 272
  natural 271
  perishable 271
  resurrected 293
  spiritual 271
Body of Christ 39
bond-servants 214, 303
bondage 8, 79, 137
bonds 14, 29, 32, 105, 107, 136-7, 172-4, 176-94, 196, 198-202, 219-21, 261-2, 273, 300, 311-12, 321
  break 221
  breaking 222
  detriment 179
  existence of 177, 180, 182-3
  incorrect 178
Bonds & Vampires 6, 171, 173
bondservants 318
bondwoman 201-2
Book of Present Realities 123
Book of Promises 123, 256
Book of Realities 256
born again 23, 233
boundaries 68, 238
Bowels 306
brain 315, 320, 325
branch 124
  new 200
Braxton-Hicks 62
bread 54, 106, 196
breathes 218, 315-16, 323, 328, 332
breathing 314-16
  controlled 314
  deep 315
  slow 315
  slower 315
breathing exercises 328
bride 68, 120, 192, 216
  complete 105
bridge 193-4, 226, 308
brighter 23
  shines 23
brightness 101, 117
bronze 146
bruising 304
burial 45-7
bypasses 46, 332

C

Caleb 149, 266-7
Calvin, John 22
camp 101, 151, 204, 211, 334
  outside the 44, 204
can a nation be born in a day 189
Canaan 148-9
canopy 91, 150, 237-40, 244
capabilities 108, 148, 163, 228, 232
  great 149
  innate 229
capacity 87, 115, 136, 161, 193, 220, 226, 283, 327
  greater 188
captives 71, 158, 253, 318, 323
Captives Free 5, 85
carefulness 319
carnal Christian 292
carnal mind 31, 227, 229, 235
casting down 73, 138
casualties 23, 189, 214
catalyst 128, 259, 261
  spiritual 129
Catholic church 22
caught up 39
ceasing 47, 127, 261
  pray without 126
cedars of Lebanon 36, 84
cell 17, 320
  jail 243
century 23, 42, 225, 272, 282, 294
cerebral cortex 325
chains 38, 174, 242, 254
  long daisy 174

chakra 44, 316
changes
  accelerated 48, 157, 159
  entire 29
  greatest 150
changing 28-30, 33, 49, 72, 74, 76, 88, 93,
      126, 131, 135, 156, 160, 226, 231,
      272
channel time 275
channels 35, 39, 54, 138, 196, 216, 234,
      261-2, 300-1, 322, 324-5
  human 134
  perfect 237
  physical 260
  scientific 140
chapters, last 53, 65, 115, 145, 151, 197
cheekbone 303
child 64, 86, 115, 137, 229, 233, 252, 285,
      304
  male 64, 285
childbirth 10, 60-1, 65, 77, 286
  experienced 60
  pangs of 14, 61
children 10, 60, 75, 130, 140, 168, 184,
      199, 202, 217, 300
children of God 10, 60, 77, 79
chord, deep 257
Christ 8-11, 31-40, 79-84, 86-8, 121-4, 126-
      31, 137-9, 174-5, 177-81, 183-6, 200-
      2, 216-18, 253-5, 283-5, 289-93, 295-
      8
  authority of 98, 134-5, 159, 163, 258
  body of 100, 216
  bride of 17, 212
  crucified 196
  dominion of 151, 310
  embodiment of 54, 123
  fivefold ministry of 100
  followed 8
  full stature of 114, 128
  gospels 94
  identical with 89
  Jesus 8, 34, 248, 271
  manifestation of 81, 254, 282
  mind of 229-30, 247
  ministry of 54, 84, 151, 157, 216-18, 253,
      255, 258, 261, 273
  mystical sufferings of 218
  obedience of 158, 323
  priesthood ministry of 126-7
  raised 274
  recognized 53
  revelation of 35, 45
  ruling and reigning of 255
  the Spirit of 9, 54, 283
  unlimitedness of 89, 202
Christ company 129, 256
Christ Jesus 9, 11, 159, 214, 334
Christ living in you 88
Christ ministering 127
Christian 233
Christian believer 173, 291
Christian circles 12, 17, 99, 263
Christian world 57, 196
Christianity 41-2, 155, 237
  complacent 256
  mainstream 100
  orthodox 162
Christians 12, 34, 63

soulish 31
Christs, false 239
Christ's afflictions 216
Christ's authority 261
Christs administration 21
Christs appearance 53
Christs authority 134-6, 155, 304
  administrating 136
  manifestation of 138, 230
Christs blood 177
Christs death 67
Christs dominion 139
Christs ministry 98, 253
Christs parousia 286
Christs release 298
Christs victory 293, 298
church 12-13, 17-18, 22-3, 34, 41-2, 44, 62,
      69, 83, 104-5, 112, 134, 179-80, 195-
      6, 204, 207
  early 126
  nondenominational 334
church age 68, 120, 128, 143, 293
church hierarchy 99
church world 88, 224
cities 67, 101, 175, 270, 330
  abandoned 199
  great fortified 266
clay 78, 146-7
  common 146-7
  potter's 146
Cleanse 182
cleanser, greatest 319
cliff 124, 175
climatic changes 91
clothes 41, 46, 89, 168
Cloud 25, 88
Cloud of Witnesses 8, 18-19, 66, 70, 72-3,
      75, 82-3, 87-90, 104, 139, 159, 163,
      225, 255, 259, 261-2
clouds 18, 30, 36, 38, 55, 100, 150, 181-2,
      244, 256, 277, 320
co-creators 160, 163, 246, 323-4
  becoming 128
co-exist 115, 241
cocoon 311
coexistence 247
cognitive process, entire 232
Colossians 77, 227, 280
Come Alive 7, 279
comfort zone 219
coming 12-13, 16-19, 34-6, 38, 46, 48-9,
      67-9, 88-90, 110-11, 165-7, 212-14,
      260-2, 282-9, 295-7, 299-303, 305-7
coming judgments 72
command 67, 126, 330
commitment 60, 156, 233
  real 155
commodity 43, 187
  most precious 186
commonplace 224
communication 105, 111-12, 167, 235
  basic audible 112
  increased 111
  true 112
communion 201, 222
community, scientific 320
company 18, 277-8
  most holy 18
complacency 34-5

complaining 50, 214
completion 16, 30, 32, 48-52, 62, 64-5, 91,
    149, 160, 216-17, 228, 230, 252-3,
    255, 280, 282-3
  final 29
complexities 326
comprehending 64
comprehension 185, 232
computerization 327
computers 102-3, 106, 327
concepts 6, 28-9, 31-2, 74, 103, 109, 111-
    13, 124, 127, 155-7, 162, 171, 248,
    262, 264-5, 327-8
  common 161
  glorified 56
  religious 142
  unique 51
concert 50, 115, 145, 151, 324, 327
concerted effort 166
condemnation 9
conditioning 151, 184, 191, 193, 228, 233-
    4, 238-9, 263, 310
  deep 229, 239
  negative 242
  religious 191
  restrictive 224
  subconscious 242
conduits 177, 194
confirmation 8, 329
conflict 40, 94, 135, 252, 255, 257-61, 263
  inner 57
  internal 252
  spiritual 305, 308
conflicts, deep 211
conformity 276, 286
confound 36, 270
confrontation 130
confusion 151, 186, 275, 306
congregation 37, 253
conjunction 5, 16, 71-2, 74-5, 110-11, 294,
    314
conjunction of ages 13-14, 72, 74, 91, 109-
    10, 173
Conjunction of Ages 5, 71, 73, 75, 77, 79,
    81, 83, 85, 87, 89, 91, 93, 95
connection 82, 92, 193, 198, 282, 301, 326
  body/soul 290
  closer 92
  greater 91
  intrinsic 79
  mind/body 325
conquering 40
  great 39
consciousness 77, 90, 94, 102, 120, 166-7,
    175, 206, 224, 243, 247, 263, 282,
    292
  collective 90, 167
  global 247
  new 17, 281
  physical 281
  present 271
contacts 88, 176-7, 191, 194, 299-301, 334
  male 299
contending 28, 189, 256
context 46, 53-4, 173, 324
control 21-2, 32-3, 62, 91-3, 100, 136, 145,
    148-50, 159-60, 219, 230, 238, 242,
    314, 318, 326-7
  lost 318

real 245
convergence 173, 261
convey 60, 291
  gospels 158
convey oppression 178
conveyance 112-13
cords 157, 174, 176-7, 181, 190, 272, 312
cords of the wicked 176
Corinthians 77, 181, 270-1
correlation, direct 91, 183, 285
corruption 10, 60, 77, 79
cost 20, 41, 186, 211, 277
Council 98
country 62, 135, 147, 169, 238, 292
  high 266-7
  hill 266
couple 190
covenant 48, 130
Covet 207
Crawling & Itching 307
create concepts 262
create illusion 247
create life 323
creation 5, 8, 10, 14, 17, 19, 37, 59-63, 65,
    67-9, 72, 76-84, 86, 88-95, 160-1,
    288
  dawning of 114, 277
  new 29-30, 32-3, 213, 270-1
  order of 28-9, 94, 290
  orders of 83, 94
creation groaneth 79
creative process 162-3
Creative Word 6, 153, 155-9, 161, 163,
    165, 167, 169
cries, unspoken 99
cross dodger 50
crowns 37, 284, 301
crux 159, 183, 232
culmination 16, 24, 60, 216, 253-4
cultures 192, 224-5, 233, 237, 297, 316-17
cup overflows 169
currents 177
  electrical 177
cursory understanding 147

D

Daniel 30, 57, 115, 117, 146-7, 149-50,
    210, 263-4, 277, 318
Daniels" vision 149
dark side 173
darkness 38, 45, 63, 100, 118, 130, 135-6,
    148, 150, 166, 180-1, 185, 237, 240,
    246, 255-6
  deep 240
  great 44, 240
  pit of 150
  present 91, 148, 150, 184
  sons of 148, 150, 252
  thick 38, 100, 256
date set by the Father 252
daughters 18, 44, 104, 108, 129, 147, 173,
    178, 180, 182, 190, 219, 221, 290,
    294
David 168, 209
dawn 23, 38, 100, 209, 256
dawning 53, 167
Day of Pentecost 68
Day of Reversal 6, 153

INDEX - 337

days 18, 44, 53-5, 67, 74, 79, 126, 145-6, 148-9, 166-7, 169-70, 199-200, 252-3, 263-4, 275, 284-5
  consecutive 242
  final 8
  last 54, 83, 108, 134, 145-7, 166, 168
  reversal of 167, 169
days of Sodom 137, 166, 204
Dead Sea scrolls 272
deadness 102, 242
death 9, 11, 18, 23, 38-9, 45-6, 50-1, 74, 154, 179, 214, 265, 273, 290, 293, 323-4
  ministering 273
  physical 273, 290
  process of 47, 51, 273
the death of his godly ones 49
deception 34-5, 45, 109, 150, 166, 240, 244, 247-8, 255, 275
  great 45
  rampant 239
decision 43, 142, 155
decreasing quality 318
deeds 9, 204
  unfruitful 135
Deep Breathing Techniques 314
defenses 21, 101
delay 6, 53, 138, 171, 173, 175, 177, 179, 181, 183, 185, 187, 189, 191, 210, 248
deliverance 8, 76-7, 80, 82, 156, 190, 193, 201-2, 227-30, 233, 246, 259, 304
  complete 243
  deep 193
  deeper 235
  miracle 304
delivery 14, 63
demands 17, 48, 52, 122, 130-1, 154-5, 211, 217
  progressive 154
demonic assault 302
demons 62, 139, 173, 187, 253
demons shudder 125
demoralization 34
  progressive 166
denomination 23
departure 214
  radical 119
destiny 39-40, 69, 81, 89-90, 110, 114, 128, 148, 197, 215, 246, 258, 262, 289, 298
destroy 35, 55, 75, 136, 158, 166, 168, 179, 216, 245, 324
destroy fortresses 183
destroy humanity 148
destroy mankind 139
destroy principalities 183
destruction 50, 64, 158, 167, 317
deterrent, greatest 173-4
Deuteronomy 140
devastation 137
devils 42, 195, 286
devour 61, 64, 101, 179
dialogue 105, 167
dichotomy 62, 216, 238
diet 7, 309, 313, 317-19, 321
  vegetarian 319
difference 16, 35, 56, 135, 157, 180, 210, 238, 260, 273, 281, 325

distinct 324
diligent 106, 331
dimension 31, 44, 81, 83-4, 90, 92-3, 109, 111, 175, 227, 229-30, 235, 238
  higher 319
  physical 108
  spiritual 229
dimensional levels 175
direction 118, 143, 210, 218, 321
directives 56
  personal 330
directs 94, 324
  lord 143, 256, 264
disagree 161, 328
disarray, great 199
discern 36, 73, 82, 110, 128, 182, 231, 239, 245, 248, 259-60, 297, 310
discernment 188, 302
disciples 42, 67, 83, 94, 102, 119-22, 136, 175, 184, 264, 272, 277, 289
  early 67-8
  go and make 136
discipleship 154-5
distortions 31
distractions 138, 315, 318
divinity 161, 316
DNA 29, 276
DNA change 272
DNA structure 272
doctrine 13, 34, 42, 50, 68, 75, 186, 293
domain 227
dominion 39, 62, 79, 98, 119, 135, 160, 183, 230, 256, 258, 285
domino effect 249, 263, 318
doors 104, 243, 281, 311
  closed 73, 99, 136, 296
  open 143
dormant 273-4
  lain 56
dragon 55, 61, 64, 101, 137, 166, 255, 317
  paper 245
dreams 103, 105-6, 108, 110-11, 113, 117, 146, 211, 281-2, 318, 324, 330-1
  dream 104, 108, 294
  experiencing 105
Dreams & Visions 6, 97
drive 12, 23-4, 107, 128, 131, 143, 150, 156, 158-9, 206, 211-13, 219, 262, 265-7, 273, 283
  deep 210
  diligent 228
dross 52, 213
dual-consciousness 73
dual-existence 73
duality 243, 255
dwelling 39, 68, 81, 199, 285-6, 312
dynamic effect 217
dynamics 52, 77, 82, 93, 95, 140, 173-4, 192, 198, 225-6, 232, 281, 311, 322
  internal 123
  right 51

E

eagle, great 317
ears 167, 183, 234-5, 240, 248, 295, 300-2, 329
  tickle 256

338 – INDEX

earth 13-14, 21-2, 34-7, 60-3, 68-9, 82-8, 90-3, 114-15, 117-22, 134-40, 149-51, 165-7, 217-18, 253-5, 284-5, 317-18
  physical 14, 284
  in the 119
earth changes 14, 36, 63, 74
earth planes 138, 261
earth quakes 101
earthly bodies 271
Eden 38, 101, 256
edge of the envelope 281
effectiveness 128, 260, 298
  deep 262
effectual 257, 273
Egypt 54
elbow 304
elders 37, 99
electricity 177
electronics 106
elemental beings 83
elemental kingdom 5, 91-3
elemental world 93
elementals 71, 91-3, 139
  neutral 94
elementals approach 277
elements, last 276, 287
Elijah 99, 101, 110, 221, 277
elimination 20, 305
Elisha 99, 101, 136
embodiment 13, 55, 131-2
embracing 17, 23, 51
Emergence 18, 157
Emergence of Sonship 5, 27, 29, 31, 33, 35, 37, 39, 41, 43, 45, 47, 49, 51, 53, 55
Emmaus 289
emotional responses 178
emotions 49, 111-12, 177, 228, 232, 244, 300, 306
End of Illusion 6, 244
end-time events 275
endowment 31, 81, 159
  great 56
  greatest 259
endure 48-9, 101, 146, 213
enemy 21, 36, 39-40, 78, 124, 134, 151, 163, 169, 189, 194, 255, 258, 297-8, 300-1, 303-5
  greatest 234
  last 39
  man's 178-9
enemy"s devices 138
energy 73-4, 78, 82, 91, 111-12, 114, 129-31, 141, 150, 167, 172-4, 179, 186, 235, 320, 326
  electrical 320
  field of 174
  negative 172
  transmit 112
energy field 175
energy of Christ 130-1
energy vortex centers 44
enlightenment 106, 281
  simultaneous 297
enmity 234-5
enormity 56-7, 109
entanglements 191
entities 91, 94, 186

separate 291
entity, single 80
entrance 34, 198-9, 213, 289
  backdoor 184
entrenchment 238
environment 100
envisioning 322
Ephesians 37, 81, 98, 134, 150, 266, 325
Ephesus 112
era, new 21
eschatology 12
esoteric concept 49
esoteric theory 281
establishment 99, 101
estate, lowly 270
evangelical 187
evangelism 137, 292
  greatest 150
evangelists 23, 100, 305
Eve 8, 14, 212
everlasting Father 305
evil 35-6, 55, 73, 75, 91, 94, 109, 135, 138, 147, 149-50, 167, 173, 238, 247-8, 310
  great 149
evil entities 260
excellence 121, 329
execute 38, 149, 151, 254
execute vengeance 37, 254
execution 37, 135, 150, 305
exertion 70, 276, 287
exiles 87, 169, 230
existence 13, 32, 37, 40, 46, 78, 80, 102, 112, 116, 173-6, 229, 246, 255, 271, 289
  human 29
  new 151
  physical 32, 116
  plane of 38, 77, 102, 120-1, 123, 174, 219, 272
  present 244
  unlimited 84
  very 118
expanse 117, 175
  greatest 36
expectation 79, 121, 178, 182, 194, 272
experience 45, 50-2, 60, 73-4, 80-3, 85-8, 92, 103-6, 110-13, 120-2, 184-6, 219-22, 225-8, 234-5, 281-2, 294-7
  deeper 310
  linear 76
  present 17
  progressive 295
explosion 128-9
exponential 266
exponential release 30, 142-3
expose 135-6, 247, 296
exposing 73, 136, 296
exposure 30, 191
  child"s 233
exult 37, 254
eye of the needle 188
eye salve 46
eyes 13, 35-7, 41, 44, 82-3, 86-7, 106, 159, 221-2, 225, 232-5, 244-6, 255, 289-90, 302-3, 328-9
  given 19, 222
  physical 106
  seeing 87

INDEX - 339

spiritual 235
third 316
Eyes & Forehead 302
EYESALVE 41
eyesight 182
  given 232
  physical 194
Ezekiel 75, 101, 164
Ezekiels vision 75

F

faculties 31, 242, 302, 328
fairy folk 93
by faith 198
  just lived 126
  the just shall live 22
faith 13, 16, 18-19, 35, 50, 55-7, 72-3, 79, 83, 87, 117, 127-8, 162-3, 212, 229-30, 240-1
  fight of 56, 252
  having 230
  household of 111, 201
  time frame 230
faithfulness 330
familial relationships, close 300
fascination 173
father 86, 98, 178, 180, 182, 190, 194, 200-1, 219, 221, 253
Father 37-9, 67, 80-3, 86-7, 91-3, 98-9, 116, 121-4, 129-31, 134, 138-9, 148, 160-2, 221-2, 256-8, 290
Father's house 94, 102, 138, 175, 285
Fathers family 72, 213, 221
Fathers fulfillment 214
Fathers house 35, 81, 83, 94, 106, 137, 175
Fathers inheritance 221-2
Fathers kingdom 80, 83
Fathers plan 18, 83
fear of the Lord 221
fearfulness 310
feats 108
  great 148
feeding 179, 182, 195-6, 327
feeding life 196
feeling 244, 306
fellowship 180-1, 185, 212, 333
  true 333
female contact 299
female servants 104, 108
fence 199, 260
filters 31, 232, 281, 292
finality 149, 263
finances 168, 245
fingers 276, 305
finishing 24, 52
first Adam 200-2
flame burns 38, 101, 256
flesh 8-9, 16, 19, 45, 50, 52-3, 56-7, 85, 88-90, 127, 179-80, 199-200, 237, 257, 270-2, 276
  basic 270
flesh and blood 272
flesh nature 48, 50, 52, 193
flow 82, 110, 116, 131, 140, 157-8, 164, 168, 174, 177-8, 235, 265, 322
  downward 102
  upward 167, 169
fluttering sound 302

flux 118, 145, 205, 226, 244, 246
focus, soft 328
foods 54, 75, 107, 245, 318, 320-1, 326
  high-vibration 320
  plant-based 320
  processed 319
  solid 310
  supply 54
foolishness 110
foot 102, 168, 261, 283, 304
footstool 125, 258
forearm 304
Forefinger 305
foreheads 43-5, 195, 263, 301, 303
forgive 312
fornication 195
  committed 195
fortresses 35, 158
framework 130, 227-8
free world 326
freedom 10, 33, 60, 64, 77, 81, 91, 93, 100, 156-7, 172, 185, 189, 198, 238, 253
  glorious 8
  progressive 183
  total 293
freeing ourselves 234
freewill 154-5
frequencies 141-2, 229, 314
  electronic 141
  lower 229, 319
  resonant 141-2
  spiritual 143
  unique 174
front line 5, 15, 17, 19, 21-3, 25, 40, 57, 189
  the 21
Front of Neck 301
fruitfulness 70
fruition 154, 287
fruits 31, 48
  based 320
  first 10, 38, 60, 77, 201, 284, 286
fulfillment 18, 54-6, 62, 64-5, 82-3, 147-50, 157, 210, 212-14, 222, 228-9, 244-5, 248-9, 263, 284, 322-3
  deeper 227
  external 183
fullness 84, 98, 123-4, 126, 128, 133-4, 139, 150, 154, 261, 266
  day of his 87
fullness of Christ 128, 229, 257
fullness of the times 135
function 45, 91, 102, 105-6, 114, 127, 130, 134, 139, 178, 180, 182-3, 235, 254, 282, 291-2
Functioning Priesthood 6, 97, 126
Fuse 7, 251, 258
futility 8, 10, 14, 60, 65, 77, 81, 93, 156, 163, 168, 265
future tense 263

G

Galatia 179
Galatian church 179
garden 241-2
garden of Eden 38, 101, 256
garments, white 41, 46
gate 78, 164, 260, 298
  north 164

outer 164
genealogy 200-1
generations 13, 38, 56, 62-3, 69, 82, 100, 113, 135, 166, 210, 256, 264, 278, 280, 294
  hostile 216
  last 262
Genesis 53, 147, 304
Gentiles 82, 280
geophysical level 12
gifts 24, 177, 207, 212, 227, 259, 329
  greatest 186, 259
Gifts of Revelation 188
glass dimly 77
globe 81, 237
  entire 68
gloom 38, 100, 256
glorification 47, 49, 57, 65, 67, 156-7, 196, 230, 262, 278, 294, 307
glory 10, 22, 28-9, 45-6, 54-6, 63-4, 76-7, 79, 82, 88, 121-2, 187-9, 228, 270-1, 275-6, 280
glory of God 20, 126, 300
goal 69-70, 148, 292, 312
God 8-14, 16-28, 30-58, 60-6, 72-90, 102-24, 126-32, 138-52, 154-64, 184-94, 196-202, 204-8, 224-40, 252-8, 260-6, 280-92
God-head 156
God of peace 280, 288
Godhead 13, 122, 255, 290
godliness 116, 121, 196, 243, 257, 328-9
God's creation 102
God's movement 155
Gods 17, 21, 24, 35, 39-40, 53-4, 57, 70, 109-10, 168, 192-3, 233, 252-3, 262-3, 283, 310-11
  minds of 190, 248
  preceded 104
Gods agenda 155, 254
Gods army 87
Gods completion 30, 88
Gods creation 81, 90, 92-3, 95
Gods dealings 79, 212
Gods instruments 63
Gods intent 8, 56, 85, 274
Gods involvement 283
Gods joy 36
Gods judgment flows 197
Gods kingdom 72, 80, 92, 103, 138, 237, 295, 333
Gods kings 14
Gods message 35
Gods outpouring 108
Gods plan 145, 243
Gods process 49
Gods restoration 13, 310
Gods seers 160
Gods sons 30-2, 35-6, 43-5, 53-6, 62, 64-5, 86-7, 126-9, 135-6, 148, 151, 167, 172-3, 195-6, 221, 236-7
  awaited 286
  awaiting 98
  hearts of 64, 85
  limited 30
Gods Spirit 109-10, 154, 294
Gods truth 22
Gods Word 56, 210, 225
Gods worshippers 192

gold 41, 46, 49, 146, 195, 213
golden cup 195
Gomorrah 137, 166, 204
gospel 23, 55, 90, 102, 151, 272
gospel of the kingdom 151
governments 62, 145-7, 149, 238, 247, 304
grace 54, 56, 159, 266, 277, 289
grave-clothes 89
gravity 140, 243
Greek lore 148
groan 286
groaning 10, 12, 19, 60, 64, 83, 91, 122, 128, 190, 254, 257
  deep 64
ground 73, 141, 154, 167
  new 53, 197, 235
guard 93, 135, 182, 189, 323
guardians 86, 98, 253

H

habits 242
HARLOTS 195
harmonics 141
harmony 180-1, 185, 194
harness 108, 291, 324
harvest 36, 84
has been judged 253
hasten 14, 48-9
hastening 51, 106
Hawaiian Islands 94
head 63, 169, 194-5, 246, 300-1, 304
healing 89, 108, 112, 304
heart pains 298
heart-sickness 245
hearts 11-13, 16-17, 19-22, 39-40, 45-6, 67-8, 85-6, 98-9, 111-12, 154-7, 162, 189-90, 193, 205, 207-9, 219-21
  depicts God"s 222
  human 257
  openness of 13, 204
heat 174
  intense 174
Heavenly Father 147
heavens 16, 21, 36, 39, 55, 67, 76, 78, 81, 83-5, 101-2, 136-7, 175, 248, 261-2, 286
  passed thru the 175
heaviness 307, 319
Hebrews 16, 18, 72, 83, 85, 104, 116, 127, 168, 222, 230, 243
Hebron 266
heightened level 296, 316
heightened time 117
heirs 10, 86, 201, 217, 252
  fellow 10, 217
heirs of God 10, 217
helicopter 141-2
Helper 116
heritage 124, 198-9, 201, 222
High Energy Lifestyle 320
high priest 200
  great 127
highest plane 113, 206
  life on the 102
  living on the 321
hinder 138, 168, 173, 181, 183, 186-7, 189, 248, 301,
hindrances 85, 137, 189, 198

great   177
greatest   172
hip   307
at his coming   283
history   41, 67, 79, 109, 276, 310
  annals of   30, 65
holiness   237, 284
holy prophets   22, 114
Holy Rollers   23
holy sacrifice   332
Holy Spirit   23, 31, 55, 61, 67, 80, 103, 114, 116, 122, 136, 161, 226, 280, 295-6, 299
honor   19, 38, 48, 106, 254
horns   149, 195, 263
Hosea   16, 209, 213
host   116, 178
  great   277
house   67, 89, 101, 115, 138, 164, 166, 168, 177, 241, 265, 286, 289
  strong man"s   137
household   178-9
housing   29, 80, 271
hovering   55, 124, 207
human beings   82, 314
human soul   105
hunger   6, 23-4, 203-4, 206-7
  insatiable   63, 206, 208
  never-ending   206
hungering   206-7
hurdle   109
  greater   18
  last   228
hurt   43, 188
Huss   22
  John   22
hypocrisy   12

I

Ichabod   126
idols   180-1
ignites   259-60
illumination   300
illusion   6, 17, 158, 162-3, 223-5, 227, 229, 231, 233, 235, 237, 239-49, 255, 273, 277, 297
  creating   244
  passing   244
  the spirit of   245, 248
illusion of separation   17, 86
image   8, 11, 28, 43, 76, 146, 179, 232, 276
  creating   322
  last   146-7, 149
image of God   161
imagery   162, 322
imagination   322, 324-5
  sanctified   322, 324
immortality   18, 229, 276, 285, 290
immunity, great   315
impart   112, 207, 311
impartation   113, 117, 196, 220, 303
  vicarious   112
impasse   168, 210
imperceptible change   266
imperfection   163
implementation   322
impressions   232
inability   29, 44-5, 131, 150, 193, 239

incarnation, present   115, 161, 163, 262, 285, 311
incorruption   290
indifference   158, 204-5, 207
indoctrination   224
indwelling   290, 323
  complete   122, 290
infinity   76, 80, 142, 174, 177
inhabitants   38, 100, 195, 256, 302
inheritance   6, 36, 72, 78, 98, 107, 109, 115, 139, 199, 203, 210, 219, 221-2, 255, 277
iniquity   34, 74, 135, 137-8, 166, 173, 204, 233
innate ability   75, 161-2
innate capacities   233, 243
inner as the outer   282
Inner Nervousness   307
inner visualizations   323
input   75, 102, 224-5, 232, 326
  soul's   31
insecurities   182
instant   185, 189, 261
Instant Sons   189
instruments   39, 128, 148, 210
  financial   174
  human   145
integration   7, 279, 288-9, 291
intelligences   37, 81, 83, 94
intensity   156, 158, 265
intent   79, 111-12, 127, 148, 161-3, 172-3, 226, 252, 322, 324
  true   110-11
intention   84, 98, 134, 161, 312
inter-connectedness   76, 79, 82-3
interact   75, 88, 94-5, 233, 286
interaction   83, 92-3, 104, 116, 145, 172, 229, 260
  greater   14
  increased   91
intercedes   10-11, 99, 124, 127
  ever lives to   127
interceding   127
intercession   6, 97, 119-22, 124-5, 127-9, 160, 210, 301
  best   129
  greatest   131
  unspoken   128
  viewed   119
intercessor   197, 301
interest   89, 147, 322, 326
  growing   93
  heightened   94
internet   112, 147
interpenetration   122, 161, 283
  complete   122
intersecting   74
interwoven   161, 238
intimidate   138, 179
iron   146-7
  fetters of   38, 254
  rod of   64, 254, 285
iron crushes   146
Isaiah   29, 33, 46, 63, 69, 113, 115, 168, 189, 230, 253, 304, 330
Isle of Patmos   156
it is Finished   124, 293

J

jab, sharp   307
jabbing, sharp   303
Jacob   166, 168
James   67, 117, 182, 241
  King   94, 106
jaws   55, 61, 303
Jehovah Jireh   70
jeopardy   41, 181, 185, 193, 197, 211, 240
  great   180
Jephunneh   266
Jeremiah   101
Jerusalem   168
Jesus   9, 21, 24, 34-5, 37, 43, 121-2, 136,
    184, 195, 209, 214, 265, 272, 291,
    294-5
Jews   265
Job 38:4a   114
Joel   12, 36, 87, 101, 104, 108-11, 117, 143,
    169, 173, 256, 282, 294
John   3, 22, 48-9, 67, 94, 113, 116, 124,
    138, 156, 158, 178, 184, 198, 213,
    277
Joseph   53-6
Joseph company   54
Joseph ministry   53-4
Josephus   67
Joshua   18, 75, 148-9, 266, 304, 330
journal   330, 332
Journaling   7, 309, 313, 330
journey   48, 307, 311
  present   264
joy   37, 114, 117, 214, 234, 254, 284
  great   243
Judah   168
Judas   67
judgment flows   264
judgmental   237
judgments   35-9, 42-3, 46, 62-3, 139, 145-
    51, 166, 186, 192-3, 195-7, 253-5,
    258-9, 261-6, 273, 285, 304
  bringing   136
  commensurate   62
  effective   157
  final   216
  ministry of   259, 273
  the time of   150, 253
judgments of God   35-6, 150, 263
juncture   69, 77, 119, 135, 143, 187, 198,
    216, 230, 255
just men made perfect   18
  spirits of   116, 277

K

keys   49, 84, 311-12, 318-19, 322, 326
  most powerful   327
king ministry   305
kingdom   6, 21-3, 38-40, 70-1, 92, 99-100,
    119-21, 126-9, 133-7, 139, 145-7,
    149, 155-9, 183-5, 263-6, 272-3
  divided   146
  down   101
  external   173
  final   147
  last   6, 133, 145, 147, 149
  mighty   147
kingdom age   104
kingdom changes   76

kingdom governance   157
kingdom level   126, 129
kingdom of God   21, 40, 62, 99, 119, 135,
    173, 175, 270, 272, 276
kings   37-8, 98-100, 102-3, 124, 135, 146,
    151, 192, 195, 200, 245, 253-4, 275,
    305, 311, 318
Kings and Priests of God   40, 245, 275
knee   21, 39, 134, 164, 304
knee bow   135
knocking   283
knowing   19, 85, 127, 129, 131, 181, 211,
    213, 228, 230-1, 239, 243, 327
knowing Christ Jesus   212
knowledge   6, 33, 97, 100, 103, 114-18,
    207, 281, 302, 327
  release of   114-15, 117
  spiritual   118
  true   121, 329
knowledge of God   158, 323

L

Lamb   18, 43, 154
land   18, 38, 65, 75, 100-1, 108, 136, 148-
    50, 248, 256, 267, 302, 304-5, 312
  distant   285
  new   312
Laodicea   204, 207
lap, last   19
Latter Rain   23
law   9, 126, 161, 168, 212, 235
  the law of God   9, 235
lawlessness   180-1, 185
layers   85-7, 89-90
  peeling   86
  removing   85
Lazarus   273
leaders   187
  electronic church   187
  preeminent   148
learning   228, 232-4, 281, 328, 331
learning curve   226
leaven   19, 36, 84, 217-18
leaves and branches   206
Lebanon   36, 84
legs   213, 266, 322
  last   19, 88
lens   220, 224, 239
  conditioned   232
let go   123, 228, 327
letter   112, 193
  physical   112
letting go   327
level
  deeper   30, 41, 62, 80, 104-5, 121, 142,
    201, 224, 227, 302, 314, 325
  higher   121
leverage   50, 156, 238, 245, 255
Levi   49, 74, 213
liberty   33, 79, 238
  commensurate   156
  proclaim   253
life   8-9, 13, 48-51, 106-7, 183-4, 186-8,
    194-6, 205-7, 243-4, 255-7, 272-4,
    284-6, 290-2, 294-7, 326-9, 332-3
lifestyle   159, 318
  spiritual   321
likeness   9, 45, 161, 214, 228

glorious 68
limitations 17, 22, 32-3, 85, 89-90, 123-4, 157-8, 169, 177, 179, 185, 202, 232-4, 237-9, 242-3, 311
limited understanding 108
lineage 199-202
  new 200
  personal 200
linear level 261
link 201-2
  missing 84
link arms 324
link hands 261
literal outpouring 294
Little Finger 305
liver 319-20
liver functions 319
living 9, 20-1, 30, 32, 40, 69-70, 73-4, 162-3, 217, 220-2, 239-40, 254, 261-4, 292, 294, 332
living expectation 70
living experience 222, 235
living expression 262
Living Father 119
Living God 36-7, 148, 157, 180-1
living reality 28, 247, 281
living temple 289
living word 85, 89-90, 158, 162-3
living worship 332
Logos 121, 241, 272, 291
long sojourn 168, 233
  very 16
longing 64, 286
  anxious 8, 10, 60, 77, 86
Lord 18-20, 28-30, 36-46, 48-53, 68-70, 105-6, 114-17, 185-96, 203-22, 264-7, 275-7, 282-5, 288-91, 303-7, 322-4, 329-32
Lord Almighty 180, 182, 190, 219, 221
Lord GOD 253
Lord Jesus 284
Lord Jesus Christ 21, 34, 39, 123, 202, 280, 288
Lord's return 275
Lordship 34, 39-40, 130, 248
Lords arm 303
love 11, 18, 63, 98, 135, 154, 157, 173, 194, 197, 204, 211, 222, 265, 329, 332
Lucifer 237
Luke 63, 119-20, 129, 137, 175, 253, 289, 303, 330
lukewarm 204, 207
lukewarmness 204
lust 180, 240
  spirit of 306
Luther 22
  Martin 22, 210
lyre 37, 254

M

magnitude 75, 109
Maker 37, 253
Malachi 29, 49, 154, 213
Man 166, 178, 270
man-child 13, 39, 55, 61, 64, 72, 101-2, 129, 168, 188, 216, 230, 245
managers 86, 98, 253

manifest 18, 20, 31-2, 55, 64, 79, 82, 89, 92, 123, 125, 137, 148, 173, 231, 233
manifestation 4-6, 8, 22-4, 44-6, 60-4, 72, 78-82, 88-90, 94-6, 118-20, 122-4, 134-6, 138-42, 172-4, 182-4, 294-6
  absolute 137
  direct 122
  external 156
  false 168, 310
  final 55
  full 256, 270
  greater 138
  internal 156
  outward 211
  physical 174, 246, 292
  progressive 79-80
manifestation of the kingdom of God 119, 173
manifestation process 314
manifesting 30, 275
manifesting changes 33
manipulation 93, 138, 146, 238, 240
mankind 8, 12, 23, 93, 104, 108, 110, 117, 161, 238, 294
mansions 94, 138
  many 106
mantle 35, 79, 135, 159, 210, 273, 312
mantras 162
mark 33, 41, 43-7, 128, 188, 194, 239, 317
mark of Gods sons 43, 45
Mark of Sonship 5, 27, 41
martyrs 18, 22, 195
Mary 194
mass 30
  critical 120
  greater 229
mass confusion 326
master craftsman 78
matrix 81-2
Matthew 40-1, 67, 136, 252
maturing 49, 98, 128, 149, 174, 184, 253-4
maturity 14, 56, 69, 85, 100, 189, 310
Mayan prophecies 13, 275
measure
  deeper 185
  full 222
medieval world 310
meditating 282, 323
meditation 107, 314-16, 323-5, 329
  deep 282, 316
megahertz 320
Melchizedek 200, 202
  order of 84, 200
Meneheune 94
mentality 30, 190, 196
  fire escape 39
  limited 190
merge 105, 108, 147, 291
messenger 48
Messiah 36
metamorphoo 28-9, 290
metamorphosis 5, 27-8, 271, 276
Micah 167
microcosm 162, 196, 233
Middle Finger 305
mind 5, 9, 11, 28-9, 31-2, 82, 108-11, 113-14, 162, 225-30, 232-5, 237-45, 247-8, 273-4, 303, 314-15
  sub-conscious 241

344 – INDEX

subconscious   242
mind functions   325
mind set   9
mindedness, double   182
mindset   190, 219, 284
minister   62, 280, 291, 296, 306
ministry   5, 27, 53, 98, 163, 206, 211, 218, 298
  deep   273
  effective   261
  fold   23
  kingship   305
  personal   55, 259, 298
  true   79
miracles   28, 140, 187
miraculous works   225
mirror   28-9, 76, 266
mirror image   213
mis-information   247
mis-perceptions   236
mis-understandings   193
misconceptions   190
misperceptions   184, 190
missionaries   151
modality   120, 239
modes   112, 127, 162, 180, 205, 265, 329, 332
  constant   163
  creative   163
  new   129
  static   205
molecules   131, 229
  knit   229
momentum   30, 33, 73, 104, 190, 247
moon   101, 175, 271
moorings   183, 327
morning stars sang   114
Morningstar   209
mortal   270, 276, 286, 290
mortal body   7, 9, 274, 279, 281-5, 287, 289, 291, 293-5, 297, 299, 301, 303, 305, 307
  quickening of the   283
mortality   285
Moses   126, 140
Most High God   200
mother   178, 194, 200, 233
MOTHER of HARLOTS   195
Mount Zion   43
mountains   30, 36, 38, 72, 84, 94, 100-1, 146-7, 166, 168, 241, 256
  great   289
  holy   38, 100, 256
mouth   22, 36-7, 45, 56, 114, 162-4, 166, 169, 204, 207, 210, 254, 302, 315, 317
mouth of God   164
movement   23, 81, 104, 160, 167, 324
  metaphysical   104
  power of positive thinking   160
  spiritualist   109, 310
Murray, Andrew   155
myriad   12, 18, 232, 262
mystery   37, 64-5, 81-2, 84, 98, 134, 195, 216, 222, 252, 266, 270, 280, 290, 318
mystery of Christ   82, 86, 222
mystical   197, 216, 291
mystical body of Christ   217

mystical union   140
mystics   310
  eastern   224
  great   318
mythical creature   179

N

nakedness   11, 41, 46
nations   37, 47, 64, 69, 136-7, 150, 166, 168, 213, 254, 285, 289, 304, 312
  mighty   124
Natural Left Side   299
natural level   32, 324
natural plane   32, 73, 99, 141, 147, 173, 255, 264, 292, 297, 299, 310-11
natural world   13, 73, 115, 140, 163, 325
nature
  creative   161
  human   173
  stimulant   320
  triune   161
Nebuchadnezzar   318
neck   194, 300-1
neck area   300
negative identification   197
Nephilim   147-9, 266
nerve centers   306
new age modality   167
new age movement   12-13, 34, 104, 108, 322
New Testament   22, 35, 56, 100, 334
nose   302, 307, 315
nose itches   302
Nostradamus   13, 275
nuclear holocaust   317

O

obligations   9, 178-9, 182, 184
occult   112, 173, 310
  the   42
ocean   116, 174
oil   112, 169
Old Testament   53-4, 99, 101, 140, 148, 192, 305, 318
omnipotence   316
omnipresence   84
omniscience   127
oneness   6, 37, 80, 82, 87, 102, 104, 122, 127, 130, 133, 140, 142-3, 182, 213, 221-2
  absolute   80, 290
  mystical   140
  power of   141, 143
  resonating   143-4
  spiritual   181, 211, 219, 222, 295
openness   130, 189, 194, 301
  great   301
oppressions   137, 151, 177, 181, 184, 186, 233, 239, 307-8, 325
order   17, 37-8, 41, 64, 77, 81, 93-4, 139, 156, 161, 169, 175, 220, 222, 239, 276
  base   91
  new   17, 29, 33, 271, 290
  next   16
  old   186, 191
  religious   192, 196

INDEX - 345

spiritual 37
organs 319-20
Oriental religions 44
outpouring 42, 68, 108, 117, 143
  progressive 108
Outreach Ministry of Christ 305
over-stimulation 317
  excessive 102
overflow 169
overpowering 149, 263

P

pains 60-1, 79, 306-7
  false labor 62
  sharp 301
pains of childbirth 10, 60, 65, 77, 286
palms 306
paradigm 123, 126-8, 191, 196, 228, 237-8
  common 247
  personal 224, 262
paradigm shift, entire 220
parents 229, 233
parousia 76, 221, 283-4, 288
  the 80
partakers 31, 186, 191, 193
partaking 215, 218, 289
participation 94, 261-2
  deeper 261
  greater 91
partnership 180-1, 185
passing 16, 45, 47, 167, 175, 231, 234, 244, 297
passive 131, 323
Passover 67, 275
pastors 23, 62, 99-100, 305
patterns 109, 242, 331
  weather 91
Pauls drive 212
peace 9, 35, 178, 200, 207, 241, 280, 288, 305
peace and safety 93
pearls 195, 214, 300
penetration, deeper 137
Pentecost 42, 67-8, 275
Pentecostal movement 23
perception 12, 28, 34-5, 41-5, 65, 83, 93, 102, 109, 156-7, 224-5, 227-8, 296-8, 302, 317, 319-20
  deep spiritual 296
  deeper 261, 303
  delicate spiritual 316
  inaccurate 229
  limited 156
  modes of 224, 332
  personal 246
  real 147, 182
  real spiritual 103
perceptive qualities 296
persecuting 23, 42
persecution 11, 42
  greatest 24
perseverance 10
personal concepts 17
Peter 55, 67, 121, 124, 257, 329
Pharisees 161, 196
Philip 67
Philistines 187
physical act of sight 232, 234

physical body 18, 31, 74, 122, 261-2, 270, 280, 282, 293, 297
physical expression 224
physical functions 319
physical incarnation, present 271
physical level 54, 245-6, 293, 297, 299, 319
physical world 110
pit 266, 306
pivotal 17, 107
pivotal point 189, 226
plagues 191, 193
plan of God 65, 189
plane 17, 28, 40, 105, 150, 227, 238, 258, 265, 292
  deepest 292
  higher 319
  human 137
  physical 29, 61, 229
planet 36-7, 151, 176, 318
platitude 102, 211, 295
plumbline 211-12, 244, 259, 299
pollution 318
  growing 318
portals 18, 24, 49, 51, 144, 202
position 18, 51, 70, 100, 206
possessions 149, 198, 263
pottery 146
poverty 119, 199, 231
power 11-12, 20-1, 24, 34-5, 39-40, 91-4, 134-5, 140-3, 155-9, 162-3, 210-12, 237-8, 246-8, 256-9, 304-5, 322-5
  day of his 156
  demon 252
  demonic 306
  devil 138, 300, 307
  divine 116, 121, 329
  latent 108
  resurrecting 326
  satanic 150, 183, 192
power of God 129-30, 143, 151, 260
Power of Oneness 6, 133, 140
PRACTICE LAWLESSNESS 187
praise 37-8, 253-4
pray 10, 124, 129, 156, 197, 208, 221, 260
prayer 82, 119-22, 125-9, 167, 177, 282, 314, 323-5
  kingdom level of 122, 127
prayer in the spirit 128
prayer level 128
praying 127, 260
pre-destination 8
preaching 22, 280
precious stones 195
preparation 13, 54, 64, 68-9, 318
  commensurate 45
  deep 212, 220
  real 54
presence of God 116, 130
Pressure 306
pressures, daily 56
prey 36, 266
price 65, 154, 205, 211, 219
  great 214
pricks 302
  sharp 302
Priest & King 6, 97, 99, 101, 103, 105, 107, 109, 111, 113, 115, 117, 119, 121, 123, 125
Priest/Kings 251

priesthood 49, 202
  royal 56, 124
priests 14, 37, 40, 98-100, 102-3, 124, 135,
    200, 245, 275, 305, 311
Prince of Peace 305
principalities 11, 21, 40, 79, 91, 93-4, 98,
    119, 137, 148, 150, 258, 273, 304-5
  bringing down 264
principles 34, 112, 129, 137, 140-3, 178-9,
    259-60, 281, 311-12, 319, 325, 330
  basic 141
  compromised 191
  established 140
process 31-2, 36, 45, 48-52, 60-1, 73-4,
    121, 163-4, 189-90, 226, 228, 232-3,
    271, 303-4, 321-3, 331
Process of Sight 6, 223, 232
progressive change 287
projections 112, 163
promises 16, 18, 24, 29, 31, 55-6, 63-4, 67,
    69, 102-4, 123, 167-9, 209-10, 214-
    15, 256, 329
  greatest 57
prophecies 31, 53, 55-7, 87, 108-10, 115,
    117, 123, 126, 150, 169, 209-10, 212-
    13, 230, 253, 275
prophesy 104, 108, 115, 187, 294, 302
Prophesy & Speaking Anointing 302
prophet 6, 18, 23, 29, 33, 46, 54, 56, 97,
    99-101, 103-5, 107, 109-11, 113,
    115, 125-7
  false 239
prophetic fulfillment 150
protection 63, 149, 316
proverb 23, 162, 300, 323
provision 43, 52-4, 72, 98, 103-4, 109-10,
    119-20, 123, 125, 129, 142, 230, 243,
    290
Psalms 35-7, 49, 56, 139, 151, 154, 161,
    169, 176-7, 233, 254
  quoted 161
psychic 34, 56, 292, 300
  termed 102
psychic bonds 194
psychic emanations 74
psychic warfare 300
punishment 38, 254
purification 49, 73-4, 105, 154, 217, 319
purifier 74
purify 49, 182, 213
purifying work 255
Purity 219
Pursuit of Resurrection Life 7, 269, 271,
    273, 275, 277

Q

quantum physics 246
quickening 7, 279, 281-5, 287, 289, 291,
    293, 295, 297, 299, 301, 303, 305,
    307
  gradual 282

R

race 18-19, 88, 117, 148, 183, 185, 192,
    210, 237-8, 252, 277-8, 292, 297
  human 201, 233, 237, 240
  new 17, 288

radiating effect 80
raging 257, 265
rain 169, 209
rapture 12, 34, 39, 46
rapture theory 30, 39, 285
rate 110, 315-16
  accelerated 111
  exponential 30
reality 6, 12-13, 31-2, 56-7, 87-90, 116,
    120-1, 123, 173-5, 223-5, 227-39,
    241-7, 256-7, 259-62, 283-5, 292-3
  paradigm of 119, 191, 225, 234, 239
  perception of 224-5, 234
  present 283
  substantive 247
  unlimited 51
reality of sonship 28, 31, 62, 110, 125
realization 32, 90, 123
realms 82, 91, 111, 173, 231, 260-1
  spiritual 34, 260
reasoning process 232
recesses
  deep 78
  hidden 243
reconditioning 242
redemption 8, 10, 14, 31, 60, 77, 90, 105,
    120, 167, 280, 282, 286, 288, 295
  absolute 293
  full 24, 288
  total 280
refinement 51, 154
reformation 22
regeneration 234, 239
  progressive 233
reign 39, 61-2, 134, 188, 240, 254-5, 258,
    285
rejoice 169, 216, 295
relationships 93, 105, 115, 128, 172, 176,
    179-80, 182, 184, 186, 193-4, 198,
    212-14, 219-21, 224, 300
  deep 212
  direct 63
  functional 102, 178, 258, 281, 296, 301,
    324
  intimate 219
  marital 300
  natural 300
  spiritual 300
  yoked 179
release 14, 19, 31, 54-5, 62, 75-7, 79-83,
    88, 93, 123-4, 127-9, 135-7, 139,
    142-3, 150-1, 163
  commensurate 80
  complete 106
  great 63
  initial 65
  physical 314
  progressive 79-80, 91
release creation 89
release of power 140-1
religions 162, 224, 237-8
  eastern 13, 162, 244
  organized 12
  social 218
religious circles 12
religious community 34, 145, 284
religious institutions 192
religious spirit 154, 237-9
religious world 30, 196, 218

INDEX - 347

remembrance 114-16, 118, 277
remembrancers 70
remnant 22, 36, 47, 193, 196, 218
renewal 74, 226, 228, 230-1, 273, 296
  deep 235
  progressive 296
renewing 29, 225-8, 230, 233-4, 237, 243-4, 274, 303
  commensurate 240
  complete 243
  deep 235
  deeper 234
renown 266
  men of 148
Repent 312
repose 120, 272
reproach 56, 109, 204, 310, 315
resentment hitting 307
resistance 22, 40
resonance 141
  harmonic 142
responsibility 278, 312
  great 55, 156
restoration 21-3, 42, 68, 110, 114, 134, 169, 243, 294
  progressive 21-2
restore 110, 169, 205
restraints 22, 137, 150-1, 157
  learned 191
restrictions 90, 198, 238
resurrection 18, 38, 45-7, 51, 67, 201, 210, 212, 271-3, 290, 295
  first 294
  the 295
resurrection life 7-8, 49, 51, 57, 123, 139, 198, 213, 229, 248, 269-71, 273-5, 277-8, 287, 289, 295
  pursuit of 276, 334
  release of 137, 273
revelation 13-14, 17-18, 23, 35-6, 38-40, 44-6, 55-6, 72-3, 110, 127-9, 137, 156, 188, 204-5, 259-60, 285
  dawning 209
  deep 220
  new 85, 195
  personal 264
  word of 118, 206
reversal 6, 53, 102, 153, 166-9
rhythm 314-15
rhythmic breathing 314
  slower 316
Rib 307
riches 82, 221, 280
Ridgeline area 301
right now 62, 263
  the God of 70
righteous 23, 50, 79, 177, 197, 237
righteousness 9, 49, 117, 177, 180-1, 185, 200, 212-14, 284
Ring Finger 305
ripple affect 80
risen 75, 108, 164
rituals 12, 212
  dead 12
river 75, 164-6, 317
rocks 8, 63, 94
Romans 2, 5, 8-9, 14, 29, 31, 60-1, 79, 86, 95, 225-6, 228, 238-9, 242-3, 284-6, 332

fulfillment of 122, 185, 189
room 142
  single 68
  upper 67-70
root 201, 209, 260, 332
root level 29
roots, deep 263
rule 39, 61-2, 64, 134, 161, 188, 254-5, 258, 273, 281, 285
rulers 91, 98, 148, 158, 160, 184, 237, 266, 330
ruling 39, 72
rumors 74, 103

S

saints 7, 11, 82, 134, 149, 177, 183, 190, 195-6, 221, 251, 253, 255, 257, 263-5, 296-7
Salem, king of 200
salvation 37, 54, 254, 304
  eternal 200
  full 288
Samson 187
Samuel 101
sanctify 280, 288
satan 307
Satan 35, 55, 109-10, 137-8, 146, 149, 192, 216, 227, 237
satan, domain of 227
Satan, most direct accesses 184
satanic 30, 148, 216, 237-8, 262
satanic activity 166
satanic cunning 136
satanic infiltration 22
satanic influence 73
satanic level 106
satanic plot 317
satanic worlds 104, 168
Satans rule 135
Saul 168
saving souls 136
scars 214
scenario 283, 323
school 69, 139, 143, 157
Scofield approach, traditional 46
scribe 196, 296
scriptural 13
scriptural level 142
scriptural references 280
scriptures 28, 39-46, 87-8, 114, 116-17, 120-1, 131-2, 134, 136-7, 154-6, 175-7, 194-5, 198, 204-6, 227-8, 322-3
sea 100, 117, 241, 248, 303, 315
seals 43, 86, 117, 222, 303
  final 120
searches 11, 54, 142, 208, 300
searchlight 154, 188
season 13-14, 17, 33, 46-7, 51, 60-2, 64, 69-70, 76-7, 80, 87, 91, 93, 141, 275-6, 288-9
  extended 294
  long 64, 273
  short 277
secret 73, 135
secret coming 275
seeing auras 329
seeing the Lord 183
seer ministry 99-100, 105

seer ministry function 33
seer prophet 6, 97-101, 103, 105-6, 136, 159
seer prophet ministry 98-9, 107
seers 102, 159, 255, 311, 328
Seers 309
selective awareness 92
self, higher 281
self-enlightenment 12
selfish 129, 207
sensation 206, 307
  burning 303
  crawling 306
senses, physical 111, 235
sensitivity 102, 107, 180, 319, 326
  greater 311
  spiritual 181, 317, 330
separation 17, 86, 111, 237, 241, 245, 297
  man"s 242
sequence 209, 263
serpent 317
servants 48, 92, 99, 265, 318
service 85, 318
  spiritual 332
set the captives free 81
severing 229
  absolute 219
shackles 150, 159
shadows 106, 149, 207
shaken 85
shaking 85, 89
shame 41, 46, 284
shed light 295
SHEEP 11
shepherds, early 326
shift 31, 72-4, 82, 92-3, 105, 119, 135, 139, 143, 159-60, 167, 175, 227, 235, 274, 308
  negative 135
  upward 103
shine 19, 117
shining 118, 244
  lamp 209
shockwaves 42
shoulder 19, 87, 261, 304-5
shouts 281, 289
shrink 50, 284
sickness 245, 319
sight 6, 44-5, 49, 87, 103, 105, 121, 128, 136, 182, 185, 187, 220, 232, 234-5, 296-8
  act of 232
  natural 75
  window of 105
Sign of Resentment hitting 307
signals, conflicting 241, 314, 316
signposts 53, 264, 283-4
signs 36, 44, 53, 62, 68-9, 74, 93, 103, 106, 110, 145, 156, 194, 211, 225, 295-307
  anointed 302
  great 301, 303-4
  oppressive 301, 306
  physical 297, 302
  sympathetic 298
  symptomatic 298
  unique 284
signs manifest 295, 299, 302
signs pointing 74

silent coming 289
silver 49, 146, 213
  purifier of 49, 213
Simon 67
Simplicity 7, 309, 313, 326
simplification 327
sinful flesh 9
sing 37, 253-4
sins 9, 18, 105, 177, 186, 191, 193, 233, 236, 242, 284, 333
sister 127, 186, 329
slave 43, 86, 252, 330
slavery 10, 53, 60, 77
sleep 51, 187, 290, 325
slough of despond 323
smelter 49, 74, 213
Smith Wigglesworth 225, 326
snare 188, 196
snowball effect 30
soap 48-9, 213
society 207, 233, 263, 327
  sterile 317
Sodom 137, 166, 204
sojourn 16, 19, 86, 102, 184, 191, 219, 224
  personal 312
  present 69, 86, 229
Solomon 212, 222
Son of God 200
son of man 137, 166
Song 212, 222
song, new 37, 253
sons 8-11, 35-7, 39-41, 46-9, 53-7, 60-8, 76-7, 79-86, 88-93, 102-8, 147-50, 154-61, 213-14, 252-8, 272-8, 285-8
  beloved 227
  first 230
  mature 78
  spiritual 31-2
  true 147
sons experience 290
sons of God 8, 10, 21, 39-40, 60-3, 72-3, 76-7, 79-82, 86, 92-3, 102-3, 123, 147, 172-4, 238-40, 253-5
Sons of God 2, 4-6, 8, 10, 12, 14, 16, 18, 20, 26-8, 52-4, 142-4, 150, 188-90, 228-30, 258
Sons of Light 6, 118, 199, 203, 219, 222, 331
sonship 5, 13-14, 19-21, 27-9, 33-5, 43-5, 47-9, 51-3, 55-7, 59-62, 64-5, 68-70, 122, 197-8, 211-12, 235
  complete 64
  experience of 13, 160, 293
  full capacity 157
  fullness of 78, 289
  manifestation of 35, 68, 72, 122, 173, 212, 328
  mark of 46-7
  ministry of 77, 84
  path of 20-1, 154, 247
  realities of 24, 285
  release of 24, 68
  transformation of 18, 69, 100, 289
soul 31-2, 45, 48-51, 74, 111-12, 128, 142-3, 178-83, 232-5, 238-41, 243-5, 271, 280-2, 288-9, 291-3, 300-1
Soul & Body 7, 279
soul bonds 186
soul-bonds 179, 185

INDEX - 349

soul flesh   63, 191-2
soul flesh nature   240
soul level   87, 178, 219, 293
soul level relationships   183
soul nature   45, 51, 193
  un-regenerated   237
soul/physical   290
soul plane   88
soulish   23
soulish Christian   292
sovereign event   35
species, new   37
speculations   158, 323
Spine   307
spiral   45-6, 121
in the spirit   127, 156
spirit   9-11, 108-9, 142-3, 147-51, 154-61, 172-80, 193-9, 233-48, 253-5, 257-63, 279-84, 288-97, 299-302, 310-12, 323-4, 326-9
  days of   126, 281
  elemental   92-3
  free   291
  higher planes of   138, 229
  man"s   282
  plane of   68, 129, 239, 248, 292
  separate   291
  teachable   204
spirit age   294
spirit hitting   301
spirit hovering   55
spirit level   286, 293
The spirit of delay   248
the spirit of God   31, 216, 283, 323
the Spirit of God   9-10, 31
spirit/soul   177
spirit world   157, 167, 173, 186-7, 245-6, 252, 265, 286, 295, 297
  entire   217
spirit world functions   178
spiritual attack   303
spiritual Christian   292
spiritual forces   237
spiritual hearing   31
spiritual hierarchy   262
spiritual interpretation, correct   235
spiritual level   112, 128, 318-19
  higher   294
spiritual life   321
spiritual muscles   157
spiritual planes   31, 92, 292, 299, 324
  higher   229
spiritual sight   181
  greater   234
Spiritual Walk   317
spiritual warfare   56, 183, 259, 297, 304, 325
  effective   183
spiritual world   32, 110, 241
spring rain watering   209
stagger   56-7
staggering   57, 138, 199
standing shoulder   261
stars   101, 117, 175, 271
state   68, 72-3, 78, 105, 116, 131, 160, 175, 204-5, 207, 230, 243, 296, 314, 323-4, 326
  alpha   325
  beta   325

constant   226-7
dream   92
ever-changing   205
humble   68, 276, 286
minded   247
new   74
present   271
theta   325
vibrational   39
stature, full   14
step   6, 22-3, 29, 32, 47, 49, 52, 55, 79, 113,
  first   107, 228, 301
  greatest   70
  last   70
  next   70
step-by-step changes   28
stewardship   210, 280
stomach   45, 306
strangers   87, 169, 230
stretch   20, 113, 176
stronghold, last   229
strongholds   265
struggles   78, 237
  greatest   226
subconscious level   154
subliminal level   206
submission   41, 304
  total   51
substance   229, 245
  given   246
  physical   112
  real   292
sufferings   10, 212, 216-18
sufferings of Christ   54, 216-18
sun   101, 181, 244, 271
superstitions   310
supplicating   127
supplications   120
surrender   20, 211
survival   54, 252
sustain   127, 159, 190
sword   11, 35, 168, 178
  two-edged   37, 254
sympathy   178-9, 186, 193-4
symptoms   298, 300
  physical   296
synergy   83, 92, 143, 163

T

takeover   31
  absolute   283
  great   31
tape   66, 183, 242, 263, 278, 289
  break the   19
teach   103, 113, 116-18, 166, 168, 311
teachers   23, 100, 305
Teeth   303
television   107, 317, 326
temple   29, 48, 70, 80, 180-1, 271, 303
  earthen   130
  earthly   32
  heavenly   89
temple of God   180-1
tent   286
  earthly   89, 286
tentacles   190-1, 220, 237
testifies   10, 209
testimony   23, 41-3, 154, 211

thankfulness 214
Thessalonians 126, 288
thief 101, 289
Thomas 67, 119-20, 241, 255, 272, 291
thoughts 109, 112-13, 124, 161, 172, 177, 181, 301, 315, 323
  another"s 193
  innermost 78
thousand cubits 164
threads 331
  common 306
threshold 69, 139, 144, 164, 275, 294-5
throne of God 72, 188
thrones 37, 43, 52, 64, 79, 81, 119, 160, 164-5, 183, 258, 285
Thumb & Toe 305
thumbs 305
timeline 13, 62, 72, 170, 195, 209-10, 275, 280, 282-3, 285-6, 288
tip 14, 72, 190, 304-5
tipping point 120, 166
toes 146
toil 61
tongues 39, 67, 162, 332
  cloven 68, 143
tool of God 109, 139, 149
tools, unwilling 55
top floor 35
top stone 289
topic 172, 298, 326, 328
  negative 258
torment 139, 253
torrent 34, 249
track 82, 151, 258, 281, 295-7, 311, 330-1
  fast 205
  ingrain 242
  lost 277
tragic event 150
transfer 112, 186-7
transference 136, 171-2, 176-8, 185-6, 189, 192, 197, 200, 261, 306-7, 311
  most detrimental 178
  negative 178
  principle of 178, 185
transformation 8, 45, 49, 52, 60, 68, 70, 80, 150, 154, 196, 198, 228, 230, 271, 276
  final 275, 287
transition 13, 17, 28, 31, 51, 64, 67, 69-70, 74, 106, 126-8, 230-1, 234-5, 289-90, 292, 327-8
  difficult 245
  next 143
transitioning 14, 54, 179
translations 147, 200
transpiring 14, 76, 99, 103, 299, 305
travail 5, 8, 13-14, 24, 57, 59-65, 67-9, 72, 76, 79, 91, 120-3, 125, 129, 160, 257
  body experiences 60
  deep 24
travail of sonship 13, 61, 65, 122
Travail of Sonship 5, 59-60
travail pangs 61-2
travailing 91, 254
travesty 36, 42, 206
trees 8, 33, 43, 47, 128, 206, 227, 231, 239, 244, 303
  as trees walking 208
  men 159, 247

trend 12, 167
  downward 166-7, 169
tribulation 11, 36, 39
  great 63
  very intense 54
True Left Side 299
True oneness 142
trump, last 287, 290
trumpet 38, 100, 256, 275, 290
trust 113, 123, 247
truth 12, 23, 34-6, 39, 45, 110, 116-18, 122-5, 129, 184-5, 224-5, 228-30, 234-5, 239, 245-8, 315
  deep 175
  deeper 17
  new 42
  partial 34
  realized 102
  un-applied 253
  your 124
tune 102, 108, 141, 332
tuning 35, 104, 291
tuning fork 174
turmoil 72
  greater 16
twinkling 271, 290
Tyndale 22
  William 22

U

ulterior motives 111
un-learning 233
unawareness 86, 111, 175
  absolute 102
unbelief 34-5, 50, 224, 233, 241-2, 274
  learn 224
unbelievers 104, 110, 180-1, 185-6, 194
unbelieving 207
UNCLEAN 180, 182, 190, 192, 219
unfolding 12-14, 34, 44, 54, 61, 73, 75, 82, 90-1, 93, 100, 113, 260-1, 283-4, 292, 294-6
  events 331
  progressive 33, 164
union 104, 147-8, 192
unison 49-50, 75, 242
unlearn 224, 228-9
unlimited-ness 127, 290
unseen 73, 99, 283, 286, 295
unseen world 284
unveiling 17, 41, 86, 257
unwrapping 89-90
upheaval 72, 108
Upper head area 300
Upper Shoulder 304
uttermost 24, 191, 282

V

Vampires 173, 179
vegan-vegetarianism 319
vehicle 14, 121, 160, 216
veil 6, 18, 51, 75, 111, 115, 117, 150, 179-80, 222-3, 227, 237-8, 260-1, 276-7, 289-90, 295-7
veil of separation 237, 241
vessels 254
  earthen 37, 85, 131

INDEX - 351

humble 222
very 86
vibrating 141-2, 174, 229, 319
vibration 73-4, 78, 88, 92, 94-5, 102, 104-6, 129-31, 138, 167, 174-5, 260, 308, 314, 319-20, 331-2
  bodily 316
  conflicting 315
  higher 106, 320
  personal 111
  spiritual 311, 313
  unique 129
vibration lifter 319
vibrational levels 93, 175, 236
vibrational shift 39, 73, 88, 283-4
vibratory activities 316
victory 40, 78, 257-8, 262, 266, 298, 304-5
  bringing 304
violence 158-9, 240
violent 40, 158
virgins 154
  foolish 69-70, 115, 207
  wise 248
visionaries 324
visions 28, 53, 57, 63, 68, 92, 103-5, 108, 110-11, 113, 117, 129-30, 146-7, 197-9, 281-2, 329-31
  open 103, 105, 128, 188, 296, 307
  spiritual 113, 136
visitation 17, 43, 46, 67, 69-70, 110, 115, 140, 143, 145
visualization 176, 314-15, 322-5
  first 182
  power of 322, 324
Visualization & Imagination 7, 309, 313, 322
visualize 176-7, 194, 282, 314, 316, 322, 328, 332
visualizing 162, 314, 322-5, 328
  practice 325
voice 22, 43, 99, 101, 124, 161-3, 191, 193, 275, 325, 329, 331

W

walls 25, 52, 57, 101, 158, 175, 246
wanderings 72, 315
war 7, 38, 74, 137, 167-8, 173, 251-2, 254, 257, 262, 264, 296
  nuclear 317
  waging 149, 263
war horses 101
warfare 7, 57, 148-9, 158, 251, 253, 255-7, 259, 261-3, 265, 267
warring Kings 40
Warrior 251
Warrior Priest/Kings 7, 263
water 54, 75-6, 80, 100, 106, 117, 155, 164, 175, 195, 205, 226-7, 272, 318
  new 113
  poured 317
  treading 155
wave 63, 65, 69, 80, 100, 241
  first 65, 69, 278
weaknesses 10, 255, 271
wealthy 187, 204-5
weights 105, 236, 277, 297, 311, 327
  massive 229
Wesley

Charles 22
John 210
western mind 224
wheat 48, 169, 270
wheat grass 320
whole man 261
whore 172, 190-6, 219, 221, 273
  great 195
  the 191
wickedness 35, 62, 167, 237, 275
  increasing tide of 138
  spirits of 149-50
  spiritual 34
wilderness 168, 195, 212, 317
  desolate 38, 101, 256
wilderness wanderings 212
wind 19, 241, 315
  violent rushing 67
wine 43, 169, 195, 318
  new 41, 139
wineskins, new 41, 139
wisdom 84, 110, 115, 118, 188, 214, 302, 315
  manifold 266
witchcraft 109, 136, 138, 302, 306-7
within you 119
withstood 40, 258, 265
Witness, true 204
Witnesses 18, 42, 138, 277
  cloud of 18, 210
  final 166
witnessing 16, 91, 119
woman 64, 112, 119, 129, 137, 166, 194-5, 317
  free 201-2
womb 14, 60-3, 65, 230, 278
women 18, 46, 60, 148, 154
word 45-6, 53-7, 87-90, 98-9, 111-12, 117-18, 126-9, 134-6, 156-8, 160-6, 187-92, 205-7, 251-2, 256-62, 322-6, 329-32
  all-inclusive 154
  buzz 180
  greater 207
  prophetic 209
  single 173
  unspoken 128
word admonishes 185
word of god 162, 225, 326
word of God 43, 256, 264, 280, 326
word-workers 89
work, greater 49, 52, 56, 122, 143, 213, 219, 230, 292
Workshop for Seers 7, 309-11, 313, 315, 317, 319, 321, 323, 325, 327, 329, 331, 333
in the world 178, 183
world governments 146
World of Christ 5, 76, 83
world system 21, 147, 150, 224, 297, 327
worm 28, 290
worship 7, 43, 92, 308-9, 313, 332-3
  devil 138
wounds 214
wrath 43, 197
wreath, perishable 259
wrestling 56, 307
Wrist 306
writer 112, 118

Wycliffe 22
  John 22

Y

yoke 182
  unequal 178, 186
yoking, unequal 172

Z

Zealot 67
Zechariah 102, 289
zenith 22, 91
Zerubbabel 289
Zion 38, 40, 44, 64, 87, 100, 149, 167-9, 188, 256, 312
Zwingli 22, 210

Scriptural Index

A

Acts 1:13 67
Acts 2:1 68
Acts 2:1-3 67
Acts 3:21 22, 114
Acts 28:3-9 273

C

Co 13:9-12 115
Co 14:20-22 201
Co 15:24-25 258
Co 15:51-53 290
Co 15:52 290
Col 1:16-17 160
Col 1:17 77
Col 1:24 216
Col 1:25-27 280
Col 1:26-27 82
Col 2:14 126
Col 3:3-4 212
Colossians 77, 280
Colossians 1:13 227
Cor 28, 270, 290
Cor 2:9 329
Cor 5:1 89
Cor 5:1-4 286
Cor 6:14-18 180, 182
Cor 6:17-18 190, 219
Cor 6:18 221
Cor 10:11 55, 252
Cor 15:35 270
Cor 15:39-44 271
Corinthians 77, 181, 270-1
Corinthians 15 270

D

Dan 210, 318
Dan 2:40-45 146
Dan 7:21-22 149, 263
Dan 12 277
Dan 12:10 30
Dan 12:3-4 117
Daniel 30, 117, 146-7, 150, 210, 263-4, 277, 318
Daniel 7:21 149
Daniel 12:10 57
Daniel 12:34 115
Deu 32:30 140
Deut 29:5 168
Deuteronomy 32 140

E

Eph 100
Eph 1:18 221
Eph 1:3 120
Eph 1:8b-10 84
Eph 1:9-10 134
Eph 3:9-10 266
Eph 4:8 305
Eph 5:12-13 135
Eph 5:13 73
Eph 5:3 296
Eph 6:12 237
Eph 6:13-18 325
Ephesians 37, 81, 98, 134, 150, 266, 325
Ephesus 112
Eze 47:1-5 164
Ezekiel 101, 164
Ezekiel 37:5 75

G

Gal 3:11 79, 126
Gal 4:1-2 86, 253
Gal 4:2 98
Gal 4:30-31 202
Gal 5:16 240
Galatians 5:15-16 179
Gen 1:27 161
Gen 15:16 173
Gen 32:25 307
Genesis 147
Genesis 3:15 304
Genesis 39-41 53

H

Heb 4:3 129, 197
Heb 5:14-6X1 310
Heb 5:9-10 200
Heb 7:1-3 200
Heb 7:25 127, 282
Heb 8:11 100
Heb 10:13 258
Heb 10:38-39 50
Heb 10:7 197
Heb 10:9 220
Heb 11 277
Heb 11:13 87, 230
Heb 11:13-16 169
Heb 11:38-40 73
Heb 11:39-40 87
Heb 12:1 18, 236
Heb 13:13 204
Heb 14:4 175
Hebr 44
Hebrews 18, 72, 104, 168, 222, 243
Hebrews 7:25 127

Hebrews 11   83, 230
Hebrews 11:39-40   16
Hebrews 12   18, 116
Hebrews 12:26-29   85
Hos 6:3   294
Hosea   209, 213
Hosea 6:1-3   209
Hosea 6:3   16

I

Isa   100, 312
Isa 2:1-4   168
Isa 5:20   248
Isa 9:6   305
Isa 30:20   106
Isa 45:23   304
Isa 52:10   304
Isa 55:8   109
Isa 61:1-2a   253
Isa 61:2b   253
Isa 66:16   145
Isa 66:8   312
Isa 66:9   63
Isaiah   29, 33, 46, 63, 69, 113, 168,
    189, 230, 253, 304, 330
Isaiah 11:9   115

J

James 1:6-8   241
James 4:2   117
James 4:8   182
Jas   162
Jas 1:8   182
Jdg 16:20   187
Jer 29:12-13   208
Jn 1:7   333
Jn 3:20   73
Jn 14:2   81, 102
Jn 14:2-3   175
Jn 14:9   122
Jn 16:24   117
Jn 19:26   194
Jn 19:30   120-1
Job 13:15   211
Job 38:4a   114
Joel   87, 104, 108-11, 117, 143, 173,
    256, 282
Joel 2:1-11   101
Joel 2:1-3   256
Joel 2:11   36
Joel 2:23-25   169
Joel 2:28   294
Joel 2:28-29   104, 108
John 2:24   178, 184
John 3:30   213
John 5:19   238
John 7:38   306
John 8:36   198
John 12:24-26   48
John 14:1-3   94
John 14:2-3   138, 285
John 14:26   116
John 14:3   124
John 14:30   184
John 14:6   49
John 16:11   253
John 18:36   265
John 21:18   113
Joshua 1:3   304
Joshua 1:8   330
Joshua 13:1   18
Joshua 14:12-13   266
Judges 1:7   305
Judges 7:7   36
Judges 16:20   207

L

Logos 22   241, 291
Logos 48   241
Logos 48-51   272
Logos 51   121
Logos 108-113:   272
Logos 114   121
Lu19:26   207
Luk 6:35   194
Luke 4:19   253
Luke 4:29-30   175
Luke 8:44   129
Luke 17:21   119, 175
Luke 17:26   137
Luke 18:3-6   120
Luke 18:5   303
Luke 19:17   330
Luke 21:28   63
Luke 24:13-31   289

M

Mal   216
Mal 3:1   70
Mal 3:2   74, 154
Mal 3:2-3   49, 213
Malachi   29, 154, 213
Malachi 3:   49
Mark 3:35   194
Mark 8:24   33, 128, 239
Mark 13:20   317
Mat 7:22-23   187
Mat 10:34-36   178
Mat 13:12   188
Mat 24:22   148
Mat 24:40-42   46
Matt 5:45   197
Matt 5:8   43, 287
Matt 8:24   208
Matt 8:4   185
Matt 11:12   158

INDEX - 355

Matt 12:29 137
Matt 24:12 173
Matt 28:18-19 136
Matthew 67, 136
Matthew 9:17 41
Matthew 11:72 40
Matthew 24:22 252
Mic 4:1-2 166
Micah 167

N

Num 13 149
Number: 2010913340 2
Numbers 33:55 302, 307

P

Pe 1:3 120
Peter 67, 257
Peter 1:10-12 55
Peter 1:3 121, 329
Peter 2:9 124
Phi 289
Phil 19, 334
Phil 2:10-11 134
Phil 2:5-8 214
Phil 2:7 204
Phil 3:12 124
Phil 3:21 276, 287
Phil 3:8-10 212
Phil 5:11 135
Php 3:21 276
Prov 13:12 244
Prov 23:7 123, 323
Proverbs 4:18 23
Proverbs 23:7 162
Proverbs 25:2 300
Ps 37:23 79
Ps 72:16 84
Ps 82:6 161
Ps 110 155
Ps 149 135, 149, 298
Ps42:7 64
Psa 78
Psa 23:5 169
Psa 36:9 333
Psa 51:5 233
Psa 103:7 140
Psa 105:19 56
Psalm 110 154
Psalms 23:5X 169
Psalms 51:5 233
Psalms 72:16 36
Psalms 82:6 161
Psalms 105 56
Psalms 116:15 49
Psalms 129:3-4 177
Psalms 129:4 176
Psalms 149 139, 254

Psalms 149:5-9 35

R

Rev 7:3 303
Revelation 12 13
Ro 33, 57, 78, 122, 128, 273
Ro 1:7 79
Ro 6:5 289
Ro 8:17 217
Ro 8:19 86
Ro 8:19-23 60, 77
Ro 8:26 122
Ro 8:34 127
Rom 7:15 243
Rom 8:1 9
Rom 8:10 9
Rom 8:11 9
Rom 8:12 9
Rom 8:13 9
Rom 8:14 10
Rom 8:15 10
Rom 8:16 10
Rom 8:17 10
Rom 8:18 10
Rom 8:19 10
Rom 8:2 9
Rom 8:20 10
Rom 8:21 10
Rom 8:22 10
Rom 8:23 10
Rom 8:24 10
Rom 8:25 10
Rom 8:26 10
Rom 8:27 11
Rom 8:28 11
Rom 8:29 11
Rom 8:3 9
Rom 8:30 11
Rom 8:31 11
Rom 8:32 11
Rom 8:33 11
Rom 8:34 11
Rom 8:35 11
Rom 8:36 11
Rom 8:37 11
Rom 8:38 11
Rom 8:39 11
Rom 8:4 9, 180
Rom 8:5 9
Rom 8:6 9
Rom 8:7 9, 235
Rom 8:8 9
Rom 8:9 9
Rom 12:2 226
Romans 2, 5, 8-9, 14, 29, 60-1, 86, 91, 95, 122, 147, 156, 167, 185, 189, 238-9
Romans 7:19 242
Romans 8: 286

Romans 8:10-11   284
Romans 8:11   295
Romans 8:14   31
Romans 8:17X   216
Romans 8:19-22   79
Romans 12   228
Romans 12:1   332
Romans 12:2   225-6, 234

S

Solomon 8:5   212

T

Thess 4:17   36
Thessalonians   288
Thessalonians 5:17   126
Tim 3:5   155

Z

Zech 2:5   64
Zech 4:6-9   289
Zechariah   102, 289

Romans 8

Rom 8:1 Therefore there is now no condemnation for those who are in ChristJesus.

Rom 8:2 For the law of the Spirit of life in Christ Jesus has set you free from the law of sin and of death.

Rom 8:3 For what the Law could not do, weak as it was through the flesh, God *did:* sending His own Son in the likeness of sinful flesh and *as an offering* for sin, He condemned sin in the flesh,

Rom 8:4 so that the requirement of the Law might be fulfilled in us, who do not walk according to the flesh but according to the Spirit.

Rom 8:5 For those who are according to the flesh set their minds on the things of the flesh, but those who are according to the Spirit, the things of the Spirit.

Rom 8:6 For the mind set on the flesh is death, but the mind set on the Spirit is life and peace,

Rom 8:7 because the mind set on the flesh is hostile toward God; for it does not subject itself to the law of God, for it is not even able *to do so,*

Rom 8:8 and those who are in the flesh cannot please God.

Rom 8:9 However, you are not in the flesh but in the Spirit, if indeed the Spirit of God dwells in you. But if anyone does not have the Spirit of Christ, he does not belong to Him.

Rom 8:10 If Christ is in you, though the body is dead because of sin, yet the spirit is alive because of righteousness.

Rom 8:11 But if the Spirit of Him who raised Jesus from the dead dwells in you, He who raised Christ Jesus from the dead will also give life to your mortal bodies through His Spirit who dwells in you.

Rom 8:12 So then, brethren, we are under obligation, not to the flesh, to live according to the flesh--

Rom 8:13 for if you are living according to the flesh, you must die; but if by the Spirit you are putting to death the deeds of the body, you will live.

Rom 8:14 For all who are being led by the Spirit of God, these are sons of God.

Rom 8:15 For you have not received a spirit of slavery leading to fear again, but you have received a spirit of adoption as sons by which we cry out, "Abba! Father!"

Rom 8:16 The Spirit Himself testifies with our spirit that we are children of God,

Rom 8:17 and if children, heirs also, heirs of God and fellow heirs with Christ, if indeed we suffer with *Him* so that we may also be glorified with *Him*.

Rom 8:18 For I consider that the sufferings of this present time are not worthy to be compared with the glory that is to be revealed to us.

Rom 8:19 For the anxious longing of the creation waits eagerly for the revealing of the sons of God.

Rom 8:20 For the creation was subjected to futility, not willingly, but because of Him who subjected it, in hope

Rom 8:21 that the creation itself also will be set free from its slavery to corruption into the freedom of the glory of the children of God.

Rom 8:22 For we know that the whole creation groans and suffers the pains of childbirth together until now.

Rom 8:23 And not only this, but also we ourselves, having the first fruits of the Spirit, even we ourselves groan within ourselves, waiting eagerly for *our* adoption as sons, the redemption of our body.

Rom 8:24 For in hope we have been saved, but hope that is seen is not hope; for who hopes for what he *already* sees?

Rom 8:25 But if we hope for what we do not see, with perseverance we wait eagerly for it.

Rom 8:26 In the same way the Spirit also helps our weakness; for we do not know how to pray as we should, but the Spirit Himself intercedes for *us* with groanings too deep for words;

Rom 8:27 and He who searches the hearts knows what the mind of the Spirit is, because He intercedes for the saints according to *the will of* God.

Rom 8:28 And we know that God causes all things to work together for good to those who love God, to those who are called according to *His* purpose.

Rom 8:29 For those whom He foreknew, He also predestined *to become* conformed to the image of His Son, so that He would be the firstborn among many brethren;

Rom 8:30 and these whom He predestined, He also called; and these whom He called, He also justified; and these whom He justified, He also glorified.

Rom 8:31 What then shall we say to these things? If God *is* for us, who *is* against us?

Rom 8:32 He who did not spare His own Son, but delivered Him over for us all, how will He not also with Him freely give us all things?

Rom 8:33 Who will bring a charge against God's elect? God is the one who justifies;

Rom 8:34 who is the one who condemns? Christ Jesus is He who died, yes, rather who was raised, who is at the right hand of God, who also intercedes for us.

Rom 8:35 Who will separate us from the love of Christ? Will tribulation, or distress, or persecution, or famine, or nakedness, or peril, or sword?

Rom 8:36 Just as it is written, "FOR YOUR SAKE WE ARE BEING PUT TO DEATH ALL DAY LONG; WE WERE CONSIDERED AS SHEEP TO BE SLAUGHTERED."

Rom 8:37 But in all these things we overwhelmingly conquer through Him who loved us.

Rom 8:38 For I am convinced that neither death, nor life, nor angels, nor principalities, nor things present, nor things to come, nor powers,

Rom 8:39 nor height, nor depth, nor any other created thing, will be able to separate us from the love of God, which is in Christ Jesus our Lord.

For
Supplemental Teaching
to this book

Please go to:

Www.SonsOfGod.com

Quantity discounts
are available for your
church or prayer group.

Please contact Edward at
Edward@sonsofgod.com

Made in the USA
Lexington, KY
06 February 2014